Nine Lives of William Shakespeare

Shakespeare Now!

Nine Lives of William Shakespeare

Graham Holderness

continuum

Continuum International Publishing Group

The Tower Building
11 York Road
London SE1 7NX

80 Maiden Lane, Suite 704
New York
NY 10038

www.continuumbooks.com

British Library Cataloguing-in-Publication Data
A catalogue record for this book is available from the British Library.

ISBN: 978–1–4411–51858 (hardback)

Library of Congress Cataloguing-in-Publication Data
A catalog record for this book is available from the Library of Congress

Typeset by Fakenham Prepress Solutions, Fakenham, Norfolk NR21 8NN
Printed and bound in India

Contents

For Marilyn
'Witty above her sex'

General Editors' Preface to the Second-Wave of the Series

We begin with the passions of the critic as they are forged and explored in Shakespeare. These books speak directly from that fundamental experience of losing and remaking yourself in art. This does not imply, necessarily, a lonely existentialism; the story of a self is always bound up in other stories, shared tales of nations or faiths or of families large and small. But such stories are also always singular, irreducible to the generalities by which they are typically explained. Here, then, is where literary experience stops pretending to institutionalized objectivity, and starts to tell its own story.

Shakespeare Now! is a rallying cry, above all for aesthetic immediacy. It favours a model of aesthetic knowledge as *encounter*, where the encounter brings its own, often surprising contextualizing imperatives. Implicit in this is the premise that art is as much a subject as an object, less like aggregated facts and more like a fascinating person or persons. And encountering the plays as such is unavoidably personal. Much recent scholarship has been devoted to Shakespeare *then* – to producing more information about the presumed moment of their inception. But this moment of inception is in truth happening over and over, again and again, anywhere that Shakespeare is being experienced anew or freshly. For the fact is that he remains, by a country mile, the most important *contemporary* writer – the most performed and read, the most written about, but also the most remembered. But it is not a question merely of Shakespeare in the present, as though his vitality is best measured by his passing relevance to great events. It is about his works' abiding *presence*.

In some ways criticism needs to get younger – to recover the freshness of aesthetic experience, and so in part better to remember why any of us should care. We need a new directness, written responses to the plays which attest to the life we find in them and the life they find in us.

Ewan Fernie and Simon Palfrey

General Editors' Preface

Shakespeare Now! represents a new form for new approaches. Whereas academic writing is far too often ascendant and detached, attesting all too clearly to years of specialist training, *Shakespeare Now!* offers a series of intellectual adventure stories: animate with fresh and often exposed thinking, with ideas still heating in the mind.

This series of 'minigraphs' will thus help to bridge two yawning gaps in current public discourse. First, the gap between scholarly thinking and a public audience: the assumption of academics that they cannot speak to anyone but their peers unless they hopelessly dumb down their work. Second, the gap between public audience and scholarly thinking: the assumption of regular playgoers, readers or indeed actors that academics write about the plays at a level of abstraction or specialization that they cannot hope to understand.

But accessibility should not be mistaken for comfort or predictability. Impatience with scholarly obfuscation is usually accompanied by a basic impatience with anything but (supposed) common sense. What this effectively means is a distrust of really thinking, and a disdain for anything that might unsettle conventional assumptions, particularly through crossing or re-drafting formal, political or theoretical boundaries. We encourage such adventure, and base our claim to a broad audience upon it.

Here, then, is where our series is innovative: no compromising of the sorts of things that can be thought; a commitment to publishing powerful cutting-edge scholarship; *but* a conviction that these things are essentially communicable, that we can find a language that is enterprising, individual and shareable.

To achieve this we need a form that can capture the genuine challenge and vigour of thinking. Shakespeare is intellectually exciting, and so too are the ideas and debates that thinking about his work can provoke. But published scholarship often fails to communicate much of this. It is difficult to sustain excitement over the 80–120,000 words customary for a monograph: difficult enough for the writer, and perhaps even more so for the reader. Scholarly articles have likewise become a highly formalized mode not only of publication, but also of intellectual production. The brief length of articles means that a concept can be outlined, but its implications or application can rarely be tested in detail. The decline of sustained, exploratory attention to the singularity of a play's language, occasion or movement is one of the unfortunate results. Often 'the play' is somehow assumed, a known and given thing that is not really worth exploring. So we spend our time pursuing collateral contexts: criticism becomes a belated, historicizing footnote.

Important things have got lost. Above all, any vivid sense as to why we are bothered with these things in the first place. Why read? Why go to plays? Why are they important? How does any pleasure they give relate to any of the things we labour to say about them? In many ways, literary criticism has forgotten affective and political immediacy. It has assumed a shared experience of the plays and then averted the gaze from any such experience, or any testing of it. We want a more ductile and sensitive mode of production; one that has more chance of capturing what people are really thinking and reading about, rather than what the pre-empting imperatives of journal or respectable monograph tend to encourage.

Furthermore, there is a vast world of intellectual possibility – from the past and present – that mainstream Shakespeare criticism has all but ignored. In recent years there has been a move away from 'theory' in literary studies: an aversion to its obscure jargon and complacent self-regard; a sense that its tricks are too easily rehearsed and that the whole game has become one of diminishing returns. This has further encouraged a retreat into the supposed safety of historicism. Of course the best such work is stimulating, revelatory and indispensable. But too often there is little trace of any struggle; little sense that the writer is coming at the subject afresh, searching for the most appropriate language or method. Alternatively, the prose is so laboured that all trace of an urgent story is quite lost.

We want to open up the sorts of thinking – and thinkers – that might help us get at what Shakespeare is doing or why Shakespeare matters. This might include psychology, cognitive science, theology, linguistics, phenomenology, metaphysics, ecology, history, political theory; it can mean other art forms such as music, sculpture, painting, dance; it can mean the critical writing itself becomes a creative act.

In sum, we want the minigraphs to recover what the Renaissance 'essay' form was originally meant to embody. It meant an 'assay' – a trial or a test of something; putting something to the proof; and doing so in a form that is not closed off and that cannot be reduced to a system. We want to communicate intellectual activity at its most alive: when it is still exciting to the one doing it; when it is questing and open, just as Shakespeare is. Literary criticism – that is, really thinking about words in action, plays as action – can start making a much more creative and vigorous contribution to contemporary intellectual *life*.

Simon Palfrey and Ewan Fernie

Introduction

In the film *Shakespeare in Love*, Lady Viola de Lessops, already in love herself, asks the Bard: 'Are you the author of the plays of William Shakespeare?'[1] 'Are you William Shakespeare?' would have been simpler. But Lady Viola knew and loved the plays before she knew and loved the man. She is a fan, a groupie, one who hangs round stage doors in search of an autograph. Like her original, Viola Compton in the comic novel *No Bed for Bacon,* she is in love with the theatre, enamoured of the stage.[2] She doesn't want just any man, even one as dashing and soulful and sexy as Joseph Fiennes. She wants the author of the plays of William Shakespeare; who happens, of course, to be William Shakespeare himself. And fortunately for her, Shakespeare is, in the film, dashing and soulful and sexy, and not, for example, as he might have been in life, fat, balding, snobbish, mercenary or even gay.

In Lady Viola's innocent inquiry, the plays precede the author, and Shakespeare stands in a secondary relation to the works he is known to have originated. The man Shakespeare is of prior interest to her, on account of the poetry he has already written. The author derives from his work. And this is, of course, an accurate explanation of the origins of literary biography, as Nicholas Rowe stated clearly in the first Shakespeare biography, *Some Account of the Life &c. of Mr. William Shakespear,* published in 1709, in preface to his edition of Shakespeare's *Works.* Out of the 'respect due to the memory of excellent men' arises a 'Curiosity' regarding the 'personal story.'[3] The life is of interest because of the works; which means, in practice, that the biography of a writer is always the life of an 'author,' a narrative that seeks to explain the relationship between writing, and the self who writes.

This assertion seems so obvious as to be virtually invisible: no-one could be interested in a poet who didn't write any poems, or a general who never served in a war, or a cabinet minister who never made it into government. But the obverse side of this opaque truth is that the writing, or the military campaigns, or the political achievements mediate between the observer and the person whose life is embedded in them. The man or woman is already lost inside his or her life-story, 'subdued' in Shakespeare's own words, 'to what it works in, like the dyer's hand.'

Students of literature recognize another meaning in Lady Viola's question. Major schools of criticism in the twentieth century have decreed that our relationship with poetry, or novels or drama need take no account of the writer and his life. Literature is a public property the writer no longer controls, and it is the reader who decides what it means. French theorists Roland Barthes and Michel Foucault declared that 'the author is dead,' reduced to a mere function of the text (that is, we construct an image of the author from our reading of the work). For decades students were warned off paying any attention to a writer's life, since it had no bearing on what the 'work' might be capable of saying to its readers.

Shakespeare in Love of course seems innocent of such highbrow theory, and presents the man behind the work, living the romantic life that can be imagined to have inspired the poetry. The author here is anything but dead. The idyll of love and loss embedded in *Romeo and Juliet* is really a side-effect of Shakespeare's passionate affair with a young noblewoman. But the film is also self-conscious enough to acknowledge just how fictional this exercise really is. Early in the film we see close-up shots of Shakespeare's hand, in the act of writing. We assume he's dashing off a scene or a sonnet. On closer inspection it turns out that he is trying out different spellings of his own name. The joke is stolen from *No Bed for Bacon:* 'He always practised tracing his signature when he was bored. He was always hoping that one day he would come to a firm decision upon which of them he liked best.'[4] The jest is a bit of donnish wit, typical of co-writer Tom Stoppard, derived from the fact that among the surviving specimens of Shakespeare's signature, the name is spelt differently. But the scene in the film also gestures towards the problems of literary biography. Here we see Shakespeare, comically trying out different identities, as if he was already preoccupied with the difficulties later encountered by people trying to work out exactly who he was.

†

Biographers in pursuit of Shakespeare's 'personal story' are constrained by a lack of personal data. While Shakespeare the 'author' is ubiquitously visible via his works, Shakespeare the private man remains largely mysterious and unfathomable. People often say that very little is known of Shakespeare's life. Scholars retort that in fact a great deal is known, for a literary figure from that period, though there are yawning gaps such as the so-called 'lost years,' 1585–1592, from which period no documentary evidence has survived. The problem is not lack of information, or even its lack of comprehensiveness, but the kind of information we do have. The main deficiency in the available data consists in the fact that is public and not private. 'There is nothing,' states Bill Bryson, 'that gives any certain insight into Shakespeare's feelings or beliefs as a private person.'[5] There remains not a single letter, or diary entry or reported conversation, except for a court record from 1612, discussed below, documenting Shakespeare's oral deposition, which in itself is tantalizingly opaque and self-effacing.

We know when and where Shakespeare was baptized, who his parents and siblings were, whom he married and when, how many children he had and when they died. We know about his success as a writer, and much about his professional career. We know about his property dealings and the contents of his will.

But we do not know exactly (only approximately) when he was born; where, when or even if he went to school; what he was like as a child; if his family was very poor, or reasonably well off. We do not know if he worked for his father as a young man, or did something else; what happened to him in the 'lost years'; how he became an actor and writer; if he stayed in London to keep away from his family in Stratford. We don't know for sure if he had to get married; if he loved his wife; if he ever lived anywhere but Stratford and London; if he had sexual relations with other women, or men; if he was religious, and if so of what persuasion; if he loved his children; how much he cared about his writing. We know when and where he died, but not what he died from. We know nothing for certain about the relationship between his writing and his life. We do not know what he believed in; what he cared about; what he thought about anything at all.

'A shilling life,' as W.H. Auden said, 'will give you all the facts,'[6] but is likely to omit what biography really wants most of all to know, the interior life, the secrets of the private man: what he believed, how he felt, whom he loved. If we set aside the idea that the plays and poems are autobiographical, the Shakespeare biography consists entirely of historical records. But as biographer Katherine Duncan-Jones admits, historical records deal only with public events, social interactions of law and property, baptisms and burials:

> Surviving documents don't take us very far in answering the kinds of questions that many post-Romantic readers may want to ask – did he love his wife? who was 'the dark lady'? what was his religious position, if any? Or his overall vision of the world?[7]

A brief life of Shakespeare, based purely on these historical documents, and drawing no inferences at all about any autobiographical content in the writing, would look like the following biographical sketch. Here I have not entered into any detail about these historical records, as they are all discussed more fully in the chapters that follow. But these are the inferences that can reasonably be drawn from the historical evidence. These are the facts.

†

A son William was born to John and Mary Shakespeare of Stratford-upon-Avon, and baptized on April 26 1564. Their other children were Gilbert, Joan, Anna, Richard and Edmund. We do not know exactly what Shakespeare's father John did for a living. He is described variously, in different documents, as a farmer, a tanner and a glover. In 1557 he married Mary Arden, daughter of a local farmer, Robert Arden, who bequeathed her £6 13s. 4d. in money, and a house with 50 acres of land. John Shakespeare rose through various municipal offices to the position of bailiff, or mayor, of the town, in 1568. Afterwards his career faltered, he lost his civic offices, and there is evidence that the family may have experienced financial difficulties.

In 1582, Shakespeare married, in some haste and with some irregularity in the formalities, Anne Hathaway, also from a farming background. He was 18, she was 26. Within six months of the wedding, a daughter, Susanna, was baptized, on May 26 1583. Shakespeare's other children, the twins Hamnet and Judith, were baptized in February 1585.

There follow the so-called 'lost years,' 1585–1592, for which there is no documentary evidence at all about Shakespeare's life. By 1592 he had become a successful actor and playwright, and by April 18 1593, a published poet. Both his narrative poems *Venus and Adonis* and *Lucrece* were dedicated to the Earl of Southampton. He was an actor in the Lord Chamberlain's Company by 1594, involved for example in the presentation of two comedies, before the Queen, at Greenwich Palace, in the Christmas season of that year. He acted in Ben Jonson's plays, and in his own. On Elizabeth's death, his company became the King's Men, servants to James I, and Shakespeare is mentioned in official documents as a member of the company.

On August 11, 1596, his only son Hamnet was buried. The following year, he bought New Place, one of the largest houses in Stratford. He acquired land in 1602 and 1610, and a cottage adjoining his house in 1602. In 1605 he acquired a lease of the Stratford tithes, a purchase that involved him in litigation. In March 1613, he bought a house near the Blackfriars Theatre in London. Between 1600 and 1609, he prosecuted several suits to recover small sums of money from debtors, while at the same time the tax collectors in London were seeking unpaid taxes from him. John Shakespeare had earlier tried to secure the coat of arms for which he was eligible, but had failed to achieve it, possibly because of his money troubles. The application was renewed in 1596, probably by William, and this time was successful. The motto 'Non Sanz Droict' ('not without right') was attached to the application.

From 1598 to 1604, he lodged in the house of Christopher Mountjoy, a wigmaker, at the corner of Muggle and Silver streets near Cripplegate. This association brought Shakespeare into court on 11 September 1612 as a witness to an alleged breach of promise between his landlord and the landlord's apprentice, Stephen Bellott. Bellott was claiming a dowry of £50 he claimed was promised by Mountjoy when the apprentice married the landlord's daughter. The court record is the only instance of Shakespeare's own words having been written down. But they throw very little light, either on his character, or on the affair being prosecuted. He said he could not remember the sum agreed on for the dowry.

Letters from the Stratford archives from around this period show Shakespeare being regarded by local businessmen as someone who might be interested in becoming a partner in the purchasing of land, or who might lend money to his friends and neighbours.

The quarto editions of *Richard II* and *Love's Labour's Lost* were the first plays to put his name on the title page, after which publishers of the plays usually gave him credit as author. In about 1599, he became, a 'sharer,' with John Heminge and Henry Condell (fellow actors and later Shakespeare's editors), and others, in the receipts of the Globe Theatre, erected in 1597–8 by Richard and Cuthbert Burbage. In 1610, he became a sharer also in the smaller Blackfriars Theatre, after it had been acquired by the Burbages.

On June 5 1607, Shakespeare's elder daughter Susanna married Stratford doctor John Hall. His younger daughter, Judith, married Thomas Quiney on February 10 1616, also with some haste and informality. In March 1616 Shakespeare signed his will. He died on 23 April 1616, was buried in Stratford Church, and on his grave appeared a monitory epitaph:

> Good friend, for Jesus' sake forbeare
> To dig the dust enclosed heare ;
> Bleste be the man that spares these stones,
> And curst be he that moves my bones.

Seven years later, thirty-six of Shakespeare's plays were collected by his former colleagues of the theatre, John Heming and Henry Condell, whom he had remembered in his will, and published in the famous First Folio of 1623.

Of Shakespeare's handwriting, nothing has survived except six signatures and a passage of the manuscript play text *Sir Thomas More*. The signatures show variations in spelling: Shakspere, Shakespere, or Shakspeare.

Knowledge of Shakespeare's personal appearance is limited and uncertain. The bust on the monument in the church at Stratford was cut, apparently before 1623, by a Dutch stonecutter, Gheerart Janssen. It was originally coloured, later whitewashed, then re-tinted. The frontispiece to the First Folio was engraved by Martin Droeshout. Neither image is very much admired; and neither (though they are the only sources for Shakespeare's appearance) is universally acknowledged as a good likeness.

†

Many of these facts were discovered by scholars through the eighteenth and nineteenth centuries; the details of the Bellott-Mountjoy lawsuit as late as the early twentieth century. When Nicholas Rowe set out to gather material for his *Some Account of the Life &c. of Mr. William Shakespear* (1709), there existed only a few anecdotes, available in writings by men such as Ben Jonson, Thomas Fuller and John Aubrey. Rowe also relied on a kind of oral history of Stratford tradition, drawing on the actor Thomas Betterton's conversations with local people and their reminiscences. Rowe recorded some verifiable facts with accuracy. But most of what he managed to gather in the way of Shakespearean 'Remains' was an assortment of stories that modern biographers regard as legendary and mythological.

Rowe for example tells us that Shakespeare had to leave Stratford because he was caught poaching deer in the park of local magnate Sir Thomas Lucy. Scholars have pointed out that at the time Lucy had neither park nor deer, and that this story sounds about as historical as Robin Hood and his Merry Men. Shakespeare is perhaps being fitted here into an archetype, the unruly young man whose nocturnal adventures bring him into trouble with the law. The story had to be completed with some reference to writing, so we get the tale that he penned a 'bitter ballad' of satirical contempt against Sir Thomas Lucy, and had to flee Stratford to avoid serious consequences. Most modern biographers treat this as little more than a fairytale. But there is more to it than that.

Like historians, biographers of Shakespeare depend on a basic distinction between 'fact' and 'tradition.' Fact is documentary evidence that can be verified, or has in the past been expertly tested, or is reliably corroborated by other evidence so as to render it persuasive. Fact is evidence, dated and proved, and beyond all reasonable doubt genuine. I can walk into the Public Record Office in Kew and look at Shakespeare's Last Will and Testament of 1616. I may doubt that Shakespeare drew up the text himself; I may question the meaning of the various bequests in it; I may even believe that the man who signed the will was not the man who wrote the plays. But I cannot argue against the indisputable historical fact that this piece of parchment in front of me is the Last Will and Testament of William Shakespeare, Gent., of Stratford-upon-Avon in the county of Warwickshire, and that the shaky signature, the trembling autograph of a dying man, is his. This is a fact.

The outline of Shakespeare's life is marked out by a number of recorded 'facts' like this: birth, marriage, children, acting, publication, theatre management, business dealing, property acquisition and speculation, death. 'Traditions,' in the favoured language of Shakespeare biographers, may be facts, but their relevance to Shakespeare's life is not factual. Traditions appear later in time than facts, are further away from the actuality; they derive from anecdotes and annotations rather than legal documents; they are in the manner of stories and legends rather than pieces of concrete documentary evidence.

But this distinction is a relative latecomer to the Shakespeare biography scene. In Rowe's biography, details now confidently regarded as factual are freely interwoven with 'traditions.' The few facts listed by Rowe include: Shakespeare's baptism and those of his siblings, his marriage to Anne Hathaway, the authorship of *Venus and Adonis* and *Lucrece* with their dedications to the Earl of Southampton, his retirement to Stratford, the marriages of his daughters and his death in 1616. All these can be verified from the historical record. Most of Rowe's account, however, is taken up with traditions that are unsupported by facts. That Shakespeare attended the local grammar school, but had to leave to work in his father's business; that he had to quit Stratford for London on account of the deer-stealing episode; that he arrived in London's theatre-land as a poor young man, and entered the playhouse in a servile capacity:

> It is at this Time, and upon this Accident, that he is said to have made his first Acquaintance in the Play-house. He was receiv'd into the Company then in being, at first in a very mean Rank; But his admirable Wit, and the natural Turn of it to the Stage, soon distinguished him, if not as an extraordinary Actor, yet as an excellent Writer.[8]

Rowe goes on to assert that Shakespeare was favoured by the Queen; that the Earl of Southampton lent him £1000; that he helped Ben Jonson get a play accepted for performance. None of these assertions can be found in the documentary record. There is no evidence of Shakespeare's early education, no trace of when or why he left Stratford, no record of how he entered the theatrical profession, and no particular mark of any personal royal favour.

Some of these details are nonetheless generally accepted as probable: e.g. the author of the plays and poems must have had an education, and the local grammar school was the obvious place to obtain it; or plausible, e.g. Shakespeare and Ben Jonson certainly had a professional relationship, so he may have done him a favour. Other details have gained less credence: Rowe couldn't believe the loan of £1000 from the cash-strapped Southampton; and although we know Shakespeare's company played before the Queen, that touch of personal royal favour from Queen Elizabeth seems too good to be true.

†

Yet to any historian, such early records would necessarily claim our attention, and may even hold priority over the modern analyst's opinions. It is not merely that these traditions, written down in the seventeenth and early eighteenth centuries, lie much closer to Shakespeare than do the experiences and assumptions of a twentieth-century scholar. The traditions themselves derived from sources – some verifiable and others not – that can be traced back very closely indeed to the historical moment they describe and interpret. Rowe took his data from actor Thomas Betterton, who had undertaken a field trip to Stratford to research Shakespeare's life:

> I must own a particular Obligation to [Mr. Betterton], for the most considerable part of the Passages relating to his Life, which I have here transmitted to the Publick; his Veneration for the Memory of *Shakespear* having engag'd him to make a Journey into *Warwickshire*, on purpose to gather up what Remains he could of a Name for which he had so great a Value.[9]

John Aubrey collected fragments of information for his *Lives of the English Poets* from Restoration actors such as William Beeston and John Lacy. Beeston succeeded to the management of the Cockpit Theatre in Drury Lane when his father Christopher Beeston died in 1637. Christopher Beeston is named among the actors who, with Shakespeare, took part in the first production of Jonson's *Every Man in His Humour*. Lacy, leading Restoration actor and dramatist, and author of an adaptation of *The Taming of the Shrew*, was a member of the Caroline theatre troupe, the King's and Queen's Young Company, colloquially known as 'Beeston's Boys' since it was created by the same Christopher Beeston. What would a modern biographer give for information acquired from the son of an actor who played alongside Shakespeare in a Ben Jonson play? Or from one who served as a boy player in that same actor's company?

In place of the crude historicist notion of 'tradition' as little more than inauthentic invention, later accretion, myth and legend, we need something more like the meaning 'tradition' holds in religion. Jewish, Islamic and Catholic Christian scholarship all give priority to the holy scriptures, Torah, Qur'an and Bible, but also give weight to the subsequent interpretations and supplementations of the scriptures in Midrash, Hadith and Tradition. In Shakespeare's time the Christian Reformers tried to insist on the Bible as the only source of truth ('*sola scriptura*') against the Roman church's reverence for Tradition. In the same way many biographers have dismissed the assertions of Rowe and Aubrey, because they are late in the day, second-hand, unverified and improbable. In Shakespeare biography it is possible to view 'tradition' as in its own way authentic. Rowe's life incorporated information derived by Thomas Betterton from the people of Stratford. Aubrey took his data from men like Lacy and Beeston, the very people who were best placed to have received information about Shakespeare, handed down through the theatres and the acting companies he worked with and wrote for. A certain Mr. Dowdall visited Stratford in 1693, conversed with an elderly parish clerk whose life might have overlapped with that of Shakespeare himself, and wrote down some of his findings in a letter. Stratford neighbours, parish clerks, local gossips, actors and theatre managers of the seventeenth century – where else would we go for reliable information about the life of Shakespeare? On the other hand these 'traditions' are obviously telling a story as well as citing a fact, so the information they provide may well be both factual, and yet to some degree already partly fictionalized.

†

Shakespeare scholars since Rowe have tried to construct a biography based on the historical evidence, and to explore links between the man and his works. Self-evidently there is much more of Shakespeare's work, in terms of texts, documentary evidence, commentary and critical analysis, than there is of his life, but the two are notoriously difficult to connect. Hence biographers use Shakespeare's poems and plays as repositories of hidden or extant information about the poet's feelings and attitudes and beliefs. But every single word in the plays is spoken by a dramatic character, and may have no personal origin at all. Even Shakespeare's famous *Sonnets* may not be as confessional as many readers like to believe. Data from the 'life' and the 'works' are then invariably supplemented by the use of the biographer's imagination, in order to deliver to the reader those speculations essential to disclosing the things we really want to know.

Notwithstanding these difficulties, in the last few years there has been an explosion of interest in the life of Shakespeare: according to Anne Barton's count, at least one formal biography of Shakespeare has appeared every year since 1996. From Nicholas Rowe to Peter Ackroyd, innumerable 'Lives of Shakespeare' have been written, by scholars and academics, by professional novelists and biographers, and by creative writers. All are in quest of what Rowe called the 'personal story,' but they tell it in different ways.

Scholars typically approach the life on the basis of an extensive knowledge of the actual textual works and their critical literature; of Renaissance history, local and national; of the Tudor and Stuart theatre; and of Shakespeare's many afterlives, in drama, criticism, film and the broader culture. The works precede the life, and it is the works that speak of the man.

Professional biographers have a more difficult task, since the confessional material that is their stock-in-trade is virtually absent: there are no letters, diaries or directly reported conversations; no testimony from family, friends and neighbours about 'the common accidents' of Shakespeare's life. They depend on the same materials as the scholars, but typically seek to supplement these by what scholarship would regard as unlicensed imaginative speculation.

Creative writers give free reign to the imagination, and produce, out of the raw biographical facts and the mysterious connections between life and works, overtly fictional biographies that nonetheless demonstrate a surprising plausibility, and exercise a curious compulsion over the popular imagination. Here the 'personal story' tends to align with the impersonal patterns of myth and legend.

As interest in both popular and academic biographies of Shakespeare continues to grow, so too imaginative works about Shakespeare's life have flourished, in the form of novels, poems, plays, films, radio and television drama and artworks. There is not such a huge difference between these different biographical genres as many of their authors would like to think. Restless under the constraints of the historical record, biographers end up telling us about many things besides Shakespeare, and filling the empty spaces with their own preoccupations.

In Jonathan Bate's biography *Soul of the Age*,[10] for example, there is a strong emphasis on Shakespeare as a countryman rather than an urbanite, who emerged from, and always belonged to, the little provincial town of Stratford. London was for 'business and busy-ness,' he writes, Stratford for 'home and rest' (p. 13). This sounds as if London was the real focus of Shakespeare's life, and Stratford his dormitory-town commuter retreat. But this rural countryside of the Midlands was no mere suburb of the metropolis, according to Bate, but England's very heart, to be found 'not in Westminster, but somewhere in the midlands, deep in the shires' (p. 35). Bate displays a strong personal investment in this Midland 'heart of England,' and in this rustic Shakespeare who came from 'deep in the shires,' like some Tolkienian hobbit. Bate works at the University of Warwick, and 'I live,' he writes, 'at the edge of a cornfield three miles out of Stratford-upon-Avon' (p. 58). The life of the biographer, here unnecessarily obtruded upon his theme, and the life of his subject, are mirrored in this emphatic provincial placing.

Peter Ackroyd in *Shakespeare: the Biography*[11] also describes Shakespeare as country-bred, though his Stratford is significantly more urban than Bate's. But the real heart of his book is London. Shakespeare's life and career become part of that great metropolitan experiment that Ackroyd has enthusiastically chronicled in his earlier work *London:The Biography.*[12] Shakespeare's temperament in this biography is urban, secular, modern, rather than rural, pious and medieval. Indeed, his detachment from ideology, religion and empathy make him sound more like a modern professional writer than an early modern dramatist; more like Peter Ackroyd himself, than like William Shakespeare.

All biographers of Shakespeare, whether they realize it or not, supplement the facts with their own speculations, and their speculations are inevitably to some degree subjective. Consider, as a case-study, how a number of major biographers of Shakespeare deal with the poet's death. There are virtually no data to work with, other than the facts that he made a will, died on 23rd April 1616 and was buried in Holy Trinity Church, Stratford. Jonathan Bate baldly states the meagre record: 'the only solid facts are the record of the burial,' the gravestone and the monument.[13]

A seventeenth-century tradition, noted in his diary by Stratford vicar John Ward, is that Shakespeare had a 'merry meeting' (i.e. a booze-up) with Ben Jonson and Michael Drayton, and contracted a fever from the after-effects.[14] Park Honan surmises that the 'fever' Shakespeare died of was typhoid, and speculates about some of the symptoms he may have experienced. 'He would have suffered incessant headaches, lassitude and sleeplessness, then terrible thirst and discomfort.'[15] Stanley Wells permits himself to mention this speculation as a reasonable hunch: 'The best guess – it is not more – is that he was suffering from typhoid fever.'[16]

Peter Ackroyd agrees about typhoid, for him a conveniently urban disease arising from water-borne infection. Ackroyd then goes on to narrate, as if factually, a typical seventeenth-century ritual of embalming, winding and viewing the corpse:

> He was wrapped in a linen winding sheet and two days later he was carried down the well-worn 'burying path' to the old church.[17]

Ackroyd doesn't actually know that this happened, of course, but assumes that Shakespeare died and was buried according to respectably Protestant rites and services: he was buried in the church because of 'his status as a lay rector.' So it *must* have happened like this. On the other hand Michael Wood, whose biography promotes a 'Catholic Shakespeare,' speculates that dying, the poet was 'drawn to his childhood certainties at the end,' and received extreme unction from a Catholic priest.[18]

While all these male biographers like to think of Shakespeare as carried off by an infection, female biographers prefer the tradition that Shakespeare died of tertiary syphilis, contracted in his youth from prostitutes. Katherine Duncan-Jones believes that Shakespeare probably was drinking to excess, as John Ward recorded, but that would have been to palliate his pain, since he was already severely ill from the symptoms of the pox. 'My own guess is that heart and circulatory troubles were now added to latent syphilitic infection.'[19] This disease could have made the dying Shakespeare mad and 'furiously angry with those around him.' She speculates that the final scene of Ben Jonson's play *The Devil is an Ass*, in which the protagonist Fitzdotrell feigns mortal illness, actually portrays details from the real death of Shakespeare.[20] Fitzdotrell

… is apparently mad and apparently dying. He laughs crazily, abuses his wife as a whore, foams at the mouth, uses foul language to an eminent lawyer, and comes out with childishly obscene fragments of English doggerel and bad Greek, Spanish and French (p. 276).

Duncan-Jones' 'ungentle' Shakespeare dies hating his wife: the curse on his gravestone was designed to prevent her from ever joining him in 'his angry and unshared deathbed.'

Germaine Greer, writing a biography not of Shakespeare but of Anne Hathaway, agrees that Shakespeare had tertiary syphilis, but argues that he died from the cure not the disease: poisoned by the mercury then freely used as treatment for syphilis.[21] Greer speculates that, as a consequence of being clinically poisoned by mercury or arsenic, Shakespeare became increasingly detached from society, reclusive, confused and helpless. This assumed decline created a dependence, which enabled his wife Anne to become the heroine of the story, nursing him to his end. 'In those quiet hours in the sickroom, husband and wife may have drawn closer together' (p. 309).

Here we see a clear pattern in the ideological inflections of these biographical stories. Some scholars respectfully stay away from the deathbed, invoking as their excuse a lack of evidence. Others argue that Shakespeare died a fairly ordinary death, carried away by a common infection. Some see him dying a Protestant, others a Catholic. These accounts are all partly fictional. The most inventive interpretations come from the female scholars, Duncan-Jones and Greer, who build up imaginary cases for seeing Shakespeare either as raving mad, or as prematurely senile. In the former case the wife is the victim, abused and vilified; in the latter she is the angel of the house, who lovingly cares for her helpless husband.

We scarcely need to remind ourselves that 'the only solid facts' are the record of the burial and the tomb,[22] to appreciate just how inventive, fictional, speculative and opinionated such biographical writing really is. Often, it seems, the biographer is like God, creating the subject in his or her own image. 'Trying to work out Shakespeare's personality,' wrote Samuel Schoenbaum, is 'like looking at a very dark glazed picture in the National Portrait Gallery: at first you see nothing, then you begin to recognize features, then you realize that they are your own.'[23] A biography of Shakespeare can be a thinly disguised self-portrait of the biographer.

†

Often this manifest similarity between the biographer and his/her image of Shakespeare seems mainly unconscious. But in one of the most successful – and controversial – of modern Shakespeare biographies, written by one of the world's foremost Shakespeare scholars, this subjective investment is rendered explicit, and developed via an overtly speculative and imaginative method of composition.[24] Stephen Greenblatt's *Will in the World: how Shakespeare became Shakespeare,* is a formal biography, using the established facts and traditions, reading the plays and poems in the light of them, and producing potential explanations of how the life and the works might be interrelated. But the book was strenuously attacked, despite the author's reputation, for investing more in speculation and invention than in historical evidence.[25]

Now as I have argued, there is no such thing as a speculation-free biography of Shakespeare. Greenblatt's challenge to orthodoxy was to be much more overtly fictional, or meta-fictional, in his method, much more self-reflexive in declaring the conjectural and speculative character of his writing: to admit that at times he was making it up. The best-known example is a possible meeting Greenblatt provisionally stages between Shakespeare and Jesuit martyr Edmund Campion, which he invents as a possible event in Shakespeare's 'lost years.' Campion was a Jesuit missionary executed in 1581. There is evidence that William's father John Shakespeare was a devout Roman Catholic: a document of Catholic profession, known as 'John Shakespeare's Spiritual Testament,' was unearthed from the house in Henly Street in the eighteenth century. Some scholars have argued that William Shakespeare and an actor in a Lancastrian Roman Catholic household called 'Shakeshafte,' were one and the same person, and that the dramatist was therefore probably himself a crypto-Catholic. This in itself is speculative, as no-one can prove that Shakespeare was Shakeshafte, and some scholars regard the identification as spurious. So the meeting with Edmund Campion is speculation based on speculation, indeed little more than a fantasy. But Greenblatt is fully aware of this, and clearly signals that the imaginary episode he is narrating is a piece of story-telling. He even begins with 'Let us imagine the two of them sitting together ...'[26] Here the biographer is not dealing in fact, or even tradition, but fleshing out an argument by the use of imagination. 'If Shakespeare had met Campion, this is what it might have been like ....' His narrative and dramatic method is closer to Shakespeare's than it is to the conventions of literary biography.

Moreover, the biographer's imagination is expressive of his personal experience as well as his engagement with Shakespeare. Take Greenblatt's chapter called 'Speaking with the Dead,' which again presupposes that Shakespeare's father was a recusant Roman Catholic. The biographical basis of the chapter rests on a few documentary facts. Shakespeare's 11-year-old son Hamnet died in 1596. His father John Shakespeare died in 1601. Between these two deaths Shakespeare wrote *Hamlet*. Greenblatt tells a story (adumbrated earlier by James Joyce in *Ulysses*) that aspires to explain the play that lies between these two momentous bereavements. Shakespeare 'undoubtedly' returned to Stratford for Hamnet's funeral.[27] There he heard the words of the Protestant burial service from *The Book of Common Prayer* that echo eloquently in the play. But there, Greenblatt suggests, he became acutely aware of how much he and his family missed in being deprived of Catholic rituals for the dead: the Latin memorial prayers, the candles, bells and crosses, the alms-giving and requiem masses. Shakespeare wanted, Greenblatt suggests, to mourn his son in the traditional pattern of worship, and was unable to do so.

Greenblatt goes even further and suggests that John Shakespeare may have pleaded with William, 'appealed urgently to his son' (p. 316) to have masses said for the soul of Hamnet. This is of course the anguished pleading we also hear from the Ghost in *Hamlet*, who comes from Purgatory, a doctrinal place outlawed by the Church of England, but still a vitally important article of faith for Roman Catholics. From these sources Greenblatt imaginatively creates a vivid drama in which a father, perhaps nearing death, appeals to his son to maintain a practice of traditional piety; and the son is perhaps unable, or unwilling, to do so. Now this is clearly not just about Shakespeare: it is also about Greenblatt himself.

In the 'Prologue' to his earlier book *Hamlet in Purgatory,* Greenblatt wrote about *his* father, who died in 1983. Scarred by the painful death of his own father, Greenblatt Sr lived in a perpetual denial of death. Yet, 'when we read his will,' Greenblatt says, 'we found that he had, after all, been thinking about his death. He had left a sum of money to an organization that would say Kaddish for him – Kaddish being the Aramaic prayer for the dead, recited for eleven months after a person's death and then on certain annual occasions ... the prayer is usually said by the deceased's immediate family and particularly by his sons ... Evidently my father did not trust either my older brother or me to recite the prayer for him.'[28]

Kaddish is a central Jewish prayer, praising the power and glory of God, one version of which is used as a memorial prayer for the dead. So all this talk of bereavement, and maimed rites, and fathers appealing for ancient observances, and speaking with the dead, is certainly about Shakespeare, and about *Hamlet*. But it's also about Stephen Greenblatt. John Shakespeare and other

Catholics, he says, in requesting requiem masses 'were asking those who loved them to do something crucially important for them.'[29] Greenblatt's father did not ask him to say Kaddish, and that in itself was clearly doubly painful for the son. But he says it anyway, 'in a blend of love and spite,'[30] and ends the preface to *Hamlet in Purgatory*: 'this practice then, which with a lightly ironic piety I, who scarcely know how to pray, undertook for my own father, is the personal starting point for what follows' (p. 9).

Greenblatt, says Gary Taylor, has 'mined his own life to supply the emotional raw materials that energise this book.' 'What purports to be an image of Shakespeare is only an idealized image of the biographer himself.'[31] So there is a 'personal starting point' for this exercise as well as a starting point in the author, and innumerable others in the historical context. By the end of this chapter in *Will in the World*, Greenblatt has merged all these together:

> Shakespeare drew upon the pity, confusion and dread of death in a world of damaged rituals (the world in which most of us continue to live) because he himself experienced those same emotions at the core of his being.[32]

The world of damaged rituals is that of Protestant early modernity, which killed off the old Catholic consolations of purgatory and efficacious prayer for the dead. But it is also the world of secular modernity, in which the son of a pious Jew involuntarily absorbs his culture's agnosticism and feels a consequential loss. Shakespeare lived in this world, *Hamlet* lives in that world, and so too does Greenblatt. All experience these fundamental emotions of irreparable loss, aching nostalgia and the desire to speak with the dead, 'at the core of ... being.'

Like all of Shakespeare's work, this is a story that can't be proved (or disproved). It's a story woven between the pegs of certain documentary facts: the death of Hamnet, 1596; the death of John Shakespeare in 1601; the composition of the play *Hamlet*, first published in 1603; John Shakespeare's 'Spiritual Testament.' But it's also a story mapped between certain poles of emotional truth: first, what we read in the play, the anguish of the father, the grief of the son; and secondly Greenblatt's own sense of bereavement and obligation. These two points are then triangulated against a third that cannot be known in the same way, the condition of the author's heart and soul: what was passing in the core of the Shakespearean being. Of course we have no access to that realm. So the critic has recourse to his imagination, and creates a narrative consistent with the documentary facts, and with the emotional truths embedded both in the writing and in the heart of the critic. As one critic puts it, he 'lets his imagination loose in the fields of his knowledge.'[33]

In trying to account for the effect great literature has on him, the critic is to some extent making it up as he goes along. But this is not just a sort of opportunistic appropriation of the work, perverting it from its original meaning, since the motivation for doing it comes from a very deep source, what Greenblatt calls the 'core of being.' Literature touches us so deeply that we're driven to presuppose the author must also have been touched in some comparable way, depth calling to depth.

Now this method can be challenged: we can say, as many readers have, that this is nothing to do with the author of Shakespeare's plays, and that the critic is just writing about himself. In defence of the method we could say that the documented facts of Shakespeare's life are so sparse that it is impossible to avoid filling the gaps they leave with invention. If the result is a consistent and plausible way of explaining the evidence – the poems, the facts, the traditions – then it will do; it's the nearest we ever really get to the truth. But clearly this opens up other possibilities as well. If what happened at the core of Shakespeare's being to generate *Hamlet* was much the same as what happened at the core of Greenblatt's being at the death of his father, then there is nothing unique about the experience. Similar things obviously happen at the core of everybody's being. And if we reach out from our own being to complete a story that lies dormant among the tattered traces of historical fact, then there are many other stories that we could tell, stories that might equally convincingly, or even more convincingly, account for the evidence.

Many scholars lined up to castigate Greenblatt's imaginative method. Alistair Fowler was unclear as to whether the book was 'fact or fiction, criticism or history.'[34] *Will in the World* is just a 'biographical fiction,' said Colin Burrow.[35] The book is 'entirely Greenblatt's fiction,' said Richard Jenkyns, and indeed 'an improbable fiction.'[36] Alistair Fowler, in one of the most hostile reviews received (in *TLS*), suggested that Greenblatt might have been better off making 'a crossover into historical fiction' where he could freely have fomented conjecture with even less respect for evidence. This should not be the case in a literary biography: here the 'subject veers too much between Shakespeare's imagination and Stephen Greenblatt's own.'[37]

On the other hand, plenty of reviewers lined up to praise Greenblatt's imaginative and inventive approach to his subject. The book should be read as 'imaginative writing.'[38] Greenblatt's 'chief allegiance is to imagination,' says Lois Potter, and the book rightly stresses 'the importance of imagination in our approach to this supremely imaginative writer.'[39] Charles Marowitz calls the book an 'extended flight of fancy,' but of a valid kind: 'a speculative leap into the murky life of Shakespeare, using one's knowledge of the period, hints from the collected works and a creative use of conjecture, is a perfectly legitimate endeavour.'[40] In writing this book I have taken considerable encouragement from these testimonies, and from Stephen Greenblatt's personal example.

†

Every subject of biography is two things: an outer world of social behaviour, theatrical display and cultural performance, and an inner, secret world of 'private life.' The former, in the case of a celebrity life, is likely to be well documented and recorded; the latter is likely to remain elusive to the inquirer, even where there is autobiographical and confessional material, and testimony acquired from close relatives, friend and colleagues. Normally, in order to access the private, the biographer must use data derived from the public sphere. In the case of an author, the writing clearly lies between public and private, but is unlikely to be a straightforward map of the interior (think of Shakespeare's *Sonnets*). The quest for the private takes the biographer into realms of personal intimacy which have often been kept secret and concealed, in cases where, for example, the subject was a closet homosexual, or a crypto-Catholic, or just obsessively averse to being known.

Biography deals in secrets. Many biographers avoid the pitfalls of the exercise by not confronting the domain of the secret, the concealed, the unacceptable, and producing bland and neutral narratives that avoid personal offence to any custodian of the artist's reputation. These are what W.H. Auden called 'shilling lives,' that list the external facts, and miss the mystery and uniqueness of the person. But biography must tamper with this realm of the personal, with the hidden life of the subject, and with the efforts of those who try to own and define that life. Biography is a violation of privacy. Biography pursues the elusive personality of the subject, and the biographer needs to have the skills of a novelist, rather than those of a diplomat. Biography should be emotionally involved, not dispassionate; self-reflexive, not neutral; experimental and innovative, not realist and documentary. In addition a biography should be metabiographical, explicitly telling the story of the biographer's engagement with the subject.

This imposes on the biographer of Shakespeare an almost impossible brief, since there is so little of the personal, and so much of the public, in the subject. The writer and his work were separated at a very early stage. The 'First Folio,' the first collected works of Shakespeare, published posthumously in 1623, gave the Shakespearean oeuvre its characteristic shape of comedies, histories, tragedies. The editors, Shakespeare's friends and fellow-actors Heminge and Condell, wrote of the collection as an exercise in putting the now dead Shakespeare back together again. But the writer himself was both invoked and distanced by the Droeshout portrait, and Ben Jonson's famous poem on the facing page. Look not on his picture, Jonson advised, but his book. The writer is already inside the work: Shakespeare has become 'Shakespeare' before we reach the first page. And the author himself, with his famous cloak of invisibility, seems to have spent a lifetime resisting the legible clarity of a manifest personality. In other words, the question of 'how Shakespeare became "Shakespeare"' seems to have arisen almost as soon as pen touched paper.

Biography requires exhaustive and detailed research into the intensive evidence bordering on an individual literary life; an honest and searching power of analysis; a boldly intrusive curiosity that targets the most closely guarded secrets; and the recognition that a literary life is as much an external performance as an expression of what is hidden within the inner sanctum. The life of a major writer, a 'literary biography,' requires a deep critical and historical knowledge of literature and theatre; a thorough acquaintance with Shakespeare's afterlives in different historical cultures; and a vigorous and independent polemical approach to tradition. In combination these methods can produce the kind of empathic speculation necessary to penetrate Shakespeare's personality, with the additional critical and satirical detachment essential to distinguish between genuine revelation and narcissism in the biographical form.

†

This new biography of Shakespeare identifies and expound some of the many possible 'lives' that can reasonably be drawn around the basic facts, traditions and literary remains of the Shakespeare legacy. This is to some extent a scholarly and historical initiative, taking a hard and fresh look at the facts, the traditions and the possible relationships between a life and the works that life created. Biographical narratives intended for a general readership usually suppress their sources in favour of interesting and compelling exposition. I have assumed that my readers will want to understand exactly what we know about Shakespeare, what we do not know, and how we have attempted to fill the gap between those positions. I also want to interrogate and reassess the very distinctions between 'fact,' 'tradition' and 'speculation' in biographical writing, so the work has a theoretical dimension, though it is not formally a work of theory, and the reader is not expected to absorb complex and abstract theoretical paradigms. But the most unconventional feature of this study is that it deliberately exploits the manifestly fictional character of much biographical writing, and takes that mode to its natural conclusion in the form of explicitly imaginative compositions. This is the first scholarly biography of Shakespeare to embrace freely the imaginative and fictional processes that are always at work, though hidden and unacknowledged, in the activity of life writing.

Nine chapters supply nine 'lives' or micro-biographies of Shakespeare, each based on specific facts and traditions, each drawn from the documentary record and from biographical interpretation, and each supported by a body of critical and biographical work. Each chapter employs the same formulaic pattern, dividing its contents into 'Facts,' 'Traditions' and 'Speculations.'

Each 'factual' section sets out the historical evidence from which that particular version of the life history is drawn. Most of these documents lie in archives or specialist collections, accessible mainly to the scholar. But they are discussed, described and often pictured in most Shakespeare biographies, and facsimiles of the relevant sections are widely available on the internet. For convenience I have referred the reader directly to Samuel Schoenbaum's *William Shakespeare: a Compact Documentary Life*, which attempts to construct a biography entirely from the surviving documentary material, and in which all the relevant records are fully represented.

Each 'factual' section is then followed by a section tracing the later 'Traditions' that bear upon that particular micro-biography, recognizing that this evidence is different from 'fact,' but nonetheless acknowledging that it may, in many cases, contain both historical veracity and the capacity for true imaginative interpretation. 'Traditions' often bridge the gap between the baldly factual and the boldly speculative in Shakespeare biography.

Lastly, each chapter reviews contemporary biographical commentary on a particular life-scenario under the heading of 'Speculation.' Here I have undertaken to review and appraise the existing literature, analysing aspects from a number of modern biographies, and in each case exposing in the text personal bias, ideological inflection and unconscious attachment to certain questionable assumptions. There are so many biographies of Shakespeare, not to mention counter-biographical works arguing that someone other than Shakespeare wrote his plays and poems – and the number grows every year – that even specialist academics have difficulty keeping up and keeping track. Since this book is to some degree written for the general reader, I have focused mainly on fairly recent biographical works available to the mainstream market, especially those by Peter Ackroyd, Jonathan Bate, Bill Bryson, Katherine Duncan-Jones, Stephen Greenblatt, Stanley Wells and Michael Wood. In reassessing this literature, I will question existing paradigms for mapping Shakespeare's works back onto his life.

The works considered here have been produced by leading professional writers, and leading Shakespeare scholars, and they clearly stand as significant monuments of biographical writing. But in my view, the very fact that they seek to construct a holistic and integrated totality out of essentially heterogeneous material renders them vulnerable to question. My intention is to take advantage of a 'disintegrationist' movement growing up alongside these dominant biographical paradigms, to show that the Shakespeare 'life' can in reality be broken down into its constituent parts. In parallel with these major contemporary biographies, a number of works have recently been published that adopt a similarly peripheral view. I am thinking of Charles Nicholls' *The Lodger: Shakespeare on Silver Street*, which employs a 'thick description' of the district Shakespeare lived in for a brief period of his life; of Germaine Greer's *Shakespeare's Wife*, which approaches the Shakespeare biography from the perspective of Anne Hathaway's life story; and James Shapiro's *Contested Will*, which throws light on the Shakespeare biography by studying attempts to prove that someone else was, in fact, responsible for producing Shakespeare's works.[41] *Nine Lives of William Shakespeare* is, on the other hand, the first biographical study to proceed on the assumption that Shakespeare's various lives are multiple and discontinuous.

The preceding introduction has shown that Shakespeare biography began simultaneously with a search for facts, and the impulse to invent a story. The later biographical traditions, in my view, present us with facts already elaborated into imaginative form, and already extrapolated into narrative exposition. Modern scholars have convinced themselves that their methods are capable of supplanting such 'myths' and 'legends' with solid fact and historical accuracy. But as I have shown, every attempt to write a life for Shakespeare again embroiders fact and tradition into a speculative composition that is, at least partly, fictional. 'Fiction' here does not mean the opposite of fact, only a different approach to truth, and one which is in many ways more properly suited to the exploration of a creative life. Each of my chapters is paired with an original work of fiction, exploring that particular life-context, employing a variety of literary and narrative styles. Some of these are stories, set in different times and places. Some employ the form of an imaginary 'memoir.' Some purport to be reconstructed 'historical' documents, and some are best described as 'fables.' The creative pieces also draw on other literary sources, as detailed in the prefatory notes. In each case, the basic facts of the Shakespeare biography are worked up into a fictional composition that takes the argument of the chapter forward, albeit by alternative and overtly speculative methods.

The fictional pieces that make up the 'imaginative' component of *Nine Lives of William Shakespeare* are diverse and varied in form and style, and in their orientation towards the Shakespeare biography. Some of the stories and fables constitute a direct extension of the biographical essays, since they dramatize historical details from the biography and recreate them in narrative form. Other fictions reflect less on the historical 'life,' and more on the extended biography represented by Shakespeare's 'afterlife': his reputation, his mythology and the independent life of his dramatic and poetical works. This distinction could be illustrated from the two great Shakespeare stories of Jorge Luis Borges, 'Everything and Nothing,' and 'Shakespeare's Memory.'[42] The first is a fable that reinterprets Shakespeare's personality in the form of a biographical fantasy. The second, a story about a man gifted or cursed with Shakespeare's memory, focuses rather on how the Shakespeare biography lives and works in other people.

For example the fictions in this book that accompany the chapters on Shakespeare as actor, businessman and Roman Catholic adopt methods drawn from historical fiction, and imaginatively narrate the 'might-have-been' of speculative history. Other pieces focus more directly on the 'afterlife,' and explore issues arising from the process of biographical writing itself. The imaginative texts that accompany the lives of Shakespeare the butcher's boy and Shakespeare the husband consider what exactly it is that documentary sources such as Rowe's life, or the observations of Victorian antiquarians, have to tell us about Shakespeare. These fictions should be described as 'metabiographical' rather than strictly biographical, concerned with the means by which a life is written, as well as the nature of the life itself.

Other fictions range more widely, and depart from the territory of biography proper, in those cases where the historical record is remarkably deficient in terms of concrete evidence. Examples include the stories that circle around the legends of 'Shakespeare in love' with the Earl of Southampton and the

'Dark Lady of the *Sonnets*.' There is no evidence, beyond the dedications to two poems, the narrative expounded in the *Sonnets* and a cryptic allusion in Rowe that Shakespeare did in actuality enjoy and suffer these relationships. Hence it seems legitimate for a fictional commentary to take the form of invention, and to operate by parallelism and contrast rather than by historical narrative. The legend of Shakespeare as lover to the Earl of Southampton is approached via the historical parallel of Oscar Wilde and Lord Alfred Douglas, and mediated through an imitation of Sir Arthur Conan Doyle's Sherlock Holmes stories, specifically *The Hound of the Baskervilles* and 'The Adventure of the Final Problem.' There are implicit parallels to be made between the forensic methods of the famous fictional detective and the analytical speculations of the literary biographer. I have addressed the 'Dark Lady' myth via a modern parallel set in Italy in the First World War, and written by way of an imitation of Ernest Hemingway's *A Farewell to Arms*. Hemingway's great tragedy provides a framework for a modern reworking of the legendary Shakespearean ménage-a-trois, applying the language of the *Sonnets* to a narrative that reflects on the past via similarity and difference. The final story employs the medium of satirical fable invented by Jonathan Swift to comment on the cultural phenomenon of 'Bardolotry'; while the sequence of fictions opens with an imitation of Dan Brown's pseudo-historical romance form, 'The Shakespeare Code,' which explores issues arising from the scholarly quest for 'originality.' The biographical essays have the normal scholarly apparatus of endnotes, while each fiction is prefaced by a brief contextualising note explaining the relationship between the imaginative and biographical components of each individual chapter or 'life.' Here I have indicated sources of quotations, though not citing their specific origins.

This book therefore ruptures some of the boundaries that normally corral academic and scholarly discourses separately from creative and imaginative writing. What this means is that the book operates on two discrete 'tracks,' running in parallel and intersecting, but operating by different sets of rules or signals. In the creative works, the historical facts and traditions are implicit, but the normal disciplines of scholarly writing do not apply. Here some of the facts are invented; traditions are offered as facts; speculation is presented as manifest knowledge. Although one of my intentions is to blur the boundaries between scholarly and imaginative writing, I think it important that the reader is engaged in the process from a position of knowledge. Shakespeare did not, for example, leave any 'Instructions to the Actors,' as these are expounded in Chapter 2, and Nicholas Rowe did not produce a third revised edition of his 1709 biography, of the kind that appears in Chapter 3. So there is no point in going to the library to look for them. But if they had, one might imagine that this is pretty much what the end results would look like.

†

Why 'nine lives'? Every other biographer of Shakespeare has written one life, and each has sought to argue that his or her particular way of putting together of facts and traditions is the best way of interpreting the evidence. Perhaps one of them has got it right, and managed to produce a definitive, 'authorised' biography of Shakespeare. Or perhaps there are as many lives as there are biographers, since each act of biographical definition mediates fact and tradition through the labyrinthine web of speculation, and produces a new Shakespeare in every new iteration. I have provided nine lives of Shakespeare, not because that is the right number, but because there are manifestly innumerable such interpretations, and these are just a few of them. Shakespeare has many more lives than a cat, and nothing can kill his endlessly regenerating life stories. The greatest of originating story tellers, and yet the greatest of plagiarising imitators, Shakespeare himself would I think appreciate the cocktail of fact and fiction here arranged around his many lives.

I have made it clear throughout this book that in my view all biographical writing is to some degree autobiographical, always inflected by personal, ideological and subjective considerations. In which case, surely, my own attempt at recreating a new Shakespeare biography can be no exception to this rule? What is my own personal investment in this project? What are the unconscious ideological parameters framing my analysis? What is the subjective core of my interest in the many lives of William Shakespeare? If everyone creates a Shakespeare in his or her own image, what is the image in which I have created mine?

The answers to these questions lie in the pages that follow, and are for the reader to decipher. But here, by way of introduction, is my William Shakespeare. He was born into a poor family in the northerly part of England. His father was a tanner. One of his earliest childhood memories was of sitting in the corner of his father's workshop, surrounded by pungent piles of animal hides, watching his father scraping the bristles from the skin of an ox. He grew up speaking with a broad regional accent, which was softened by education and social advancement, but never entirely left him. He was a gifted, child, and despite his family's poverty, was admitted to the local grammar school on the basis of merit. He began writing poetry, and realized straight away that this, more than anything else, was what he wanted to do. Patient and strenuous attempts to develop his interest in other areas of the curriculum came to nothing, and he persistently followed only his own natural bent for literature and drama. He married young and prematurely, and produced children who always remained dear to him, though at that stage of his journey married life with Anne Hathaway in Stratford-upon-Avon was not for him. Following some trouble with the authorities, he had to leave town, and found his way to London in search of employment. He found work in the theatre and became a successful actor, but soon proved his extraordinary abilities in writing and became a dramatist. Feeling the power of his pen, writing became his means of living, and his raison d'être. Nothing else in his life mattered as much to him.

He attained wealth, fame, some measure of cultural authority from his work in the theatre. But for him true happiness lay in the exercise of that absorbing craft of writing. In time it became an obsession, in which he would forget himself, putting the real world at a distance, and losing himself in the cold snows of his dream.

He found his way, by talent and industry, into a cultural élite, a milieu that fascinated and dazzled him, but in which he never felt entirely at home, never quite himself. He was an internal émigré, adrift from his social roots, disconnected from the professional context in which he was nonetheless very successful, in exile from his own plebeian origins. Not that there was any going back to those roots in any direct, unmediated way, since he had changed too much, and his eventual return to his origins could only be accomplished by an act of self-recreation, the assumption of a different role.

At times the worlds created in his writing seemed far more real to him than the world he lived in, the characters in his plays more living than the people around him. In his writing, as on stage, he assumed a multiplicity of attitudes and opinions that were not truly his, as if he were a scientist experimenting on himself, or a man constantly recreating himself in response to occasion and to the pressure of other needs. Hoping to find for himself a real and consistent personality, and desperate to liberate himself from the clinging, shaping presence of other people, he pursued pleasure and experience to the ultimate, careless of how many people he wounded and damaged, recklessly defying the laws of God and man in the quest for absolute freedom. All these experiences he cast into the forge of his dramatic and poetic creativity, where they assumed moving and compelling forms. In his plays he provided solutions to the problems he found intractable in real life. But eventually this tension between life and art became stretched to the point of painful rupture, and his poetry burst into the beauty and violence of a tragic flowering. He himself was spent, exhausted, finished, a burnt-out case. He looked inside himself, and found an emptiness; he attained self-knowledge, only to learn that he had no self at all to speak of. He who had been everyone was no-one at all.

In a moment of Pauline ecstasy, one day on an empty road, he had his vision, the thunder and the lightning, the fall into abjection, the momentous realization of what he had been, was, and must thereafter become. He went back home to Stratford, and rejoined his family, as a new or reconstructed person, entering what was in effect a second marriage to another wife. He knew that the only thing that could fill that emptiness at the core of his being, the only thing that could give him back himself, was love: love of wife and children, love of the earth, love of God. His writing blossomed into new and happier forms, that told some of this story. In truth it became less important to him, since the centre of his gravity had shifted in favour of living and away from artifice. Everything that had delighted him in life – beauty, music, poetry, faith – merged into a new homogenous totality. Everything that had been discordant became unified; everything that had been broken became whole.

In this new life he came to regret profoundly many things he had done, and to confess them as sins: things done to others' harm, things said and written that he had only half intended, but had been the cause of pain to those who deserved better of him. He tried thereafter, in everything he did, to do, say and think harm to no-one.

He and his wife entered a new companionship, and she became a partner in all his enterprises. To be what he had been, apparently open to all experience, he had in reality shut himself off in a kind of personal closure, a sealing off of the self against the world, and especially against those who loved him. Now he was able to open himself, and to live, not wholly but to a far greater degree, in and for others. He found himself, in other words, in the costly openness of a life lived not for himself alone.

His writing accompanied him throughout this pilgrimage. It was the means of his awakening to consciousness, and the route of his social advancement. It was the instrument of his descent into the inferno of sin, and the route by which he found a way through hell to look once more upon the stars. Writing was his innocence and his experience, his pride and his passion, his heaven and his hell, his sin and his redemption. Through it he knew what it was to be in love with the world, and to arrive at a bleak disenchantment; what it was to be bound upon a wheel of fire, and what it was to be delivered into a state of grace.

My story? Of course not: who would have the temerity to compare himself to Shakespeare? Oldcastle is not the man. My Shakespeare? Yes, and as good as anybody else's. Better, in fact, since there are more of him: my Shakespeares. Nine lives for the price of one. And we begin with Shakespeare the writer. In the beginning is the word.

LIFE ONE

Shakespeare the Writer

Shakespeare is celebrated as one of the greatest, if not the greatest, of *writers* – 'above all other writers,' as Samuel Johnson described him. Today the word 'writing' is more likely to signify the noun, 'something written,' than the verb, 'the act of writing.' Everywhere in modern culture, writing is a collective and mechanised activity; a compilation of material from multiple sources, electronically processed and stored so that everyone's 'writing' looks much the same as everyone else's.

But at one time 'writing' was shorthand for 'handwriting,' and Dr. Johnson was certainly thinking of Shakespeare as a writer like himself, a man who personally placed words on a page, with a pen dipped in ink. One of the iconic representations of Shakespeare is the image of a man writing, as in his funeral monument in the chancel of Holy Trinity Church, Stratford-upon-Avon: quill pen in his right hand, expectantly poised in the air, ready to begin, and a sheet of paper held firmly under the left hand. The image dovetails with our romantic idea of the writer, physically engaged in putting words on paper, transferring thoughts and emotions from the mind, via the muscles and nerves of arm and finger, through the writing implement that makes immediate contact with the paper. One of the most frequently reproduced images from *Shakespeare in Love* is that of Joseph Fiennes as Shakespeare, sitting at a table, holding a long, elegant feather quill, staring into space, trying to think what to put down on the blank page. Biographies of Shakespeare (e.g. those by Peter Ackroyd and Bill Bryson) often prominently feature a quill on the cover illustration. Thus the instrument that signs becomes itself the visual 'signature' standing in for the writer. *Le style, c'est l'homme.*

This is writing as a physical and intellectual process, involving the whole man, a holistic relationship between mind, body and writing technology. In their Preface to the *First Folio*, Shakespeare's friends and colleagues Heminge and Condell, who must have actually observed him in the act of composition, said that in his writing 'his mind and hand went together.'[1] In such images of the writer at work, the figure is usually seen as isolated, remote from any contact with other people or with material objects. Writing is an individual action, conducted at some distance from actual living, almost a form of contemplation.

The quill pen is the defining property of the early modern writer, and the image of Shakespeare with a feathered quill is so well established in the popular imagination that it is frequently reproduced in adverts, cartoons and comedy sketches. Yet of course we have no actual knowledge of Shakespeare's writing habits. He must have used a quill, since this was the universal implement of the period for writing with ink (though they also had lead pencils), and the quill is often alluded to in the plays. But the feathers may well have been stripped off from his pens, so they didn't get in the way. Such unattractively bald objects feature in early modern pictures of quills, but never in later representations of Shakespeare the writer.

No one ever thought to describe Shakespeare engaged in the practice of writing: where he sat, when he wrote, whether he wrote alone or in company. Most frustratingly, the sheets of paper on which his plays were written have all disappeared. There are no Shakespeare manuscripts extant, as there are for other and later writers, which would enable us to trace and infer his habits of composition. We have Shakespeare's signature on legal documents; but the 'signature' we would wish to have, the name signed on manuscripts of the plays, the endorsement that would indissolubly connect the writing with the writer, is absent.

How was Shakespeare thought of as a writer during his lifetime? He is often described by those who knew him as a fluid as well as a copious writer. Ben Jonson wrote of his 'facility.'[2] Heminge and Condell said of him, 'what he thought, he uttered with that easiness, that we have scarce received from him a blot in his papers.'[3] This detail portrays Shakespeare the writer rather as Mozart the composer is depicted in Peter Schaffer's play *Amadeus*, producing perfect original drafts of music, 'with no corrections of any kind.' The perfection of literary or musical art is simply transferred, fully formed, from the mind of the genius to the receiving paper, devoid of corrections, free from blots.

Ideally, then, this is exactly the kind of manuscript we would wish to have, preserved for posterity from the ravages of time. Antique sheets of paper, suitably yellowed with age; clear strong handwriting flowing easily across the page; the author's signature, imprinting his 'hand' on the writing it has executed; the words that have become as famous as any words in any language, by that hand set down:

To be or not to be; that is the question.

No such manuscript exists. We do, on the other hand, have a specimen of Shakespeare's literary handwriting, in the form of a scene written into the collaborative play about the sixteenth century statesman and Catholic martyr, executed by Henry VIII, *Sir Thomas More*.[4] The handwriting is indeed elegant and stylish, a 'secretary hand' that flows in neat straight lines across the page, and bursts into elaborate but disciplined flourishes for the ascenders and descenders. It is a theatrical manuscript, with speech headings in the left margin, and lines ruled under each separate speech. But this is not the work of a Shakespeare who never blotted a line. On the contrary, several passages are crossed out and revised. This is the work of a writer who was thinking while writing, quickly improving on what had already been set down. This is not a writer who simply transmitted already perfected poetry on to the receiving page. Nor does this example present us with writing as the unmediated product of an individual's private vision. The MS of *Sir Thomas More* is a collaborative work, probably written largely by Anthony Munday and Henry Chettle, to which Shakespeare was obviously asked to contribute after it had been critically reviewed by the censor. Shakespeare's handwriting lies on the page, together with the hands of several others, all writing and revising in a continuous collaborative process. Here we see Shakespeare the writer putting his pen not to a pristine sheet of blank paper, but to the pages of a text already written, and already revised, by others. We see him producing writing that flows effortlessly on to the page, but is then at moments checked, recalled, cancelled and revised. We see him not necessarily, as the classic writerly image suggests, alone and isolated, withdrawn from the world, communing only with the voices of his imagination. Instead, we see him working as a professional writer within a busy, noisy and stressful environment, where writers worked together under enormous pressures of time, censorship and theatrical practicalities to get the show on the road.

The Elizabethan dramatist's workshop must have been more like the open-plan office of a modern national newspaper, than the book-lined study of a scholarly recluse. *Sir Thomas More* was a show that never did make it to the road, as it was never performed, and was clearly not a successful collaboration. But it is an invaluable document, since not only does it preserve the only specimen of Shakespeare's handwriting, other than signatures on legal documents, but it also shows us Shakespeare the writer at work, as a member of a collaborative profession.

The image of Shakespeare monumentalised in the Stratford bust will of course continue to dominate our view of Shakespeare as a writer. The quill pen will remain the staple property of Shakespeare the literary genius. Visitors to Stratford can buy their own quill pens, which may in themselves be cheap and trashy souvenirs, but are contextually ennobled with the Shakespearean ambience. No-one however is quite sure how the funeral monument acquired that pen, since it was absent from the monument's original design. When William Dugdale printed a sketch of it in his *Antiquities of Warwickshire* (1656),[5] pen and page are both notoriously absent, and the hands of the figure rest on a cushion or stuffed sack. This was the image reproduced as one of Shakespeare's portraits in Nicholas Rowe's 1709 edition of Shakespeare's works. The sack has been thought of as a reference to Shakespeare's activities as a merchant, trading in crops such as barley and animal staples such as wool, while others have proposed that it is really a 'writing-cushion.' Some time after this seventeenth century installation, the figure was altered to that of Shakespeare the writer with paper and pen. Those who seek to prove that Shakespeare of Stratford was not a writer at all, but a landlord and merchant, and that someone else wrote the works, naturally find great significance in this transmutation. Annually on Shakespeare's birthday, a new quill pen is placed in the hand of the figure on the Stratford monument, as if to reiterate that this antique tool is also a modern interpolation, and has always been retrospectively placed in the writer's hand by others.

But we can think about writing, not via the romantic image of the writer as an isolated individual genius, but rather, in a more modern sense, as a collective cultural activity taking place in the busy professional environment in which a collaborative work like *Sir Thomas More* was messily and roughly concocted. In this context the contingency of woolsack and quill should neither surprise nor discourage. Let us rather imagine Shakespeare as a writer who wrote with others, and with others around him; who combined writing with acting, theatre management, property dealing and general trading. Let us think of writing more in the modern sense as a collective and collaborative cultural activity, a practical process that Shakespeare the writer undoubtedly led, but did not accomplish alone.

Facts

We have no idea of course how Shakespeare learned to write, since we have no record of his education. Of his handwriting we have six indisputable signatures, all on legal documents. One is to the deposition in the court proceedings of the Mountjoy marriage; one to the deed of the house he bought in Blackfriars in 1613; one to the mortgage-deed on the same house, executed on the day after the purchase; and one on each of the three sheets of paper containing his will, the last endorsed with a 'By me.' A signature that may be a seventh appears on the title-page of a book by William Lambarde, now in the Folger Shakespeare Library. The handwriting in the manuscript of *Sir Thomas More* can be thought of, in Stanley Wells's words, as 'at least compatible' with Shakespeare's.[6]

We know that by 1592 he was writing for the theatre, and had achieved enough success to arouse jealous resentment among competitors. He was scathingly attacked in *Greene's Groatsworth of Wit* as an 'upstart Crow, beautified with our feathers';[7] a plagiarist who pinched other men's ideas, an actor who stole the lines of literary authors like Greene, or a parvenu who sought to emulate the cultural cachet of university-educated poets. Shakespeare thinks he is 'an absolute *Johannes Factotum*,' master of all trades, and the only contemporary playwright worth talking about: 'in his own conceit, the only Shakescene in a country.' Henry Chettle, one of the collaborators in *Sir Thomas More*, publisher and probably author of this satire, later apologised for the diatribe against 'Shakescene'/Shakespeare:

I am as sorry, as if the original fault had been my fault, because myself have seen his demeanour no less civil, than he excellent in the quality he professes: Besides, divers of worship have reported his uprightness of dealing, which argues his honesty, and his facetious grace in writing, that approves his Art.[8]

The writer and 'his Art' are closely linked. The man is of 'demeanour ... civil,' and his literary art one of a 'facetious grace in writing.' What this circumstantial evidence shows is that already, by the early 1590s, Shakespeare, despite his humble origins and lack of higher education, was recognized as a writer by other professional writers, as well as by the public who came to see his plays.

A few months later, Shakespeare entered the public domain in person as an author. On 18 April 1593, Richard Field, who was, like Shakespeare, a craftsman's son from Stratford (his father was a tanner), entered at Stationers' Hall a book entitled *Venus and Adonis*. The dedication, which is to the Earl of Southampton, is signed by 'William Shakespeare,' and scholars have considered that the state of the text suggests that the poet himself oversaw the publication. Shakespeare's other narrative poem, *Lucrece*, was registered on 9 May 1594, and appeared also without a name on the title-page, but with Shakespeare's full signature attached to a dedication to the same nobleman. These publications present Shakespeare unambiguously as a writer: signing his work, presenting it as a gift to a wealthy patron, explicitly defining himself as an author:

> Right Honourable, I know not how I shall offend in dedicating my unpolished lines to your Lordship, nor how the world will censure me for choosing so strong a prop to support so weak a burthen, only if your Honour seem but pleased, I account myself highly praised ...
>
>   Your Honour's in all duty,
>   William Shakespeare.[9]

This is from the dedication of *Venus and Adonis* to the Earl of Southampton. The dedication explains the purpose of the work, which is to 'please' the aristocratic patron. The tone is one of false modesty, natural considering the difference in station, but misleading as to the quality of the poem, which is far from 'unpolished' (the *Lucrece* dedication similarly alludes to Shakespeare's 'untutored Lines'). In the dedication to *Venus and Adonis*, Shakespeare depicts the writer metaphorically as a farmer, planting crops and hoping for a good harvest. If the poem does not please, he will 'never after ear so barren a land, for fear it yield me still so bad a harvest.' At one level, this is a conventional pastoral language routinely used by writers who never sowed a field, and concerns the relationship of poet and patron: 'if you don't like it I won't waste my time again.' In Shakespeare's case we can see his own rural and artisanal background coming through the conventional image. Here writing really is like the labour of the fields, both exacting and risky, dependent on the accidents of climate and the vagaries of weather. Like the arable farmer, the writer must scatter his seed and leave it where it falls, hoping for the blessing of a good harvest, always conscious of the possibility of failure.

There is a significant difference, from this 'writerly' perspective, between the lyric poems published under Shakespeare's name – *Venus and Adonis, Lucrece* and later the *Sonnets* – and the dramatic works, written for performance and published by others. In the poems the writing seems, at least initially, to be of a more personal and individual kind. Shakespeare appears to have been involved in their publication. Circumstantial evidence surrounding the lyric and narrative poems reveals the poet as a young man writing for a coterie of enthusiastic readers; who was annoyed at a publisher misrepresenting his work, and quick to assert his own authorial prerogative; and who formally signed and inscribed his work in the form of personal dedications. The early published texts of the plays, by contrast, did not carry Shakespeare's name. This was not unusual, since the plays were the property of the theatre company. But in 1598 the quarto editions of *Richard II* and *Love's Labour's Lost* were the first plays to exhibit his name on the title page, and later play-texts usually bore the authorial name.

In the same year Francis Meres in *Palladis Tamia* celebrated Shakespeare both as a poet and a dramatist.[10] He compares the 'mellifluous and honey-tongued Shakespeare' with Ovid for his 'Venus and Adonis, his Lucrece, his sugared sonnets among his private friends,' but also with Plautus and Seneca for his excellence 'in both kinds for the stage; for comedy, witness his Gentlemen of Verona, his Errors, his Love Labors Lost, his Love Labours Wonne, his Midsummers Night Dreame, and his Merchant of Venice ; for tragedy, his Richard the 2, Richard the 3, Henry the 4, King John, Titus Andronicus, and his Romeo and Juliet.' Other writers similarly alluded to Shakespeare as poet and playwright; but writers more closely connected with the theatre tended to praise his 'copious industry' and his talent for theatrical writing. Seven years later, thirty-six of Shakespeare's plays were collected by two of his former colleagues of the theatre, Heming and Condell and published as the 'First Folio.' The editors claimed that the publication was based on Shakespeare's 'papers.' But the First Folio is a memorial tribute to Shakespeare who died in 1616, so the author is distinctly absent from the process of publishing 'his' work.

As far as Shakespeare's plays are concerned, apart from the fragment in *Sir Thomas More*, which was clearly not one of 'his' plays, we are unlikely ever to see an authorial manuscript. Our earliest sources are the printed texts of the plays, which already lie at some distance from the author's individual hand, and already mediated by many other parties, thoroughly contaminated by the traces of others peoples' work . In the light of eternity the poised quill and the expectant paper remain forever linked, but always separate, like the figures on Keats' 'Grecian Urn.'[11] The gap between the quill pen's point and the blank paper remains, as far as Shakespearean drama is concerned, a space that appears to be empty of all but promise, but is in fact already full of other people; people who roughly interpose their bodies between us and Shakespeare, and drown out with their loud recitations the inaudible sound of his own voice.

People like us.

Tradition

Tradition, surprisingly, has virtually nothing to add to Shakespeare's reputation as a writer, as distinct from a theatre professional. The best the compilers of 'tradition' could manage was to imagine Shakespeare penning a 'bitter ballad' of scurrilous lampoon against Sir Thomas Lucy in revenge for the knight's persecution of the young man. Efforts were later made to pass off various orally recorded ballads as originals by Shakespeare. Needless to say, as poetry they are worthless, as history even more so.

Speculations

In his *Shakespeare: For All Time,* Stanley Wells provides some informed speculations about Shakespeare's habits as a writer. The manuscript of *Sir Thomas More* shows a man writing quickly, leaving out quite important details. Names are abbreviated, initial capitals missing, spelling left inconsistent. But although the writing may have been fast, it was not entirely spontaneous. Though the preface to the First Folio edition states that Shakespeare 'never blotted a line,' this writer did 'blot' some of his work, correcting three consecutive lines. Some of the misspellings indicate a change of mind, with the writer starting one word and continuing with another.

This is a careful and thoughtful writer, revising and correcting as he goes. He wrote, Wells states, with a quill pen dipped in ink. The restrictions imposed by this writing technology kept him desk-bound. Writing with a quill pen, which requires constant sharpening and a constant supply of ink, made the writer relatively immobile:

> This means he would have been more bound to a table or desk than modern writers, who have greater freedom of movement.[12]

Where would that desk have been? Certainly, Wells speculates, after Shakespeare had purchased New Place in Stratford, it would have been there:

> Can we really imagine that ... a writer who owned a splendid house in a small and relatively peaceful town in Warwickshire would not make every possible effort to spend time there? ... Shakespeare was, I suspect, our first great

literary commuter. All his contemporaries who wrote for the theatre based themselves in London. Only he had the good sense to maintain a household many miles away (p. 37).

Shakespeare must have sought such rural solitude because

> Writing is a solitary occupation. It calls for peace and quiet. Shakespeare's plays are the product of intense imaginative and intellectual activity, deeply pondered and intricately plotted. To write them he needed space for thought (p. 36).

In addition, being a very literary writer who drew directly from books, Shakespeare must have had books by him, some of them very large and bulky tomes that couldn't have been easily transported in commuter trips between Stratford and London. What all this adds up to for Wells is that within the rural retreat of New Place, Shakespeare must have had his own more removed ground of solitude:

> We know little about the contents of New Place, but my guess is that it contained a comfortable, book-lined study situated in the quietest part of the house to which Shakespeare retreated from London at every possible opportunity, and which members of the household approached at their peril when the master was at work (pp. 37–8).

Peter Ackroyd also offers a similarly detailed account of Shakespeare's habits as a writer, based on the same meagre repertoire of facts: the manuscript of *Sir Thomas More*, the quill pen, the bulky literary sources. But his Shakespeare is an entirely different kind of writer. Shakespeare wrote, he says, 'at extreme speed and intensity.'[13] This detail is revealed by the handwriting in *Sir Thomas More*, where the writer leaves some lines unfinished 'in the rapidity and restlessness of creation.' (p. 256) There is little punctuation. Ackroyd assumes that the various corroborative descriptions of Shakespeare writing with 'facility' and 'easiness' meant that he wrote at breakneck speed, and under extreme pressure of imagination. Ackroyd then describes Shakespeare at work, in an improvised 'study' that would have been 'fitted up for himself in the sequence of London lodgings that he rented.'

> It is sometimes suggested that he returned to his house in Stratford in order to compose without noise and disturbance. But this seems most unlikely. He wrote where he was, close to the theatre and close to the actors. It is doubtful if, in the *furia* of composition, noise or circumstance affected him (p. 257).

What about his books, those bulky volumes that in Stanley Wells's view must have kept him anchored to one spot? He took them with him as he shifted from one lodging to another. 'He is likely to have owned a book-chest.' He also probably kept notes in small notebooks, that could also be transported.

> He could have jotted down notes or passages that occurred to him in the course of the day; other writers have found that walking through the busy streets can materially aid inspiration (p. 257).

In both cases, what little is definitely known of Shakespeare serves as a template for the construction of two radically different images of Shakespeare as writer. In one scenario Shakespeare the writer needs peace and quiet for the prolonged and intensive labour of literary composition. He is also firmly fixed to a particular workstation, by the technical requirements of his writing implement and the size and weight of his literary sources. So he willingly forsakes the bright lights and loud noises of London for the tranquillity of Stratford. There in his big house he retreats even further to a comfortable book-lined study, maintaining some distance from the business of family life, where his poetic and dramatic imagination can operate at the right level of undistracted concentration. He writes carefully and cautiously, revising and correcting as he goes.

In the other scenario Shakespeare the writer is far more unfixed and itinerant, since he lives not in his own house in Stratford but in a sequence of rented lodgings in London. He moves easily from place to place, taking his tools of books and pens with him in a box. He stays here to be right in the thick of cultural London, close to a teeming milieu of theatres and actors and printing presses. He wanders the crowded streets, picking up ideas and images as he goes, jotting them down in little portable notebooks. As he writes, he is surrounded by the disturbances of noise and social activity, but remains independent of all distractions. A furious torrent of inspiration absorbs him, and under its influence he writes at breakneck speed.

One of these Shakespeares sounds very much like an academic, and the other very much like a professional writer. One sounds like a man who prefers the solitude of the country, the other one who is at home in the metropolis. One is a dead ringer for Stanley Wells, and the other could easily be mistaken for Peter Ackroyd. Will the real William Shakespeare please stand up?

Story: 'The Shakespeare Code'

The fictional component of *Nine Lives of William Shakespeare* begins with an exploration of the impossible, unfillable gap between the writer and the writing. Inside that gap lies whatever we can recover, or reconstruct, of the Shakespeare biography. We know that Shakespeare 'wrote' those plays and poems, and we possess the writing itself with confidence and certainty. But we have no means of knowing exactly how the writing got written, how the trick was done. We always have to place the quill pen in Shakespeare's hand ourselves. So the story of Shakespeare as a writer is a cultural mystery, and one obvious form for its exploration is the pseudo-scientific romance thriller so successfully colonized by Dan Brown's *The Da Vinci Code*. 'The Shakespeare Code' places the mystery of Shakespeare as writer in that fictional territory, and pursues one man's imaginary attempt to solve, forever, the mystery of how Shakespeare wrote. The tale becomes a fable showing how such a quest is always inevitably defeated, since writing is never solely the product of one man's pen. The story draws on an incident in the life of pre-Raphaelite poet Dante Gabriel Rossetti, who buried a manuscript volume of poems together with the corpse of his wife Lizzie, 'between her cheek and hair,' and later consented to have the poems exhumed from her grave in Highgate cemetery. 'The Shakespeare Code' demonstrates that our approach to Shakespeare's biography always starts with the here and now, and is invariably in the manner of a contemporary quest; always has to begin initially with an address to the 'afterlife' of a centuries-old reputation; and always involves the kinds of philosophical and theological difficulties inevitably entailed in 'speaking with the dead.' The whole story is of course pure invention, but Susanna Shakespeare was buried in the crypt of Holy Trinity Church, Stratford; Baldwin Brooks the bailiff did sequester goods, including books and papers that might conceivably have belonged to Shakespeare, from New Place in 1637; and the phrases 'Witty above her sex' and 'wise to salvation' are taken from the epitaph on Susanna provided by her husband Dr John Hall.

The Shakespeare Code

†

Fitfully the flashlight illuminated broken brick and slippery stone. Water from the gutters in the street above his head dripped down the lichened walls of the Victorian conduit. Beneath his feet, the stones were smooth and treacherous, so he stumbled and slid, startling a feral flurry of scurrying sewer-rats. *It has to be here somewhere*, he thought, though the tunnel seemed to end in a blank brick wall. The old map of Stratford he had used could be misleading, or the bearings of his street-level survey a degree or two off. But where else could the sewer go, if not beneath the floor of the church?

At last he saw it, an aperture no more than a foot high, into which the trickling stream of drain-water flowed and disappeared. Here the bricks were powdery with mould, and crumbled to dust at a touch, so it was the work of a minute to clear a hole big enough for a man to squeeze through.

Lying down, he shone his torch through the hole and into the darkness beyond. The solid shaft of yellow light wavered over dripping buttresses and mouldering beams, then came to rest on a collection of ancient coffins, thick with dust, and traceried with the gossamer filaments of spiders' webs.

A chill arced down his spine like an electric shock. He was staring into the crypt of Holy Trinity Church, Stratford-upon-Avon.

Good friend for Jesus sake forbear
To dig the dust enclosed here …

His heart knocking against his ribs, he pulled himself through the gap in the wall and into the burial chamber. Standing upright, he banged his head against a low-hanging beam. Careful, he said to himself, his voice sounding hoarse and unnatural in the silence of the tomb. Don't blow it now. A moment's pause to let his racing pulse slow to a more natural rhythm. Now for the coffin. Which one was it?

Patiently he flashed his torch over the tops of the coffins that cluttered the floor of the crypt. He soon located a small group of boxes, arranged on the southern side of the burial chamber, each bearing a coat of arms: 'a falcon his wings displayed argent, standing on a wreath of his colours supporting a spear gold …'

The last resting place of Shakespeare's family: his father and mother, his daughter Susanna and her husband John Hall. In the middle of the group, one coffin displayed a more elaborate decorative scheme than the others, with some decayed remains of wood-carving, and traces of gold lettering long since eroded and effaced into illegibility. This was it. The final resting place of the Bard of Avon.

Shakespeare's tomb.

He took a deep breath, and drew a crowbar from his shoulder-bag. Standing over Shakespeare's coffin, he seemed to hesitate, as if irresolute and undecided. But he knew what he was doing. Abruptly he turned aside from Shakespeare's bier, and thrust his lever under the lid of a smaller coffin that adjoined it, on the side opposite to that of his wife Anne. The mortal remains of Shakespeare's daughter, Susanna were also buried in the chancel of the church.

Witty above her sex. Wise to salvation.

The ancient wood of Susanna's coffin splintered under his levering pressure. Soon the lid could be wrenched off, revealing a damp and blackened shroud wrapping a shapeless heap of corroded limbs. Gingerly he unfolded the shroud from around the corpse's head. Motes of dust rose and hung in the yellow torchlight. Susanna grinned at him from her detached jaw. Disgust moved his stomach and clotted with bitterness in his mouth. He had expected the vacant eye-sockets, the empty noseless vomer. But what made his gorge rise was the fact that the skull still retained the dry and dusty traces of Susanna's hair.

Slowly his hand slipped down into the space between the woman's hair and the skull's cheek-bone. His fingers closed on an object, which he carefully extracted and placed in his bag. Roughly replacing the coffin lid, he retraced his steps, crawling back through the hole in the wall and into the sewer. Minutes later he re-emerged, via a manhole cover, into the Avon fog, with the air of a hero who had braved the laws of God and man to find the treasure all men desired. He shivered, partly from cold, but also with a saving remembrance of the imprecation on Shakespeare's gravestone, which perhaps covered, like comprehensive insurance, every occupant of that umbrageous sepulchre.

Forbear to dig the dust enclosed here.

†

The telephone shrilled and fragmented the silent darkness that sealed Stephen Hawker's heavy slumbers. Disorientated, he switched on the lamp, and blinded by the light, grabbed at the phone.

'Hello?'

'This is Edward Malone.'

'Edward … who?'

The voice betrayed impatience. 'Malone. From the university.'

'Edward. I'm sorry, I wasn't sure … what time is it?'

'I have something I want you to look at,' he replied, ignoring Hawker's question. 'It's important.'

'Can't it wait till morning?'

'It is morning. It's Friday, six o'clock. I'll meet you outside your lab.'

Then the line was abruptly disconnected.

Feeling he had no choice, Hawker got up and put the kettle on. Usually on a Friday he wouldn't even think about going onto campus. As he dressed and made coffee in the kitchenette of his small flat, he tried to recall what he knew about Edward Malone, to work out what he might want at that ungodly hour of the morning, and to wonder why he had ever befriended a man so manifestly unhinged.

†

Malone seemed like a fairly typical academic of the old school, his appearance neutral and nondescript. But there was something haunted about him. His specialism was Shakespeare bibliography, his work mostly scholarly editing. His lifelong obsession was a passionate belief that somewhere, some fragment of Shakespeare's authorial manuscript lay, long hidden from the light of day, awaiting discovery at his hands.

He was often away, nobody quite knew where, rooting around in libraries and archives and private collections all round the world, hunting for that lost fragment of autograph. He apparently spent some of his time in Stratford-upon-Avon, where the university had an adult education centre. Nobody else ever went there, and Stratford was in those days so hard to reach that he might just as well have been in a Buddhist monastery in Nepal. His chronic absence, and some curiosity about the true nature of his work, generated a sense of mystery, as if he were in quest of the Holy Grail, or trying to authenticate the Turin Shroud.

His preoccupations set him at odds with most of his colleagues, who had long since abandoned the search for authorial authenticity in the autograph manuscript. For most of them the author was dead, replaced by an impersonal mechanism of cultural production. Printed texts were the only 'originals.'

'Seriously, Edward,' one of them would say to him: 'no document in the world has been sought with anything like the same persistence. If a Shakespeare manuscript existed, surely it would have been found by now?'

'No fragment of Shakespeare's manuscripts has *ever* been found,' Malone would reply. 'Not a page. Not a word. Ancient manuscripts turn up all the time. They emerge from old boxes and trunks, they fall out from between the pages of old books no one has bothered to read for hundreds of years ....'

'But we're talking about *Shakespeare* ...'

'Why not? Listen. Which are the two most famous books of Western culture? That's right: the Bible, and the Complete Works of Shakespeare. The editors of the King James Bible, put together in Shakespeare's lifetime, thought they had everything they needed to compile a definitive edition of the sacred text. Since then thousands of papyri, with textual variants and additional sources, have emerged from the sands of the desert, and the KJV is just a historical curiosity.

'Yet not one tiny scrap survives of Shakespeare's autograph manuscripts, of which there must have been hundreds. And that's the most compelling proof that they didn't just disappear. If you lose a book, you assume it's mislaid. It'll turn up. Lose hundreds, and you know something strange has happened to them.

'Shakespeare's manuscripts weren't lost. They weren't destroyed. They weren't burned in the Globe fire of 1613. They're still out there. Somewhere. I'm sure of it. All I have to do is find them.'

Hawker wasn't part of Malone's circle, as he was a research scientist working on genetics in the Biology Department. But he found these loud common room altercations about lost manuscripts fascinating, and far more interesting than the saturnine taciturnity of his own colleagues, bioscientists who lived meagrely from one research grant to another, and were afraid to speak openly about their work for fear of plagiarism and poaching. These people from the English Department seemed to be talking about nothing, yet they did so with a passion for inquiry and a sincerity of interest that opened doors and widened horizons to a scientist unaccustomed to freedom of thought.

So one day, when Malone had been left alone with his thoughts, Hawker sat down opposite him. 'Speaking as a scientist,' he began, 'the lack of evidence doesn't in any way preclude the possibility that you could be right. What exactly is it you want to find? Why is it so important?'

'The fact that no Shakespeare manuscript survives,' he explained, 'means that we can never know what Shakespeare really wrote. All our evidence derives from printed texts that we know were badly copied, censored, revised, altered by actors, edited. Shakespeare probably had nothing to do with their publication. Scholars spend their lives trying to work out, from this evidence, what the manuscript contained. But it's all guesswork. They manage to conceal this from the general public, who buy their Penguin Shakespeare plays, thinking this is just what the Bard himself wrote with that famous quill pen. But it's not – or rather we don't know whether it is or not. Imagine you're a student of painting, and you're working on the Mona Lisa. But you have nothing in front of you except copies: derivative paintings by others, photographs, descriptions in words. Because Leonardo's original painting has disappeared. Maybe that thief who stole it from the Louvre in 1912 managed to fence it to the Shah of Persia, and it was never seen again. You spend your life sorting through those imitations, knowing that they are not really "it", hungering for a glimpse of the real thing, the one true original. And that, my friend, is the unenviable lot of the Shakespeare scholar.'

'How would you know if a manuscript was absolutely genuine? From the handwriting?'

'Partly. The specimens of Shakespeare handwriting – the signatures and Hand D in *Sir Thomas More* – aren't especially consistent. One would need some context, some provenance, to be absolutely sure. His signature on a manuscript. A dedication to a patron. Some personal message ....'

'Would there be clues in the place you found it?'

He paused, leaving something unsaid. 'That depends on where it was placed, and on who placed it there. But yes, I'm hoping to find clues. In the place where I hope it will be found.'

Hawker began to realise then that what he had in mind was more than the exhaustive ransacking of libraries and archives: something wild and reckless, illegal perhaps, certainly unethical. Something dangerous enough to risk peril to the body, and even more, to the sanity and health of the mind and the soul.

Then, in all innocence, Hawker had asked him the one question he should never have asked, the question that probably tipped Malone over the edge. 'Have you thought about DNA?'

Malone stared at Hawker in silence, while behind his opaque eyes the thoughts could be seen gathering, like cumulus on a far horizon. A cloud no bigger than a man's hand.

†

In the weeks that followed that initial ice-breaker, Malone and Hawker conversed frequently, in Malone's office, or in a quiet corner of the common room. He was eager to know about DNA typing and the possibilities it offered for forensic identification. Hawker explained to him how every cell in the body carries the unique genetic code like a fingerprint, and how traces of cells could be transmitted to objects in the form of a hair or a few skin cells. He wanted to know if such traces would be left on paper by a writer? The absorbency of paper would certainly, Hawker thought, capture traces of the writer who worked with it. You couldn't know whose it was, of course, unless you had a sample to compare it with. Would it also capture prints from other people who'd handled it, such as printers, editors, bibliophiles? Hawker's hunch was that each of these contacts would leave a trace, most likely at the extremities – a corner where a leaf had been turned, or on the outside pages when the MS was conveyed from place to place. The writer, however, who was in constant contact with the pages, his writing hand resting on the page, shifting downwards as each line was completed, the other hand, with fingertips outstretched, steadying the paper, would leave a primary genetic signature all over the surface.

'So that would certainly help with your identification,' Hawker explained. 'And you'd obtain a sample of Shakespeare's DNA. Of course, unless you've got one of his teeth, or a lock of his hair, you wouldn't be able to do much with it in terms of establishing identity. But you'd have strong circumstantial evidence that one person was the primary author of the manuscript. Still, wouldn't it be a remarkable thing to have a sample of that DNA? You could try and track down some Shakespeare descendant. Maybe in the future, who knows? Replication, cloning … we might create an infant Shakespeare in the lab. But not just yet … .'

†

Malone was waiting for Hawker outside the sealed door of the Biology lab. Hawker was shocked at his appearance, and scarcely recognised him. His face was chalk-white, disfigured by a bruise on his forehead and a cut over one cheek. But in himself he was elated, jubilant, triumphant even.

Hawker let them both into the deserted lab, and waited for Malone to explain himself. Slowly he drew from inside his bag it a tattered blackened object, of rectangular shape, and about an inch thick. He placed it on the bench, and sat back to watch the other's reaction.

'That's not ... is it?'

'Yes' he said, wonder and exultation striving in his voice. 'That, I think, is it. It's a sheaf of papers that I believe to be an autograph manuscript, written by William Shakespeare.'

'Where did you get it?'

'Let's just say it was buried, and has now come to light.' Hawker started to question him, but Malone cut him off. 'I don't want to be more mysterious than necessary, but it's better if you don't know too much about how I came by this. There shouldn't be any – consequences. But if there were ... you understand. Now, to business. Can you open up the pages of this manuscript to find the writing inside it? And can you test it for DNA signature?'

Hawker examined the black tablet visually, without touching it. 'I'm not sure I have the capacity to separate the pages. They're so thoroughly oxidised, almost sealed together. And I'm not sure what we'll find inside. The decay you see on the outside might well have gone right through, so there would be nothing left on the pages anyway. Maybe the British Museum ...'

'No. No-one else is to share in this, until I'm absolutely sure. This is my life's work. It's my discovery. I'm trusting you with it. Only you. Once we've established what it really is, then we can tell the world. But not before.'

'It may take a while.'

'Of course. You can do it over the weekend. There'll be no-one else around. I know you drop in to check on your experiments. Get it back to me by Sunday night.'

†

The task was intimidating, reflected Hawker as he prepared his experiment on the Saturday morning, and not just for its technical difficulty. The object he had to work on could prove to be one of the most valuable and sought-after relics in the world. By one careless movement, he could easily destroy it. He knew nothing of the object's provenance, or of how it had been obtained. For all he knew, the CID could be waiting with Malone when he met up with him.

Gradually, patiently, he did what he could to dry the manuscript so the pages could be separated. Nothing at all was visible on the blackened outer leaves, and he feared that if this was the condition of the manuscript all the way through, then he would find nothing. What grim conditions of damp and darkness had it rested in these 400 years?

At last he was able to free up the first page from its adhesion to the next. The second page was as black and featureless as its predecessor. So was the third, and the fourth, and the fifth.

Gradually, as he penetrated closer towards the centre of the manuscript, some patches of lighter hue began to appear on the pages. They became larger and brighter, but still no words appeared. It was not until he reached a point towards the end of the sheaf of papers that he could distinctly see, within a patch of clearness, shapes that were definitely letters, blurred, indecipherable, illegible, but indisputably there. A thrill of discovery arced up his spine.

Words! Shakespeare's words!

Edward had been right all along.

He worked all night in the lab, and by Sunday morning had one page from the last third of the manuscript that clearly and indisputably held lines of verse. The effect was blurred, like writing showing through the back of the paper. He fixed the page between sheets of glass, like a specimen, to keep it from disintegrating while being examined. He knew nothing of Elizabethan handwriting, so the form of the letters held no significance for him. One line at least he could almost read, and by holding a strong light over it, managed to make out the words:

You do me wrong to take me out ath graue ...

The DNA testing was more straightforward than the preparation of the manuscript for Edward's analysis, but the results proved his hypothesis false. Hawker took samples from different points in several leaves, from corners and edges and from the centres of the pages. There was indeed a strong primary signature that dominated above the rest. This must be, had to be, the DNA of the Bard himself. The Shakespeare Code. But there were no other traces of DNA. It was as if the manuscript had been handled by only one person.

However, as he sequenced the code, it became increasingly and unavoidably obvious that something was wrong. It contained a large essentially heterochromatic X chromosome. In short, this was the genetic trace of a female subject. So unless Shakespeare was really a woman, this was not his DNA.

Hawker had no explanation for these results, but was not greatly concerned. After all, he had the manuscript. Better equipment and more time would certainly reveal more of the writing. The DNA analysis was an optional extra. He held in his hands an autograph manuscript version of a Shakespeare play. Dry-mouthed with excitement, delirious from lack of sleep, he packed his findings together to take them back to their soon-to-be-world-famous discoverer.

When he rang the bell to Malone's flat, the door opened immediately, as if Edward had been standing impatiently behind it, or nervously pacing the hall like an expectant father outside a maternity ward. He stood uneasily and watched while Hawker unpacked his results and the manuscript, now a sheet of separated leaves, with the one page of visible writing isolated and framed under magnifying glass.

No minute of Hawker's life had ever felt so long, no silence ever so profound, as the stretched-out, muffled duration of Malone's long inspection. It was impossible to tell what he was thinking, or whether his reaction was one of gratification or disappointment.

'Is it not genuine?' asked Hawker.

'Oh it's genuine all right. But it's not a manuscript. It's a printed text.' He swivelled the glass frame towards Hawker. The writing had become clearer, and the fact that it was indeed a page of print, not handwriting, showed clearly. 'See how the letters are separate, not joined, and impressed into the page. It's from the First Quarto text of *King Lear*, published in 1608. There are only twelve surviving copies, so this is the thirteenth. It's an extraordinary find ... but it's not what I was looking for. And the DNA?.'

Hawker put the printout in front of him. 'This won't mean much to you. What it shows is that the text does carry the dominant genetic signature of one person. But it can't be Shakespeare. It's that of a woman.'

'Traces of anyone else?'

'No, none. It almost seems as if one person's physical presence has wiped away all traces of the others.'

Malone began to talk rather automatically around the subject, telling Hawker about the texts of *King Lear*, explaining the significance of an additional example, even in fragmentary form. His eyes kept returning to the page of text, and the line '*You do me wrong to take me out ath graue,*' which seemed to stand out from the rest, and seemed to hold a particular message for him.

Malone sat there, amongst the ruins of his dream; and gradually, out of his fragmenting consciousness, the whole story unravelled.

†

The myth that Shakespeare's manuscripts might be buried with him had long compelled the scholarly imagination. Plenty of people had been only too willing to break open the grave in Holy Trinity Church in the hope of finding something. They were restrained by both legality and piety, but mainly by a grudging respect for the curse written on the paving above the tomb. No amount of fortune and glory was worth the risk of Shakespeare emerging, like Hamlet's father from his grave, to wreak revenge on those who had unceremoniously plundered his sarcophagus.

Malone had taken a different tack. Shakespeare's plays were in his head, and if he never even bothered to publish them, why should he want to take them to the grave with him? But there was another, the person most likely to have inherited his books and papers, his daughter Susanna. She too was buried under the chancel of Stratford church, and it was her grave that Malone set out to rob.

What he found there destroyed his dream. Edward Malone was seeking an original, and he found only a copy. He was in quest of individual genius, and he found only collaboration. He was looking for authenticity, and he found only contamination.

There can be little doubt that the book had belonged to Shakespeare, but it had been handed over to another, his daughter, and it was her decomposition that had expunged from it all traces of the parent's identity. Year upon year, in the darkness and silence of the crypt, the woman and the paper had quietly mouldered together, rotting into one another in a macabre exchange of reciprocal autolysis.

†

What became of Edward Malone? He became more and more of a recluse, and was seen less and less on campus. He took early retirement, ostensibly to concentrate on his research. Then one day he just disappeared. Nobody really cared, so there were no serious inquiries as to his whereabouts. A neighbour said he'd seen him set off, late one night, with a bag over his shoulder, like a young man in an old story, going off to sea. And that was it.

Hawker revealed nothing of his secret knowledge: what he knew of Malone's obsession, of his macabre journey into the tomb, of the Shakespeare Code. Why pursue a man so resolutely determined not to be followed? Perhaps he got lost in the labyrinth of sewers that honeycomb the earth under the old town, and wanders there still. Perhaps he returned to the crypt, and for that act of hubris, fell victim to the Shakespeare curse, and never glimpsed daylight again. Perhaps he merely chose to seek out the burial ground of his idol, and there, among the ancient scattered bones, laid to rest his disenchanted head.

He left Hawker in possession of both the exhumed text, the unanswered questions released by its recovery, and a new, unwanted vocation. Hawker must have been contaminated with Malone's obsession, since nothing else could explain why he switched careers and became a Shakespeare scholar in his own right.

In that capacity he continued to brood over those tormenting, unanswerable questions. Who knows why Susanna treasured that copy of *King Lear*, and took it with her to the grave? Perhaps it was the only remnant of her father's library not seized by Baldwin Brooks the bailiff, who broke into New Place in 1637 and carried off 'divers books, boxes … and other goods of great value' in recovery of a debt. Perhaps the play told the story of Shakespeare and Susanna, in that scene where the mad old king wakes to see his banished daughter, and thinks she's one of the blessed spirits:

> *You do me wrong to take me out ath graue;*
> *Thou art a soule in blisse, but I am bound*
> *Vpon a wheele of fire, that mine owne teares*
> *Do scald like molten lead.*

Was this the tragedy of Shakespeare and his daughter? Estrangement, followed by reconciliation? Did he go to his grave believing he would be bound upon a wheel of fire? And did she go to hers, 'wise to salvation,' sure she would join her husband in celestial bliss, but hoping that her prayers might assuage her father's purgatorial pains?

Was it wrong of Malone to rob the dead of their cherished grave goods? He obviously thought so, and felt that the text's reprimand – '*You do me wrong to take me out ath graue*' – was directed at him. Hawker wasn't so sure, and felt that in extracting the book from where it had lain so long undisturbed, he had exhumed a touching and beautiful story.

But the moral of the tale had nothing to do with originality, or authenticity, or any hermetic seal binding writer to writing, paper to pen. It was a rather a fable about how, in writing, those others invariably seem to get in the way, and obtrude on the scene. They nudge the writer's elbow, and guide his pen; they talk over him, spoil his concentration, and then take his work and tamper with it. They wrest the writing from its original purpose and meaning, appropriate and amend, or even, as in this case, literally mingle themselves with its very substance in a shared corporeal decay.

But the disinterred text, whether print or manuscript, seemed to bring those dead back to life. Forth they came from the shadows of death, like the risen dead at the end of time; blind from their accustomed darkness, blinking into the light of day:

> *Where haue I bene, where am I faire day light?*

Like the old king, waking from the dark storm of madness and cruelty, into the light of his daughter's love.

In the end, it is only the text that speaks. The Shakespeare Code unlocks nothing but itself. The writing is 'not lost,' in T.S. Eliot's words, 'but requiring.' It demands a scrutiny, and prays for a blessing: '*O looke vpon me sir,*' it says, '*and hold your hands in benediction or'e me.*'

But the text that speaks, speaks for the others – Cordelia, Susanna, even Edward Malone – as well as for the writer who made them. It is the text that has their dying voice. The rest is silence.

LIFE TWO

'An Actor's Art': Shakespeare the Player

We know that Shakespeare worked as an actor, and it is usually assumed that this is how he began his career. The very few facts that record this detail render it an especially uncertain dimension of the Shakespeare biography; which is more than a little odd, considering that every word of dramatic poetry in Shakespeare's plays was written only to be repeated by actors, and every character he created was for an actor to interpret. He may well have written his plays solely and exclusively for actors, since he seems to have placed little value on publication as a significant medium for the transmission of his works. Perhaps, for him, the dramatic poetry exhausted itself in the theatre, and every word of his writing lived and died on the actor's lips and in the audience's ears.

Facts

The first source for Shakespeare as actor is also the first source for Shakespeare as writer, namely Robert Greene's *Groatsworth of Wit*, where Shakespeare was attacked for being an 'upstart' player turned playwright. The lampoon clearly indicates that Shakespeare was initially, or primarily, an actor. So when Henry Chettle, in his subsequent apology, refers to Shakespeare as 'excellent in the quality he professes,' we can assume that that 'quality' is the profession of actor; and that therefore Shakespeare must have been thought of as an actor, and apparently a very good one.

The accounts of the Treasurer of the Chamber for March 15, 1594–5 bear record of Shakespeare's having been summoned, along with Will Kempe and Burbage, as a member of the Lord Chamberlain's Company, to present two comedies before the Queen at Greenwich Palace in the Christmas season of 1594[1]:

To William Kempe, William Shakespeare & Richard Burbage, servaunts to the Lord Chamberleyne, upon the Councelles warrant date at Whitehall xvth March 1594 for twoe severall Comedies or enterludes shewed by them before her majestie in Christmas tyme laste paste ...

In the folio edition of Ben Jonson's works, attached to *Every Man in His Humour*, appears the statement: 'This Comedie was first Acted in the yeere 1598 by the then L. Chamberleyne his servants. The principal Comedians were Will. Shakespeare, Aug. Philips, Hen. Condel, Will. Slye, Will. Kempe, Ric. Burbadge, Joh. Hemings, Tho. Pope, Chr. Beeston, Joh. Dyke.'[2]

'Comedian' was a generic name for an actor, not as it is now the term for a stand-up comic, though it is to some degree ironic that the author of *King Lear* and *Macbeth* has been documented for history as a 'Comedian.' Throughout the 1590s Shakespeare was, officially and publicly, recognized as an actor. As we have seen, other contemporary references from this period are to Shakespeare as a writer, but in some sources he is identified as an actor who wrote. In *The Return from Parnassus*, performed at St John's College, Cambridge in about 1601, Will Kempe attacks plays written by university men as insufficiently theatrical, excessively academic, too concerned to show off the playwright's learning. 'Why here's our fellow Shakespeare puts them all down.'[3] Shakespeare is a 'fellow' to the actors, which may mean a number of things – companion, friend, equal, one of the gang – but certainly puts Shakespeare in the same category as the other actors. His writing was more theatrical than the literary drama of the university wits because he had the advantage of an insider knowledge of the theatre which he acquired by professional acting.

On the death of Queen Elizabeth, the Lord Chamberlain's Company became the King's Men, servants to King James I. A patent, dated 19 May 1603, authorizes the King's servants

> Lawrence Fletcher, William Shakespeare, Richard Burbage ... and the rest of their associats freely to use and exercise the arte and faculty of playing comedies, tragedies, histories, interludes, moralls, pastorals, stage-plaies, and such other like as they have already studied, or hereafter shall use or studie, as well for the recreation of our lovinge subjects, as for our solace and pleasure when we shall thinke good to see them, duringe our pleasure.[4]

At least a dozen instances are recorded in the Revels Accounts of the Company's having acted before the King. Shakespeare's name also stands first in a list of nine actors who walked in a procession on the occasion of James's entry into London, March 15, 1604, when each actor was granted four yards and a half of scarlet cloth for cloaks for the occasion.[5]

Shakespeare is also mentioned in the Ben Jonson Folio of 1616 as playing a part in *Sejanus* in 1603.[6] His name is absent, however, from the list of the King's Men when they performed *Volpone* in 1605, *The Alchemist* in 1610 and *Catiline* in 1611, omissions that have led scholars to assume that Shakespeare quit acting around 1603–4. He is identifed as an actor in his own First Folio (1623), heading a list entitled 'The Names of the Principall Actors in all these Plays.'[7] But that list is generic and retrospective. A recently discovered list of 'Players of Interludes' in the records of the royal household, dated 1607, omits

Shakespeare's name: so while Burbage, Heminges and Armin were at this time acting at court, apparently Shakespeare was not. Bate regards this as conclusive evidence that Shakespeare the actor had by this time left the stage.[8]

The most striking thing about these contemporary records and allusions is that there is no reference, apart from the list in the First Folio, to Shakespeare acting in his own plays. For evidence of this, we have to turn to what Bate calls 'unsubstantiated theatrical traditions.'[9] In fact, as I have shown, some of these traditions have very strong historical credibility. In the seventeenth century John Aubrey recorded that Shakespeare 'did act exceeding well.'[10] Aubrey's observations came from actors such as William Beeston, whose father Christopher acted with Shakespeare, and John Lacy, men who were in a position to preserve genuine theatrical history. From similar sources comes the tradition that Shakespeare's own instructions to other actors on how to play *Hamlet* were preserved by seventeenth century actors John Lowin and Joseph Taylor.[11] Nonetheless we cannot help but wish for more evidence that Shakespeare acted in the plays he wrote for actors to perform.

Rowe admitted that he had failed to discover much information about Shakespeare as an actor, other than that he played the Ghost in *Hamlet*: 'and tho' I have inquir'd, I could never meet with any further Account of him this way, than that the top of his Performance was the Ghost in his own *Hamlet*.'[12] Sir William Oldys reported that Shakespeare's brother Gilbert, himself an actor, recalled his brother having played the part of an old man, probably Adam in *As You Like It*.[13]

An epigram published in 1610 describes Shakespeare as known for playing kings:

SOME say good Will (which I, in sport, do sing)
Had'st thou not plaid some Kingly parts in sport,
Thou hadst bin a companion for a King;
And, beene a King among the meaner sort.[14]

Finally there is a story, recorded in lawyer John Manningham's diary in March 1601, and corroborated by another source, about Shakespeare beating Richard Burgess to a one-night stand in a citizen lady's bed. Although this anecdote does not specifically state that Shakespeare was himself at that time acting, or that his sexual magnetism was that of an actor rather than a writer, this seems the most likely inference:

Upon a time when [Richard] Burbage played Richard III there was a citizen grew so far in liking with him that before she went from the play she appointed him to come that night unto her by the name of Richard III. Shakespeare, overhearing their conclusion, went before, was entertained, and at his game ere Burbage came. The message being brought that Richard

III was at the door, Shakespeare caused return to be made that William the Conqueror was before Richard III.[15]

Some have assumed that Shakespeare actually pretended to be Burbage, introducing himself as Richard III, and the star-struck lady couldn't tell them apart. It seems more likely that for an amorous groupie like this, either of the two was equally a catch, and she couldn't care less which one she had.[16] So it is natural to assume that Shakespeare scored here on the basis of his charisma as an actor, perhaps performing another role in the same play, rather than as a writer. 'William the Conqueror' is of course Shakespeare himself, taunting his rival and crowing over his bedroom triumph. Jonathan Bate suggests, however, that the anecdote would have even more point, if Shakespeare had actually played the part of William the Conqueror on stage:

> There is also a strong possibility that Shakespeare, who became known for playing kingly parts on stage, took the role of William the Conqueror in a comedy called *A Pleasant Comedy of fair Em, the Miller's daughter of Manchester, with the Love of William the Conqueror.*[17]

Speculations

Most biographies of Shakespeare have surprisingly little to say about Shakespeare as an actor. Some biographers, such as Duncan-Jones and Greer, say virtually nothing at all on this point. Perhaps the interest accorded to this dimension is simply coterminous with the quantum of knowledge: little is said, because little is known. But this does not seem to apply to other areas of Shakespeare's life, where just as little is known, but speculation still runs both deep and free.

Not all dramatists are actors, and not all actors dramatists. Some great dramatists have also been actors – Molière, Harold Pinter – but many have not. It would seem a natural assumption that the person best qualified to write for the stage would be someone who knew how a dramatic text might be performed. Certainly few people would regard acting experience as any kind of *disqualification* for theatrical writing.

But the symbiotic relationship between acting and stage writing represented by Shakespeare stumbled on very rocky ground in the eighteenth century. The Enlightenment intellectuals who began to produce scholarly editions of Shakespeare's works, men like Alexander Pope and Samuel Johnson, had a very poor opinion of the acting profession to which Shakespeare belonged. They saw their editorial role as that of rescuing Shakespeare's literary texts from the damage done to them by actors and other theatre workers. Shakespeare's literary judgement was, according to Pope, compromised by his judgement as a player, since the two were dissimilar and even incompatible:

Another Cause (and no less strong than the former) may be deduced from our Author's being a *Player*, and forming himself first upon the judgments of that body of men whereof he was a member. They have ever had a Standard to themselves, upon other principles than those of *Aristotle*. As they live by the Majority they know no rule but that of pleasing the present humour and complying with the wit in fashion; a consideration which brings all their judgment to a short point. Players are just such judges of what is *right* as Taylors are of what is *graceful*. And in this view it will be but fair to allow that most of our Author's faults are less to be ascribed to his wrong judgment as a Poet than to his right judgment as a Player.[18]

For the satirist who wrote *A Groatsworth of Wit*, actors and players were quite different animals, and Shakespeare crossed a line in trying to be both. *The Return to Parnassus* reflects the opposite view, that the person best placed to write for actors would be one of them. In the eighteenth century, when the Shakespeare text was being formulated by scholars, the more literary viewpoint was the dominant one, and this anti-theatrical prejudice has remained very strong in the modern editorial tradition.

Now most of the modern biographies of Shakespeare invoked here are written by scholars who are also editors of Shakespeare. In some cases they are, or have been, in charge of major Shakespeare editions such as the Oxford Shakespeare (Stanley Wells) and the Norton Shakespeare (Stephen Greenblatt). Thus they are inheritors of the tradition inaugurated by Pope and Johnson, with its prioritizing of the literary over the dramatic text, and its distrust of the theatrical. The exact balancing of these contraries varies from biographer to biographer, and some have tried to bring their editions closer to the theatre (e.g. the Oxford Shakespeare explicitly prioritized the theatrical text). Nonetheless one cannot avoid the impression that the Shakespeare imagined by a biographer who is also an editor is less likely to be Shakespeare the actor than Shakespeare the writer, or Shakespeare the philosopher, or Shakespeare the quasi-academic.

Most biographers assume that Shakespeare began his career in the theatre as an actor, but was not an especially good one. 'He was an actor,' writes Stanley Wells, 'not, apparently, of any great distinction.' 'He was no star.'[19] Stephen Greenblatt agrees. He presents the image of Shakespeare watching Edward Alleyn play Tamburlaine:

At the sight of the performance, Shakespeare ... may have grasped, if he had not already begun to do so, that he was not likely to become one of the leading actors on the London stage.[20]

And Jonathan Bate concurs:

Shakespeare must have swiftly realised that he was never going to become a stage colossus like Alleyn or Richard Burbage, the leading player in the company he had joined himself … [21]

All three of these biographers are impatient for Shakespeare to graduate from acting to writing. Bates' narrative is the most speculative: he imagines the young Shakespeare choosing a career his father would have regarded with horror. (p. 74) In becoming an actor, he was 'going against the grain of his background and taking a very considerable financial risk.' (p. 74) Shakespeare's 'dilemma,' says Bate, was 'to make his way as a new dramatist while remaining true to his conservative heritage.' (p. 75) So here Shakespeare himself, focused on making money and driven by a hunger for respectability and a Protestant work ethic, couldn't wait to stop being an actor and start being a writer. This he was soon able to do by putting his manifest writing talents at the service of the company. 'He did have a talent for improving the scripts in his company's repertoire – and soon for writing his own' (p. 166).

Bate constructs a summary narrative linking these facts and speculations together. Shakespeare began as a player in the late 1580s, then showed he could improve scripts, and was writing successfully by 1592. When the theatres were closed, he had a go at writing non-dramatic poetry. Subsequently, when the Lord Chamberlain's company was formed, he was part of it, but more as a writer than as an actor:

> … the fragmentary evidence suggests that his own acting parts with the new company were limited. His main role was to be their in-house dramatist …
> (p. 354)

And he gave up acting altogether around 1603–4. Michael Wood endorses this view:

> … his professional career might have begun as a jobbing actor and general dogsbody … perhaps he began as an actor, who then moved on to writing as a collaborator in a team.[22]

Occasionally these biographers return to the topic of Shakespeare's work as an actor, but with the implication that acting was always subordinate to something bigger and more permanent. Bate suggests that Shakespeare persistently gravitated towards the image of the world as a stage, and life as the enacting of a series of parts, partly because he had been an actor.[23] Greenblatt imagines Shakespeare playing the Ghost in Hamlet, and hearing his own words as the voice of his dead father.[24] In these examples, a bit of acting experience has merely served to make Shakespeare into a better philosopher, a more accomplished theologian, a better writer. Acting is always a means to another end, never an end in itself.

The one modern biographer who embraces Shakespeare the actor is Peter Ackroyd. Ackroyd sees Shakespeare as an aspiring actor from the start. This is implied by the note in John Aubrey's *Lives of Eminent Men* (1696) stating that John Shakespeare was a butcher, and that his son was a butcher's boy with distinct thespian tendencies: 'I have been told heretofore by some of the neighbours that when he was a boy he exercised his father's trade ... When he killed a calf, he would doe it in a high style and make a speech.'[25] Shakespeare would have been trained in the dramatic arts of speaking and presenting at school, and must have excelled at these skills (p. 61). Greene's attack on Shakespeare as 'upstart crow' indicates that he 'had already won some acclaim for his skills as an actor' by 1592 (p. 121).

Stanley Wells correctly affirms that 'we cannot certainly identify' any of the roles he played as an actor (p. 56). The facts give us Shakespeare acting in Ben Jonson's *Every Man in His Humour* (though we don't know which part he played); in an unspecified interlude before the Queen; and according to the Folio's 'List of the Principall Actors,' in at least some of his own plays. Tradition gives us Shakespeare playing the Ghost in *Hamlet,* and Old Adam in *As You Like It.* Ackroyd however gives Shakespeare a whole CV of plays and parts, stating (always conditionally) that he 'probably' played in the *Seven Deadly Sins, A Knack to Know a Knave, Friar Bacon, Orlando Furioso, Muly Molloco* and *The Famous Victories of Henry the Fifth;* acted in Marlowe's *Jew of Malta* and *Massacre at Paris,* and in Kyd's *Spanish Tragedy;* and in his own plays, performed the role of king in *Henry VI, King John, Richard II, Henry IV* and *Cymbeline;* and that of duke in *Comedy of Errors* and *A Midsummer Night's Dream.* He also apparently played Antonio in *The Merchant of Venice,* Malvolio in *Twelfth Night* and possibly a number of unspecified female roles.

Most scholars would retort that there is no evidence at all to support these hypotheses. This is true, yet they are not in themselves impossible or even improbable. They can no more be disproved than they can be proved. Ackroyd goes on to point out, correctly, that according to the record, Shakespeare 'remained an actor for more than twenty years' (p. 218). He must have trained and kept in training as an actor: exercising the body, being able to fence, dance, sing as well as move and deliver verse (p. 219). Since he played kings, he would most likely have possessed 'an authoritative and even regal bearing with resonant voice.' If he played old men like Adam, he would have 'impersonated dignity and old age.' He rarely played comic roles, might have doubled two or three minor parts, but probably assumed the functions of chorus and epilogue when required.

Generations of actors have testified to the user-friendliness, for their purposes, of Shakespeare's theatrical language. As Ackroyd says, his words are 'attuned to the movement of the human voice, as if Shakespeare could hear what he was writing down' (p. 250). The stagecraft of the plays has also been almost universally admired: 'There has never been a more professional or accomplished master of all the devices of the stage' (p. 250). Shakespeare also knew exactly how to communicate with an audience through language and gesture: 'he was in intimate communion with the audience' (p. 250). He

seems to have been expert enough to train other actors. The few references
to his acting that survive testify to his excellence in the craft. Though he was
described, towards the end of the seventeenth century, as 'a better Poet than a
Player,' 'Yet,' writes Ackroyd,

> He was fully employed by the most important theatrical company of his
> generation, acting for more than twenty years in parts large and small. He
> must, if nothing else, have been a resourceful actor (p. 221).

Though most biographers are confident that Shakespeare did not excel as an
actor, all the evidence actually points in the opposite direction. He was well-
known as an actor by 1592. Official records of the court and royal household
recognize Shakespeare as an actor, and nothing else, from 1594 to 1603. He
acted in the plays of theatrical giant Ben Jonson, and according to the Folio, in
his own. Henry Chettle praised him as 'excellent in the quality he professes,'
and John Aubrey wrote that 'he acted exceeding well.' He was sufficiently
accomplished and knowledgeable as an actor to train other actors in his craft.

We have to ask why anyone should feel any reluctance at all in recognising
acting as a consistent core activity of Shakespeare's theatrical life, one that ran
in parallel with his writing for the stage. Some cannot see how he had time to
do it all. Some think he gravitated towards writing because he perceived that
there, not in performance, lay his own potential greatness. But underlying
many biographical observations lies the unconscious assumption that this
greatest of all writers, who plumbed the depths of human emotion and scaled
the heights of poetic truth, should not, at the same time, have been that most
superficial and dissimulating of creatures, a player.

Yet that is exactly what he was, and any attempt to minimize the importance
of this dimension to his career flies in the face of the evidence. In one of the
surviving copies of the First Folio appear some manuscript annotations to the
list of 'Principal Actors,' which indicate that the writer had seen some of them
perform, or heard about their performances from others. Whoever owned the
book was therefore jotting notes in it not very long after its publication in 1623.
Next to Shakespeare's name is written the words 'leasse for making.'[26] Much
has been made of this cryptic phrase. 'Making' is writing, and the dramatist
was known as a 'play-maker.' But why 'leasse,' meaning presumably 'less' or
'least'? Jonathan Bate suggests that the word might actually be 'ceast' or 'beast,'
meaning 'ceased' or 'best.'[27] If 'ceased' then it means Shakespeare 'ceased
[acting] for making,' gave up acting in favour of writing. If 'best,' then he was
being acknowledged as a better poet – 'best for making' – than he was a player.
Both readings would support Bate's own version of Shakespeare: he was better
as a writer than as an actor, and he gave up acting for writing.

But to most readers the note says, quite unmistakably, 'Leasse for making.'
The obvious literal reading – that this actor was 'less for making,' less well-
known for writing than for acting – doesn't feature in Bates's list of options at

all. If it does say 'less,' or 'least for making,' he says, then it must mean that of Shakespeare's dual professions, the one he did 'least' was acting, perhaps to make room for more 'making.' Clearly these are perverse interpretations of a phrase that seems much more likely to mean the opposite of what Bate wants it to mean: that to one very early reader of the First Folio, Shakespeare was 'less for making,' better known as an actor than as a writer, better at being an actor than a writer.

There is therefore sufficient evidence to state conclusively that Shakespeare was both actor and writer. What is missing from the record is any definite explanation of the relationship between these two professions. The evidence seems for the most part to run along two separate channels. It is this hiatus that generates so much free speculation about how Shakespeare the writer and Shakespeare the actor co-existed; persuades scholars to define Shakespeare as categorically one thing or the other; and has even enabled some scholars who genuinely doubt Shakespeare's authorship of the plays to suppose that the actor of Stratford was not the writer of Shakespeare's poems and plays at all.

The interpretative options sampled above are reasonably clear. Shakespeare was either a talented actor who turned to writing, discovered that he was much better at it, and for that reason switched to writing and withdrew from acting; or he was a mediocre actor who simply couldn't wait to change his primary activity to writing. But neither of these polarized positions necessarily follows from the documentary record. It is abundantly clear that Shakespeare was celebrated as an actor, and regarded by his contemporaries as both player and poet; and the works themselves testify to an extraordinary facility and resource-fulness in theatrical writing and stagecraft, normally attainable only by one who has worked inside the theatre as actor, director or *dramaturg*. Should we not therefore accept that in Shakespeare, acting and stage writing went hand in hand, and that his career represents the most perfect symbiosis of the two discrete but closely interlaced vocations?

As the preceding discussion demonstrates, the problem here arises not from any real incompatibility between the actor and the theatre-poet, but from the difficulty literary biographers experience in seeing the two as naturally integrated. In their collective view writing is a deeply introverted activity, requiring detachment, withdrawal, even a certain reclusiveness; while acting is an extrovert craft, demanding public display, externality, showiness. Yet it is surely clear that Shakespeare demonstrated the characteristics of both these types. Stephen Greenblatt writes of him as both a 'very public man' and a 'very private man.'[28] The public man was an 'actor onstage, a successful playwright, a celebrated poet'; and the private man 'a man who could be trusted with secrets, a writer who keeps his intimate affairs to himself and subtly encodes all references to others.' In Greenblatt's view this constituted a 'double life' of paradox and contradiction, of 'public performance' and 'absolute discretion.' The co-existence of public and private can only be understood as profound self-division. Greenblatt clearly recognizes that Shakespeare was both: but he cannot rid himself of the prejudice that the two types are fundamentally dissimilar and difficult to reconcile with one another.

Let us imagine a Shakespeare who entered the theatre as an actor, acted with some of the foremost players of his day; and enjoyed a long and successful dramatic career, a Shakespeare who began theatrical writing with no sense at all that these were discrete or incompatible activities; a Shakespeare who carried his rich and varied acting experience into his writing, heart and soul, and produced the most wholly theatrical body of work ever produced, a corpus of plays universally celebrated for their stagecraft and performability. This Shakespeare wrote with the theatre in his blood and in his bones, penning every line for its rhetorical force and dramatic impact, plotting every scene for its dramatic ingenuity as well as its poetic beauty and truth. He continued to act, in his own plays and those of others, thus refining his craft and deepening the theatricality of his writing. And he was sufficiently adept and intelligent in the understanding of his actor's craft that he was able to instruct other actors, the young players of his company, and even the world-leading professionals who were his peers. Generations later, actors were able to recall his directions, passed down from father to son, so practical and useful did they prove, even for a very different kind of theatre and different methods of acting.

This Shakespeare was a born actor, and never ceased to be one. One of the tributes published in the First Folio sees his life as a performance, his death as an exit and the republication of his work as a re-entrance onto the stage of life. The perfect model for Shakespeare's life is to be found in 'An Actor's Art':[29]

> WEE wondred (Shake-speare) that thou went'st so soone
> From the Worlds-Stage, to the Graves-Tyring-roome.
> Wee thought thee dead, but this thy printed worth,
> Tels thy Spectators, that thou went'st but forth
> To enter with applause. An Actors Art,
> Can dye, and live, to acte a second part.
> That's but an Exit of Mortalitie;
> This, a Re-entrance to a Plaudite.

Memoir: 'Master Shakespeare's Instructions to the Actors'

This imaginative piece starts from the tradition that Shakespeare taught stage-craft to other actors, and that some of his advice was preserved by actors John Lowin and Joseph Taylor and handed down to posterity. The theory of acting is taken from Hamlet's advice to the Players in *Hamlet, Prince of Denmark* and put back into Shakespeare's mouth, so the story was partly written by Shakespeare himself. The attribution of these ideas to Shakespeare is, however, critically controversial. The story is informed by something that rarely makes its way into biographical speculation, a knowledge of practical drama, and of the processes involved in rehearsing a text for performance. This Shakespeare is obviously rather too knowledgeable about Stanislavski and Artaud and Brecht, and surprisingly familiar with modern methods of theatre training. But those speeches in *Hamlet,* and everything else I have said in this chapter about Shakespeare as an actor, demonstrate conclusively that theatre 'praxis' (Bertolt Brecht's term for a theoretically-informed practice) lay at the heart of the Shakespearean project. All Shakespeare quotations in these notes are taken from *The Complete Works of William Shakespeare* (London: Harper Collins, 1994) (Alexander Text).

Master Shakespeare's Instructions to the Actors

He was smaller in the flesh than he appeared when on stage. Used to seeing him play the Ghost in his *Tragedy of Hamlet Prince of Denmark*, I'd taken away from the theatre an impression of someone larger than life, aggrandized by the charisma of spectrality, and of a voice tumultuous, immense, rich with the pain of separation, deep with the anguish of betrayal. Offstage he was a surprisingly small man, with a shy smile and a habit of rubbing his bald head, as if still feeling for some long-vanished luxuriance of hair. He spoke deliberately but quietly, not projecting his voice, so that others drew nearer to hear him.

We were there at the Globe to receive direction from Master Shakespeare in the parts we were hired to play, my friend John Lowin and I, since the company had lost two members to another theatre, and the gaps in the casting had to be repaired. We had conned the parts of the Players who come to the royal castle of Denmark in *The Tragedy of Hamlet Prince of Denmark* and play an interlude before the King and Queen. The parts seemed straightforward to us, and we had quickly learned the fustian stuff written out for them. But we were soon to learn that for Shakespeare nothing was entirely straightforward.

We were both nervous, though John covered his anxiety with braggadocio, since we lacked the experience and professional distinction of the Lord Chamberlain's Men. We had played bit parts in many a comedy and tragedy enacted in inn yards and village halls, up and down the country, but we had little acquaintance with the London stage, and none with these celebrated players who strutted and fretted their hour upon it. Good report must have reached Master Shakespeare of our abilities, or we would not have found ourselves standing before him, here in this famous playhouse, hoping to play among his company, the best actors in the world. Shakespeare seemed to sense something of this apprehension, for he spoke to us kindly, and with encouragement in his voice.

'We'll have a speech straight,' he said to John. 'Come, give us a taste of your quality. Come, a passionate speech.'

'What speech, my master?' Lowin replied, stepping up onto the stage.

'Give us – Aeneas' tale to Dido, of the fall of Troy. I heard you play once in that piece. D'ye recall it now – when he speaks of Priam's slaughter?'

John assumed a heroic position, took in a breath, and began.

'The rugged Pyrrhus, he whose sable arms,
Black as his purpose, did the night resemble
When he lay couched in the ominous horse,
Hath now this dread and black complexion smear'd
With heraldry more dismal …

'And thus o'er-sized with coagulate gore,
With eyes like carbuncles, the hellish Pyrrhus

Old grandsire Priam seeks. Anon he finds him
Striking too short at Greeks; his antique sword,
Rebellious to his arm, lies where it falls,
Repugnant to command: unequal match'd,
Pyrrhus at Priam drives; in rage strikes wide;
But with the whiff and wind of his fell sword
The unnerved father falls. Then senseless Ilium,
Seeming to feel this blow, with flaming top
Stoops to his base, and with a hideous crash
Takes prisoner Pyrrhus' ear: for, lo! his sword,
Which was declining on the milky head
Of reverend Priam, seem'd i' the air to stick ...

'And never did the Cyclops' hammers fall
On Mars's armour forged for proof eterne
With less remorse than Pyrrhus' bleeding sword
Now falls on Priam.
Out, out, thou strumpet, Fortune! All you gods,
In general synod take away her power;
Break all the spokes and fellies from her wheel,
And bowl the round nave down the hill of heaven,
As low as to the fiends!'

He ran through the speech without mistaking a word, and with a natural confidence that seemed to root him to the stage. His strong tenor voice rang through the galleries. For every image in the speech, he had a corresponding gesture. When Pyrrhus lay 'couched in the ominous horse,' he bent his knees almost to the ground, and squatted in a cramped crouch; when 'Pyrrhus at Priam drives,' he swung an invisible sword in whistling circles through the wincing air. He mimed the fall of Troy, as if he felt its high towers collapsing through the ruin of his own body, the flames of its destruction flickering at his feet. For the slaughter of Priam he struck and held so long and so pregnant a pause, that my heart was in my mouth to feel its terrible end, and then, at last, *down* his phantom weapon fell on the defenceless head of the poor weak old man: 'Pyrrhus' bleeding sword now *falls* on Priam.' He raised his hands to heaven in bootless prayer for mercy, where none could be expected, and his remonstrance against the fates seemed to speak for every man crossed by destiny.

In truth I had almost forgot where we were, and now turned to Master Shakespeare to observe the effect the speech had had on him. He sat looking at the floor, his head cradled in his hands. But when he raised his eyes, it was something of a weary expression that met us.

'An honest method,' he conceded, to my relief. 'But,' he continued, 'such a method will not serve you here. Now you must unlearn everything you have been taught. Everything. All these tricks and mannerisms and affectations of the hands and voice. All this ranting and posturing and bellowing at the groundlings. You will learn to be my kind of actor. If,' he added unnecessarily, 'you wish to act in my play.'

Shakespeare's training methods were like nothing we had ever encountered. For a good hour he put us through physical exercises, like horses or hunting dogs, regimens of movement designed to relax the muscles and render the body supple and versatile. He had us bending and stretching, standing still and shaking our hands loose at the wrists, kicking our feet to loosen the ankles. He had us lying on the stage, eyes closed, breathing slowly, till I well nigh fell asleep where I lay. He had us exercising our voices by humming and growling and singing, our faces by puckering and scowling and girning, and our midriffs by alternating contractions of tension with surrenders of relaxation. He had us standing and facing one another with the instruction to copy exactly every action and gesture of the other, so each of us was a mirror-image to our fellow; leading each other blindfold around the stage; and even falling to be caught into one another's arms.

We understood nothing of this strange method, or of its intended effect, but the changes induced in our physical condition were undeniable. We both felt lighter, more agile, our bodies fluid and flexible. Only after the completion of this programme did we come to speak any words. For the rest of the morning we worked with Shakespeare through Aeneas' tale to Dido. With immense patience he explained to us exactly how the lines should be delivered, how the actor should speak them and how he should use his body, face and voice.

Under Shakespeare's training, everything we had been taught seemed merely conventional, a set of empty gestures anyone could learn and put into practice with a loud voice and a commanding figure. He taught us how to centre emotion in the body, so its expression would not depend on exterior gestures, but show naturally from the face and figure, as warmth flows from a fire, or as leaves spring from a tree. He showed us how to trust the poet's language, to express a feeling or describe a scene, so the actor should not try to duplicate what the verse had already embodied.

'Understand,' he explained to John, 'You are not Pyrrhus, so there is no need to imitate Pyrrhus's actions and gestures. You are Aeneas, narrating the story of Troy to Dido: a man telling a tale. And yet you are not Pyrrhus, but John Lowin, a player, standing here on the stage of the Globe, by the riding Thames, on a raw foggy spring morning. You must feel these characters, Pyrrhus, Aeneas, John, together at the same time, in your body; and you must understand all these states, the warrior, the narrator, the player, all at the same time in your mind. So John must speak like Aeneas, but he will not be Aeneas, but John speaking. Aeneas will describe Pyrrhus, but he will not be Pyrrhus, but Aeneas speaking. Aeneas will feel grief for Priam and Hecuba, but that sorrow will not be John's sorrow, for he but plays it. You must be Pyrrhus and Aeneas and John. You must be temperate and furious, loyal and neutral, murderous and sorrowful and detached, all in a moment.'

Then John went at the speech again, and the effect was incredible. He spoke softly, where before he had ranted aloud, and yet the suffering and the violence and the ruin of Troy came alive in his voice as it had never done before. He kept his gestures small and controlled, alluding to the grand tragic violence of his theme, but not trying to represent it physically to his hearers. The emotion was all within, inside the story he told, so we observed the far-off tragedy up close, bright and clear as an image in a mirror, and yet also immeasurably distant. The emotion was inside the tale and inside the teller, and compelled the hearer all the more that it came from John Lowin, an actor standing alone on a bare stage in London, embodied as our own hands and limbs, solid as the planks of the stage he stood on, yet transfigured by a light as real and invisible as the impalpable air we breathed.

All the grandiose and extravagant and exaggerated gestures he had formerly used I could see now as mere hyperbole, like a man betraying his uncertainty by raising his voice. Never before had I seen and heard and felt the rage of Pyrrhus, the vulnerability of Priam, the despair of Hecuba, as I felt in that performance. The salt drops that fretted his cheeks were no crocodile tears artificially induced for a mere show of grief, but as real as if Priam were his own father. His voice was broken with emotion, but this was no forcing of the actor's soul to a prescribed routine, but rather his whole function as an actor suiting perfectly, with apt and fitting forms, the lineaments of his own conception. It was if a man could stand on a stage, and bring his dreams to life.

'You see?,' Shakespeare said to me softly, and with one of his rare smiles, 'What's Hecuba to him, or he to Hecuba? Yet your friend has turn'd his colour, and there are tears in's eyes.'

Suddenly I saw John take a few paces backwards upon the stage, as if making room for one greater than himself. I became aware of another man standing behind me and talking across my head to Shakespeare. With a shock of recognition, I realized it was Burbage, Richard Burbage, Shakespeare's fellow and friend. We had watched him play great roles like Richard III, and held him in awe above all other actors. Here he was, the legendary Roscius of his day, ready to play the lead in *Hamlet*. He jumped up onto the platform for a run-through of his part. John quickly vacated his space on the stage.

This was truly the beginning of the day's entertainment for us, as we slid along a bench in one of the galleries to watch the great Burbage perform. He delivered Hamlet's speech following the departure of the Ghost, 'Oh, all you hosts of heaven!' We were watching the greatest player of our generation, and we hung on his every word. He had a presence that thrilled the very air with weight and dignity, and a voice of such power that the very pillars of the stage shook at the sound, like the door posts of the Temple in Ezekiel's vision.

Yet he had evidently studied in the same school in which we had learned our meagre theatrical craft, for he was equally prone to tear a passion to tatters, and to add to the recitation superfluous gestures that a man might play. Burbage was known as a kind of modern Proteus, whose very being would disappear into the role he was playing. He had all the parts of an excellent actor, animating his words with speaking, and his speech with action. But this method was clearly not what Shakespeare wanted, and he proceeded to subject the great Burbage to the same training regime he had visited on us. In sharp contrast to the patience he had exercised in schooling us, he became almost angry with his fellow-actor, as if believing he should know better.

'Speak the speech, I pray you,' he said to Burbage, 'as I pronounced it to you, trippingly on the tongue: for if you mouth it, I had as lief the town crier spoke my lines. Nor do not saw the air too much with your hand, thus, but use all gently; for in the very torrent, tempest, and, as I may say, the whirlwind of passion, you must acquire and beget a temperance that may give it smoothness.'

'I warrant your honour,' replied Burbage with a biting sarcasm. But Shakespeare was in full flood of remonstrance, and like the very tide unstoppable.

'Be not too tame neither, but let your own discretion be your tutor: suit the action to the word, the word to the action; with this special observance, that you o'erstep not the modesty of nature: for anything so overdone is from the purpose of playing, whose end, both at the first and now, was and is, to hold, as 'twere, the mirror up to nature; to show virtue her own feature, scorn her own image, and the very age and body of the time his form and pressure.'

Then without warning or preamble, Shakespeare leapt onto the stage, and launched himself into the same speech; and in that moment, for me, everything fell into place. Here was a poet who was first and foremost an actor. His rendering of the speech was masterful, compelling, brilliant. He called upon the hosts of heaven with the true voice of desperation, wounded humanity crying out against the world's injustice. He bid his heart hold, in accents so piercing that we could almost hear its beating. His pity for the Ghost seemed drawn from a deep well of emotional memory, as if it were some personal grief on which the actor was able to draw.

Yet never did I see Shakespeare try to lose himself in the role. Though the passion of vengeance rang to the rafters, when Hamlet fumbled for his tablet to note down what he had seen and heard, I saw the Prince, but I also glimpsed, within the illusion, Shakespeare the theatre poet, jotting down the moment of emotion, to keep it exactly and authentically remembered. And when the speech is signed with the Prince's vow of vengeance – 'Now to my word' – it was the word of Shakespeare's work that came alive in the voice of the actor. The Prince's word, his sacred oath of vengeance, and the poet's word, that he would keep faith with the holiness of truth.

I saw everything, all at once, in a single moment. Everything was separate, discrete; yet everything came together. The one and the many; the word and the action. The rough stage of the Globe, and the turreted ramparts of Elsinore. The brown sunshine of London, and the cold black night of Denmark. I saw the Prince and the player; the writer and the actor; the world and the word, folded into one single figure that leapt and flickered as a living flame. For one brief, enthralling moment, it was there. Then things started to fall back into their usual places, and it was gone. But for the duration of that moment, short as a man's life, and long as all eternity, I had seen it; I had seen it, with my own eyes.

LIFE THREE

Shakespeare the Butcher Boy

†

Shakespeare ended his days as a successful writer and a wealthy man. He had acted before monarchs, and established a reputation as a dramatist that was already spreading beyond his native shores. But how did he begin?

People have found it difficult to believe that he may have started life as the son of a small-town butcher, spent his early years slaughtering animals, and only left Stratford because he was caught poaching deer in the park of a local landowner. Yet there is a little factual evidence suggesting this, and a strong current of tradition that affirms it.

The idea that John Shakespeare was a butcher, and that his son worked in the business, assisting in the slaughtering of animals, was set out in John Aubrey's *Lives of Eminent Men* (1696). According to Aubrey's notes, John Shakespeare was a butcher, and his son a butcher's boy:

> I have been told heretofore by some of the neighbours that when he was a boy he exercised his father's trade … When he killed a calf, he would doe it in a high style and make a speech. There was at that time another butcher's son in this towne, that was held not at all inferior to him for a naturall wit, his acquaintance, and coetanean, but dyed young.[1]

The story is corroborated from another early source. It appears in a letter of 1693, written by a Mr. Dowdall, who had visited Stratford, and was told by the elderly parish clerk that 'this Shakespeare was formerly in this town bound apprentice to a butcher; but that he ran from his master to London, and then was received into the playhouse as a serviture, and by this means had the opportunity to be what he afterwards proved.'[2]

The tales of Shakespeare the butcher boy and poacher have not, however, proved a very popular explanation of the young Shakespeare's formative years.

Facts

First of all, was John Shakespeare a butcher? He was fairly typical of his time in having a finger in a number of economic pies. The records show that he was a glover. He is mentioned in various historical documents as a glover: when he was sued for £8 in 1556, and when he set his mark on a bond in 1592. An early piece of tradition, dating to *c.* 1657, places John Shakespeare in his glover's shop, a 'merry-cheeked old man' who spoke jovially of his famous son as someone he could always crack a joke with.[3]

But he is also identified in the same records as a farmer ('*agricola*'), a dealer in wool and a tanner. He is described in records of 1573 and 1578 as a 'whyttawer,' one who prepared the hides of deer, calves and sheep to make white leather.[4] A man who made his living from farming, and from processing and selling animal skins and wool, might also have slaughtered and skinned and fleeced animals he himself reared. For his eldest son to assist him in his work would have been the most natural thing in the world.

We cannot say for certain that John Shakespeare was a butcher, or that his son slaughtered animals in his youth. These factual details do however point us towards a particular view of William Shakespeare's origins, which is that they were rural and bucolic, having to do with field and cattle-market; and that they involved the rearing and exploitation of animals, which were slaughtered for their meat and for their skins. It places him in a peasant environment, where agricultural divisions of labour were not yet well established. It locates him in a context of hard and unpleasant labour that entailed what many people today would think of as extreme cruelty to animals.

Tradition

The connection with animals also colours popular explanations of how Shakespeare came to leave Stratford and set up in London as some kind of theatre professional. This tradition shows Shakespeare still slaughtering beasts, but this time as a poacher rather than a butcher. The story that he was caught poaching deer by Stratford landowner Sir Thomas Lucy, and had to flee to London to escape prosecution, first appears in some notes written by Oxford clergyman Richard Davies, around 1688:[5]

Shakespeare was much given to all unluckiness in stealing venison and rabbits, particularly from Sir — Lucy who oft had him whipped and sometimes imprisoned and at last made him fly his native country to his great advancement.

It was also narrated in Rowe's *Some Account of the Life &c. of Mr. William Shakespear.*

> He had, by a Misfortune common enough to young Fellows, fallen into ill Company; and amongst them, some that made a frequent practice of Deer-stealing, engag'd him with them more than once in robbing a Park that belong'd to Sir Thomas Lucy of Cherlecot, near Stratford. For this he was prosecuted by that Gentleman, as he thought, somewhat too severely; and in order to revenge that ill Usage, he made a Ballad upon him. And tho' this, probably the first Essay of his Poetry, be lost, yet it is said to have been so very bitter, that it redoubled the Prosecution against him to that degree, that he was oblig'd to leave his Business and Family in Warwickshire, for some time, and shelter himself in London.[6]

Thus the story begins with these two independent accounts, and appears in two other later sources dating from the eighteenth century. In each account the writer alludes to oral sources, which of course now cannot be checked and verified. It is therefore generally classified as 'tradition' rather than fact, since it has no earlier authentication, is not corroborated by other evidence, and no legal documents can be produced to prove it really happened.

Speculation

The modern view of such traditions is that they are little different from myths and legends. Samuel Schoenbaum, one of the most distinguished of modern Shakespeare biographers, prefaced the abridged edition of his *William Shakespeare: a Documentary Life* with this description of his work:

> The book remains a documentary life. In this respect it differs from most of the innumerable popular biographies of Shakespeare that augment the facts with speculation or imaginative reconstruction or interpretative criticism of the plays and poems.[7]

Schoenbaum claimed to be restricting his sources to 'the records.' Anything else is imagination and interpretation, legend and myth. For instance he refused to accept any of the evidence characterizing Shakespeare as a butcher boy, believing its source to be suspect and its content incredible:

> The seventeenth-century gossip John Aubrey... reports that John Shakespeare was a butcher, but this is unlikely... Although Aubrey was in touch with local Stratford tradition, his confusion here runs deep ... the picture of a poetical prodigy moved to extempore effusions in the shambles is sufficiently ludicrous ... Aubrey's anecdote, however, belongs not to the biographical

record proper but to the mythos: that accretion of legend and lore which comes to surround the names of famous men.[8]

Schoenbaum belittles Aubrey as a mere gossip columnist, who may have been closer to Shakespeare's historical moment than we are, but nonetheless transmitted inaccurate and misleading biographical material. It is impossible to believe the image of the young Shakespeare practising rhetoric while slaughtering livestock. This kind of material, Schoenbaum holds, derives not lineally from historical fact but backwards from invented tradition. If you juxtapose the world's greatest writer with the idea that his father was a butcher, the inevitable result is grotesque incongruity. Poetry and butchering? Literary greatness in a slaughterhouse? To suppose this is to suppose the absurd: 'Genius will out,' Schoenbaum comments, ironically and dismissively: 'even from the mouths of butcher boys' (p. 74); meaning, of course, that no butcher boy could ever be a genius.

Schoenbaum insists that John Shakespeare cannot possibly have been a butcher, because he was a glover who 'served out his apprenticeship,' and indeed probably 'undertook an apprenticeship of at least seven years.' His son William would also have served the same seven-year apprenticeship. Nor could he have mixed trades that were legally kept separate: 'stringent regulations governing the wholesomeness of meat kept the two occupations separate' (p. 14), 'Glovers ... were restrained from looking after their own slaughtering' (p. 60).

Here Schoenbaum appears to be placing a barrier of solid historical facts between 'Shakespeare and Son' and the unpleasant trade of butchering. Clearly for him it is preferable to think of Shakespeare's father as a respectable tradesman who served his apprenticeship and then worked in fine leather, a craftsman or artisan, rather than a mere tradesman, or even worse a slaughterman who slit the throats of squealing pigs and bleating calves. That merry-cheeked old man, standing in a provincial shop full of fine leather gloves, provides a safe and respectable haven for Shakespeare's youth. Here Schoenbaum claims as fact what turns out to be more like prejudice. While claiming to disperse the gossip and rumour of tradition, and replace it with hard solid fact, he in fact weaves the facts together with inventions of his own. He does this with the confidence of academic authority, convinced that his critical and sceptical analysis of the historical records is much more substantial than some of the records he is analysing.

In fact, however, there is no evidence whatsoever that either John or William served any kind of apprenticeship; and much evidence that John Shakespeare did not restrict himself to one trade. Schoenbaum does not quote the regulations he cites as keeping trades separate, but refers to an old Shakespeare biography, *Shakespeare's Family and Friends* (1911) as a reliable source of historical evidence. This earlier book mentions sixteenth century legislation that sought to maintain divisions of labour between trades such as skinning, butchery, tanning and working in leather. The existence of laws on the statute book is taken as evidence that they were scrupulously adhered to. Yet those laws existed precisely because people worked across different trades, resulting in a long history of competition and mutual recrimination between the craft guilds. And if John Shakespeare had scrupulously adhered to the laws of the land, he would have stuck to his trade of glove-making, and not dealt in wool, or lent money at interest, and got into trouble with the law quite so often.

For Schoenbaum the tale of Shakespeare the poacher is also very definitely tradition, not fact:

> The story of Shakespeare the Deerslayer ... is a picturesque relation deriving, one expects, from local Stratford lore (p. 78).

Although 'the essential story of poaching, capture, prosecution and flight has come down in four separate versions' (p. 103), all four are dismissed as 'presumably deriving from Stratford gossip of the late seventeenth century.'

It could, on the other hand, be argued that Stratford gossip of the late seventeenth century, as a form of oral history, has a definite place in the historical record. Most biographers grudgingly accept that legends often have some basis in truth, and *The Merry Wives of Windsor*, with its deer-stealing allusions and its skits against the Lucy family, would seem to be corroborative evidence of a fairly direct kind. Why is Schoenbaum so dead-set against this evidence? There is something else here making it difficult for him to countenance the possibility that Shakespeare did in fact get into trouble with the authorities for poaching venison, or to accept that, even if he did, the episode could have been any more than a bit of juvenile delinquency:

> Even if these legends embroider, however fancifully, a genuine escapade, they describe sports and recreation, not the serious occupations of life (p. 109).

Why? Shakespeare's family was at times poor, and his father dealt in leather goods. Killing deer for food, or obtaining the animal skins that were essential to the Shakespeare family's livelihood, would seem pretty central to the 'serious occupations of life' for such people. To see these activities as merely matters of sport and pastime reveals a certain patrician prejudice that prevents the scholar him from seeing Shakespeare in this transgressive and plebeian context.

†

So little credence is given to the stories of Shakespeare reciting poetry while slaughtering, and being arrested as a poacher, not in my view because they are inherently improbable, but because academic critics and biographers simply cannot imagine so close an intimacy between intellectual and physical labours. Speaking of the memorial bust of Shakespeare in Holy Trinity Church, Stratford, editor and critic John Dover Wilson insisted that he could not have looked like this: 'This might suit well enough with an affluent and retired butcher, but does gross wrong to the dead poet.'[9] It seems to have slipped Wilson's mind that Shakespeare might well in his later years have resembled his father, who very likely was an 'affluent and retired butcher.'

This plebeian background is what produced the greatest dramatists of the age, butcher-boy Shakespeare and bricklayer's stepson Ben Jonson. Closer to home in Stratford, John Shakespeare traded with a tanner called Henry Field, and took him to court for the price of some barley. Field's son Richard was apprenticed to a London stationer, and then a printer, whose business he took over (together with his French wife) when his master died. This was the Richard Field who published Shakespeare's poems *Venus and Adonis* and *Lucrece*. The stink of tanning that surrounded these country boys in their youth did not stop them from making these substantial and complementary contributions to the literature of the Renaissance. And although, as writer and printer, they worked of course in paper, it could be more than coincidental that their fathers' trade backgrounds might also have included the manufacture of vellum and parchment from animal skins.

†

There is a certain consistency then, in these early accounts of Shakespeare's life, between Shakespeare the butcher boy and Shakespeare the poacher. Rowe's statement that Shakespeare attended the local grammar school, but had to leave to work in his father's business, is credible, and corroborated by Richard Davies. No less credible is the assertion that he had to quit Stratford for London on account of the deer-stealing episode, arrived in London's theatre land as a poor young man, and entered the playhouse in a servile capacity:

> It is at this Time, and upon this Accident, that he is said to have made his first Acquaintance in the Play-house. He was receiv'd into the Company then in being, at first in a very mean Rank; But his admirable Wit, and the natural Turn of it to the Stage, soon distinguished him, if not as an extraordinary Actor, yet as an excellent Writer.[10]

We can say with some confidence that both fact and tradition identify Shakespeare as a boy from an agricultural trading family, who worked with livestock; who turned up in London looking for a job; and who set to work applying the skills he had learned in the management of domestic animals. In a later book called *The Lives of the Poets of Great Britain and Ireland* (1753) it was asserted that 'Shakespear, driven to the last necessity, went to the playhouse door, and pick'd up a little money by taking care of the gentlemen's horses who came to the play.'[11] The author traced this story back to William D'Avenant, who claimed he was Shakespeare's godson (and even perhaps his illegitimate son). Shakespeare is described as prospering in this business and expanding it, and so coming to the notice of the company, whose bosses brought him in as actor, and then writer. The story is usually regarded as a baseless fabrication. Yet the young Shakespeare, butcher and poacher, might well have possessed the professional qualifications in animal husbandry that enabled him to succeed in this vocation.

†

Suppose Rowe had had more data of this kind to work with? Suppose he had learned from Aubrey and Mr. Dowdall that Shakespeare's father was a butcher, and that the young William managed to combine play-acting with slaughtering in the abattoir? Suppose he had heard, via Sir William D'Avenant, that the young Shakespeare embarked on his theatrical career by holding horses at the playhouse door? If he had acquired such additional information, information that was obviously in existence at the time, then the following mini-biography might have been the 'third edition' of his pioneering life of Shakespeare. This imagined text incorporates all the other traditions that link Shakespeare to livestock, butchering, skinning and tanning. Here we have a young Shakespeare who not only read books and wrote poems, but also cut the throats of calves; fleeced the wool from sheep; disembowelled deer; and kept restless horses in check. Not a bad training, surely, for a career in the Elizabethan theatre?

Memoir: 'Some further account of the life &c. of Mr William Shakespear'

This piece deploys the technique of the faked historical document to provide an extension of Nicholas Rowe's life of Shakespeare. The text incorporates later traditions and subsequently discovered facts, as well as the material available to Rowe. The overall emphasis of this narrative is to strengthen the view that Shakespeare was born into a butchering business. Some of the material incorporated needs to be treated with scepticism. Sir John Plume, for instance, must have had a remarkable memory, since he was only two years old when John Shakespeare died. John Shakespeare was not an executor of Field's will, though he did help to appraise Field's goods after his death. The story about Queen Elizabeth dropping her glove on stage was published in 1825, in Richard Ryan's *Dramatic Table Talk; or Scenes, Situations & Adventures, Serious & Comic, in Theatrical History & Biography* (London: John Knight & Henry Lacy, 1825) vol. 2, pp. 156–7. Ryan's version of the anecdote ends quite differently, with the Queen 'greatly pleased with his [Shakespeare's] behaviour.'

Some Further Account of the Life &c. of Mr. William Shakespear, with Corrections Made to the First and Second Editions, and with the Supplementation of New Matter Acquir'd from Diligent Researches in the Publick Records, and from Conversations Mr. Betterton had with the people of Stratford-upon-Avon (1715)

IT seems to be a kind of Respect due to the Memory of Excellent Men, especially of those whom their Wit and Learning have made Famous, to deliver some Account of themselves, as well as their Works, to Posterity. For this Reason, how fond do we see some People of discovering any little Personal Story of the great Men of Antiquity, their Families, the common Accidents of their Lives, and even their Shape, Make and Features have been the Subject of critical Enquiries. How trifling soever this Curiosity may seem to be, it is certainly very Natural; and we are hardly satisfy'd with an Account of any remarkable Person, 'till we have heard him describ'd even to the very Cloaths he wears. As for what relates to Men of Letters, the knowledge of an Author may sometimes conduce to the better understanding his Book.

He was the Son of Mr. *John Shakespear*, and was Born at *Stratford* upon *Avon*, in *Warwickshire*, in *April* 1564. His Family were of good Figure and Fashion there, and are mention'd as Gentlemen. By his own father's Estate, *John Shakespear* was a husbandman, but the son being possess'd of that Resourcefulness that can make a Marchaunt of a Farmer, grew to be a substantial Dealer and Tradesman of the town. Husbandry being his orginall Calling, John dealt in the Carkasses of beasts, and was by the Record of one who knew the Town and its inhabitants well, a Butcher. Finding that the Cloathing of sheep and cattle afforded more Profitable and respectable Employment than the butchering of their Edible parts, he became a *whyttawer*, a species of Tanner, engaged in the Whitening and Softening of Leather, the better to adapt its substance to the Manufacture of Shoes, Belts, Purses, Satchels, Sword-hangers and Gloves, and a considerable Dealer in Wool. In this noisome and noxious Trade, the poet's Father found his Craft and refined his Art, for from the Leather cured and prepar'd in his Workshop, he fell to fashioning Fine Gloves, and soon began to prosper at the Trade. It is without Controversie that Mr. *Shakespear* is recorded and remembered as a Glover of *Stratford*. His name is subscribed as Glover in the Register and Publick Writings relating to that Town, and Archdeacon *Plume* of *Rochester* had it of *Sir John Mennis* that he well remembered *Mr. Shakespear* in his glover's shop, a merry-cheeked old Man who spoke well tho' boldly of his Celebrated son. My Will, he said, is an Honest fellow, with a place at Court, but never too Lofty to crack a Jest with his old Dad.

John Shakespear's dwelling-place in *Stratford* was long known as the Woolshop, tho' 'tis now partly an Inn, and partly a Butcher's shop in which is continued *John Shakespear's* native trade. This same inn lies under the Sign of the Swan and Maidenhead, which Emblem remembers both our Illustrious poet, and his more Glorious patroness the Queene, of whom more Herafter. A gentleman of my Acquaintance had it from the Landlord that beneath the Boards of the parlour Floor, when rais'd, were found the Remnants of Wool, and the Refuse of Wool-combing embedded with the Earth. I am told of a record in the Court of Common Pleas that has Mr. *Shakespear* suing one *John Walford*, a clothier, for negligence in payment of £21 for 21 tods of Wool, tho' I know not if't be true.

True it is that in another Court *John Shakespeare* brought Action against *Henry Field*, a tanner, for the price of some Barley. The Difference they must have Mended, for *Shakespeare* was an Executor to *Field's* will. This *Field* was father to *Richard*, who was Prentic'd to a London stationer, and afterwards a Printer, and who succeeded on his Master's death to both his Wife, a comely French woman, and his Business. 'Twas from Richard's press came our poet's *Venus and Adonis*, in which Poem there is also some little Difference of Years between the Lady and her young Man. These two School-fellows of Stratford worked each in his father's Trade, and many are of the opinion that the sons of Tanners and Butchers have so little access to Learning, that 'tis a wonder any one of them should do Well. Yet *Field* was preferr'd to a London Printer, and *Shakespeare* was advanced to the foremost Theatre of the City. It is my Conjecture that both their Fathers were wont to Supply, of their Workshops, to the London Stationers and Printers, fine Parchments and Vellums made from the skins of their Sheep, Goats and Calves. And this, tho' I own 'tis but my Belief, is how these country boys wrote their Names in History, by first writing them on Parchments made in their fathers' Shops. 'Is not parchment,' asks Hamlet, 'made of sheep-skins?' Horatio replies, 'Ay, my Lord. And calf-skins too.' That Speech of High style made by *Shakespear* in the killing of a Calf, as mentioned below, he may have committed to Writing on vellum made from the same Creature's skin. Certain it is that his Plays abound with knowledge of these Crafts: of Hides, of Calf-skins, Sheep-skins, Lamb-skins, Fox-skins; of Dog-skins, Deer-skins and Cheveril; of Neat's-leather shoes, and Sheep's-leather bridles; of Horse-hair and Calves' guts, Aprons, Bottles and Jerkins of leather, Greasy fells and White fleeces.

Though a substantial Marchaunt and Burgess of the town, John *Shakespear* had so large a Family, not ten (as I wrote in my first edition, as I had the number from Mr. *Betterton*, who has since read the record with a closer scrutiny), but eight, that tho' *William* was his eldest Son, he could give him no better Education than his own Employment. He had bred him, 'tis true, for some time at a Free-School, where 'tis probable he acquir'd that little *Latin* he was Master of: But the narrowness of his Circumstances, and the want of his assistance at Home, forc'd his Father to withdraw him from thence, and unhappily prevented his further Proficiency in that Language. It is certain that the Neighbours of Stratford heretofore told unto Mr. *Aubrey* that Shakespeare, as a boy, Practising his father's trade of Butchery, when he killed a Calf, would do it in a *high style*, and make a Speech. Whence he had these Speeches, I know not, for it is without Controversie that he had no knowledge of the Writings of the Antient Poets, as in his Works themselves we find no traces of any thing that looks like an Imitation of 'em. Some *Latin* without question he did know, and may have Employed some snatches of Cicero or Caesar, remembered out of his Grammar, in his Calf-killing. Or some fine words out of his Bible may have sèrved as Fitting accompaniment to the Slaughtering, as the words used by Abraham and Aaron, when they served so a Ram, or a fatted Calf. Certain it is that no Regularity and Deference for the ancients restrain'd that Fire, Impetuosity, and even beautiful Extravagance which we admire in *Shakespear,* and which in my Opinion furnished him with ample Eloquence with which to Beautify the Slaughterhouse, and to make a Theatre of a Shambles. See how Piteously he recalls, in his *Second Part of Henry the Sixt,* the Cruelty of the Abbatoir:

> And as the butcher takes away the calf,
> And binds the wretch, and beats it when it strays, …
> And as the dam runs lowing up and down,
> Looking the way her harmless young ones went,
> And can do naught but wail her darling's loss …

Upon his leaving School, he seems to have given intirely into that way of Living which his Father propos'd to him; and in order to settle in the World after a Family manner, he thought fit to marry while he was yet very Young. His Wife was the Daughter of one *Hathaway,* said to have been a substantial Yeoman in the Neighbourhood of *Stratford.* In this kind of Settlement he continu'd for some time, 'till an Extravagance that he was guilty of, forc'd him both out of his Country and that way of Living which he had taken up. He made a frequent practice of Deer-stealing, robbing a Park that belong'd to *Sir Thomas Lucy* of *Cherlecot,* near *Stratford.* There be some have Question'd this story, as the account of a Misdemeanour alien to the Character of our gentle Poet. But at that time *Sir Thomas* had no Royal licence to keep a park at *Charlecote,* for 'twas some years after this that his fields were Empaled. The free-warren of his land sheltered many Beasts of the chase, as Rabbits and Hares, Pheasants and Deer, and of these the good people of *Stratford* had for many years made their choice, remembering the Rights of the Free-born Englishman, and taking such prey as suited them from under the Keeper's winking eye. It is certain that the young Shakespeare took his Share, for a jolly old Parson of *Oxford* was heard to say that he was much given to Stealing Venison and Rabbits from *Sir Thomas Lucy's* lands. The Flesh of these beasts gave sustenance to his family, and the Pelts furnish'd his father's workshop with skin enough for many a fine pair of Gloves.

Sir Thomas liked this despoiling of his Land by the people so little that he resolv'd to make Example of one, and had his Keepers lie in wait for Shakespeare, one night when Moonlight whitened the Turf. Our Poet, wandering idly in the Greenwood, and Wounding the barks of trees with his

Love-sonnets, was easily Caught, and afterwards Whipped and held for a time in the County gaol. Angered beyond Measure by the Knight's tyrannical Usage, Shakespeare composed a Bitter Ballad, mocking Sir Thomas as a Covetous Cuckold, who needed not to keep Horns in his Park, since his wife bestowed them so liberally on his Head. This Ballad was writ upon a sheet of Parchment made by *Shakespear* himself from the skin of a stolen Sheep, and stuck upon *Sir Thomas's* Park gate. At this *Sir Thomas* was Angry out of all Compass, and would have prosecuted *Shakespear* even more Severely, and so he was Oblig'd to leave his Business and Family in *Warwickshire* for some time, and shelter himself in *London*. In due time he took further Revenges, for in *The Merry Wives* of Windsor, he has made Falstaff a Deer-stealer, that he might at the same time remember his *Warwickshire* Prosecutor, under the Name of Justice *Shallow*, he has given him very near the same Coat of Arms which *Dugdale*, in his Antiquities of that County describes for a Family there.

It is at this Time, and upon this Accident, that he is said to have made his first Acquaintance in the Play-house. He was receiv'd into the Company then in being, at first in a very mean Rank, as a Serviture, for what was he at this time, for all his Promise, but a Butcher's Prentice run away from his master? When he came to London, he was without Money and Friends, and being a Stranger he knew not by what means to support Himself. At that time as Gentlemen were accustomed to ride to the Playhouse, Shakespeare, driven to the last Necessity, went to the Playhouse door, and pick'd up a little Money by holding the Horses of those who had no Servants, that they might be ready again after the Performance. If this sounds too Menial an occupation for our greatest Man of Letters, then heed the witness of another, who records that *Shakespear* took good Care of the Gentlemen's Horses who came to the Play. Who better to bestow such Care on Animals, than one whose family Depended on 'em, and who from his apprenticeship knew well how to Soothe a fearful Nag, or quiet a restless Jade? Though some speak scornfully of this Tale, and cannot bide the thought of their *Shakespear* splashing in those Manured Precincts, it was no mean Craft that he assumed, there at the Theatre door, and soon became Eminent in that Profession. But his admirable Wit, and the natural Turn of it to the Stage, soon distinguished him, if not as an extraordinary Actor, yet as an excellent Writer. For he knew as well, remarked one clever Fellow, the inside of a beast as he knew the Outside, and could draw you out a sheet of Vellum as handily as he could hold your Horse for the length of a Play. And did not Shakespeare himself speak of 'a wit of cheveril, that stretches from an inch narrow to an ell broad,' as if to him the Stretching of Imagination, and the Pulling into shape of fine Leather, were actions Comparable, and not utterly Distinct?

Being come of a simple and industrious Kind, neither arrogant nor froward in their Manners, besides the advantages of his Wit, he was in himself a good-natur'd Man, of great sweetness, and a most agreeable Companion; so that it is no wonder if with so many good Qualities he made himself acquainted with the best Conversations of those Times. Queen *Elizabeth* had several of his Plays Acted before her, and without doubt gave him many gracious Marks of her Favour. She used frequently to appear upon the Stage before the audience, or to sit delighted behind the Scenes. Once when Shakespeare was personating the part of a King, she crossed the Stage when he was Performing, but he did not Notice it! Accordingly, as he was about to make his Exit, she Stepped before him, dropped her Glove, and re-crossed the Stage, which *Shakespear* noticing, immediately presented the Glove to the Queen. Her Majesty, being perhaps a little Displeas'd that the actor had paid more Attention to his audience than to his Sovereign, or rather loving (as she did) a cruel Jest even more than she loved her Poet-favourite, was heard to say: 'Gramercy, good Master Shakespeare, of the glove. Tell me, *is it one that you made yourself?*' Which shaft of Wit, glancing thus upon his Humble origins, so deeply distressed him that he left the Stage, and never again return'd.

The latter Part of his Life was spent at his native *Stratford*, as all Men of good Sense will wish theirs may be, in Ease, Retirement and the Conversation of his Friends, the Shopkeepers and Merchants, the Tradesmen and Craftsmen, the Butcher, the Baker, &c. He had the good Fortune to gather an Estate equal to his Occasion, and, in that, to his Wish. His pleasurable Wit, and good Nature, engag'd him in the Acquaintance, and entitled him to the Friendship of the Gentlemen of the Neighbourhood.

He Dy'd in the 53d Year of his Age, and was bury'd on the North side of the Chancel, in the Great Church at Stratford, where a Monument is plac'd in the Wall. How apt a Likeness this is, I know not, though many Condemn it as unworthy its great Subject. One Gentleman, visiting the Church, was heard to say, intending to the Disparagement of the Sculptor, that to his eye it looked not so much like a Poet, as like a self-satisfied Pork Butcher. But how indeed should our *Shakespear* look, this Butcher's boy become the world's greatest Poet, if not, at least a little, like a Butcher? and if not, at least a little, satisfied with himself?

LIFE FOUR

Shakespeare the Businessman

Looking coldly at the extant biographical 'facts,' it is clear that there is more material testifying to William Shakespeare's activities as what we would now call a 'businessman' than there is to any other aspect of his multifarious life and careers. As Greenblatt puts it, 'the core biographical records of the poet's adult life are real estate [property] documents.'[1] This has struck many people as strange, given the nature of the subject, and the reasons for our interest in the 'personal story' of his life. The disproportionate wealth of documentation about property and finance, contrasting with the apparent lack of literary and cultural evidence concerning Shakespeare's Stratford life, has helped to bolster the views of those who see the writer of the plays and 'the man from Stratford' as two entirely different people.

The favoured explanation for this anomaly lies in the nature of historical documentary record. What sort of thing invariably gets written down, copied, signed, witnessed? Not what we say, and think, and feel in our everyday lives, but legal transactions, such as buying and selling land and property, marriage settlements, money-lending, court actions for debt, wills. As Bate puts it, 'lawyers and court officers are better at writing things down than theatre people.'[2] It is generally assumed that more is known about Shakespeare's property dealings than about other aspects of his life, simply because such things were routinely documented, and scholars were able to locate and identify such records, while the more private domain of their subject's life-history remained unwritten, uncopied, unsigned, unwitnessed. Be that as it may, Shakespeare the actor and writer was also Shakespeare the man of property, and commercial transactions form a very large component of his life's documentary record.

Facts

Chapter 3 above describes the kind of economic background Shakespeare emerged from, which was that of a provincial and agricultural, farming, trading and craft environment. His father seems to have started out as a farmer, may have been a butcher, certainly became a tanner and glover. The records show that John Shakespeare's commercial activities were very varied, since they included dealing in wool, money-lending and the acquisition of property, as well as engaging in various processes to do with the manufacture of leather and of leather goods. John evidently prospered in these trades, rising through various municipal offices to the position of high bailiff of Stratford in 1568. He was able to buy a big house in Henley Street, Stratford in 1556. He acquired a house and land by his marriage to Mary Arden in 1557.[3]

John's financial standing had, however, apparently collapsed by 1576, and he lost his civic offices, was in debt, and obliged to sell off houses and land. He was prosecuted for illegal wool-dealing and money-lending. Meanwhile his son's fortune was on a different trajectory. William acquired early on a lifelong habit of accumulation. By marriage to Anne Hathaway in November 1582 he took possession of the house known as 'Anne Hathaway's cottage,' so his marriage, albeit possibly unplanned, nevertheless brought him the ownership of land and property. So property ran in this family. The only certain reference to what Shakespeare might have been doing during the 'lost years' (though he may not have been personally involved) is the record from 1587 of a lawsuit involving family property.[4]

Shakespeare was very much the businessman in relation to the theatre he worked for as actor and writer. About 1599 he became a sharer, with Heminge, Condell, Philips, and others, in the receipts of the Globe Theatre, built in 1597–8 by Richard and Cuthbert Burbage. The annual income from a single share was over £200, and Shakespeare may have had more than one. In 1610 he became a sharer also in the smaller Blackfriars Theatre, after it had been acquired by the Burbages.[5] This evidence shows Shakespeare operating successfully within the London cultural industry where his work was based. But it also shows him engaging in innovative economic practices that facilitated a much more substantial remuneration from his work than he could have earned as a jobbing actor and hack scriptwriter. Already by 1597, William had amassed enough money to buy for £60 New Place, the second largest house in Stratford.[6]

On his father's death in 1601 he inherited two houses in Henley Street. He invested in farm produce and land around Stratford, as well as in houses. In 1598 he was listed as a holder of malt and corn, and is also recorded as selling some of it. In 1602 he bought arable land with common pasture attached from William and John Combe for £320, and more land from them in 1610. He bought a cottage and garden in Chapel Lane, Stratford in 1602. In 1605 he paid the very large sum of £440 for the thirty-one years remaining of a lease of the Stratford tithes, a good source of regular and reliable income. It was through this acquisition that he became involved in a dispute, discussed below, over the attempted enclosure of some common fields belonging to the town of Stratford.[7]

Shakespeare also acquired extensive holdings of property in London. He bought a large house near the Blackfriars Theatre in March, 1613. There is some evidence from the records of Chancery that he owned other properties in Blackfriars.[8]

Ownership of land and property at this time frequently entailed litigation. The years 1600, 1604, 1608 and 1609 all contain records of suits by Shakespeare to recover small sums of money from debtors. Meanwhile the tax collectors in London were trying to get money out of him, seeking payment of taxes incurred on his goods while he lived in the parish of St Helen's, Bishopgate in 1593 or 1594. These claims Shakespeare satisfied some years later when he was living across the river in Southwark.[9]

Letters written by prominent townsmen of Stratford add solidity to the portrait of Shakespeare the businessman. In 1597 Abraham Sturley wrote to a relative in London about 'Mr. Shaksper' who was 'willing to disburse some money upon some odd yard-land or other at Shottery or near about us.' In the same year Richard Quiney, whose son Thomas married Judith Shakespeare, wrote from the Bell in Carter Lane, London, 'to my loving friend and countryman, Mr. Wm. Shackespere,' asking for his help with £30. A little later Sturley was confident that 'that our countryman Mr. Wim. Shak. would procure us money.' Richard Quiney's father Adrian wrote to his son, 'If you bargain with Wm. Sha., or receive money therefor, bring your money home that you may.' Clearly the businessmen of Stratford regarded William Shakespeare as a 'countryman' who could be persuaded to get involved in local investments and other transactions. We don't know of course to what extent Shakespeare complied with these requests, and the wording of Adrian Quiney's letter has been read as suggesting that getting money out of Shakespeare – 'If you bargain with Wm. Sha.' – was like getting blood out of a stone – 'bring your money home that you may [if you're lucky].'[10]

In January 1616 Shakespeare had a draft of his will drawn up by Francis Collins, a solicitor of Warwick, and after some changes this was signed in March of that year, shortly before Shakespeare died. He had evidently disposed of his shares in the theatres before his death, as they do not feature in the will. Notoriously the Shakespeare will is entirely about money and houses, property, goods and chattels, and makes no mention of books or anything else a writer might be thought likely to own.[11] 'It omits,' observes Stanley Wells, 'all mention of his books, manuscripts, and other papers which might have cast light on his life and art.'[12] It also contains nothing in the way of poetic sentiment or cultural interest, other than the bequests to actors Richard Burbage, Heminge and Condell. It is what one would expect of the Last Will and Testament of a man of property, a burgess of Stratford, but not the sort of will one might have imagined likely to have been left by the greatest writer in history. If the funeral bust in Holy Trinity church did originally display a figure with a woolsack, rather than a pen and paper, then it was commemorating Shakespeare the landowner, agricultural investor and speculator – Shakespeare the businessman – rather than Shakespeare the author.

Tradition

Tradition has little to add to this very full factual account of Shakespeare's financial and property dealings. The traditions invariably represent him as arriving in London without means, getting a job as a call-boy or horse-holder, dependent on what work he could find. Chapter 3 explored the traditional stories about his setting up, on his arrival in London, a small business looking after playgoers' horses, a tradition that depicts him as something of an entrepreneur.[13]

One anecdote that Rowe himself found hard to believe is the story that the Earl of Southampton lent Shakespeare £1000 'to enable him to go through with a purchase which he heard he had a mind to.'[14] If there is any truth in this anecdote, it shows Shakespeare borrowing money not to defray debt, or to finance a dissolute course of life, but to invest in some no doubt profitable initiative, possibly purchasing shares in the theatre, or buying property in London. So even in this anecdote about patronage of a poet by an aristocrat, the emphasis falls on Shakespeare the entrepreneur, raising capital to invest in a project.

Overall the emphasis placed by the traditions is on a young man who arrived in London without money, status, and connections, and had to make his own way financially by the exercise of his ingenuity, energy, imagination, wit and creative power. This is not necessarily a fable about a native genius: it could simply be a largely truthful account of a man whose rise from poverty to wealth can be credited to his own labours, rather than to any inherited wealth or patronage.

Speculation

There are within this history three specific financial transactions that have given rise to much debate and discussion. They all belong to Shakespeare's later years, 1612–14. These are Shakespeare's role in the Bellott-Mountjoy lawsuit of 1612, his purchase of a house in Blackfriars in 1613 and the Welcombe enclosures of 1614.

The only certain twentieth century discovery of new information about Shakespeare – the one thing we know for sure about him that the Victorians didn't – was the documentation of a law case from 1612, discovered by Charles Wallace in the Public Record Office, which includes Shakespeare's own deposition as a witness.[15] As Charles Nicholl's excellent micro-biography *The Lodger: Shakespeare on Silver Street* shows in detail, between 1598 and 1604 Shakespeare was lodging in the house of Christopher Mountjoy, a wigmaker, at the corner of Mugswell and Silver Streets, near Cripplegate. In 1604 he had apparently assisted in arranging a marriage between Mountjoy's daughter Mary and her father's apprentice, Stephen Bellott. The lawsuit was brought by Bellott against his father-in-law to secure what he claimed was an unpaid dowry and a promise of inheritance. The various depositions say quite a lot about Shakespeare's role in the marriage negotiations, since the question as to whether a dowry of £50 had been promised was central to the case. Shakespeare himself was examined on 11 September 1612, but he stated that he could not remember the details of the arrangement, and had forgotten whether or not a definite sum had been agreed upon for the dowry.

When Shakespeare bought a house in Blackfriars in 1613, the purchase of this property was effected by a complex trustee arrangement which has generated much discussion. It is not clear whether Shakespeare ever lived in the house, or intended to live there himself. He may have bought the house as a buy-to-let investment: there was certainly a tenant in occupation. But the point that has concerned many scholars is that Shakespeare chose not to buy the house outright in his own name, but purchased it through a panel of trustees. This legal mechanism had the effect of 'excluding Shakespeare's wife from any claim on it should she outlive him.'[16] Biographers have wondered why Shakespeare, who seems to have lived in rented lodgings in London throughout his professional career, chose at this late stage to buy a London town house, and to do so in such a way as to deny his wife any claim to ownership by inheritance after his death.

In 1614 William Combe, who had sold land to Shakespeare in 1602, sought together with two other landowners to enclose a large portion of arable land around Stratford, including some belonging to Shakespeare, converting it to sheep pasturage. Enclosures brought unemployment and poverty to rural communities like Stratford, raised the price of grain, and barred the people from access to the common land. The leaders of the town council opposed the plan, led by Shakespeare's cousin Thomas Greene, who sought Shakespeare's assistance in mounting a concerted opposition. Shakespeare assured Green that according to his information, the impact of the enclosure would be minimal, and it would probably never happen anyway. Greene recorded in a letter that

> My cousin Shakespeare coming yesterday to town, I went to see him how he did. He told me that they assured him they meant to enclose no further than to Gospel Bush, and so up straight (leaving out part of the Dingles to the field) to the gate in Clopton hedge, and take in Salisbury's piece; and that they mean in April to survey the land, and then to give satisfaction, and not before; and he and Mr. Hall say they think there will be nothing done at all.[17]

He may have been easily persuaded: he was indemnified against any consequent personal loss, and he stood to benefit from the enclosures through an increase in his tithe income. Combe started the work, digging ditches, but encountered direct action from the people of Stratford as well as civic resistance from the local authorities. He tried to defy the council's injunction to desist, but in the end his enterprise failed, and the land was not enclosed until well into the eighteenth century.[18]

†

Although the commercial aspect dominates the documentary record, no commensurate prominence is given to Shakespeare the man of property in the biographies. Shakespeare's purchases and investments, his borrowings and lendings, his profits and losses, tend to play a very minor role in the life-story. The biographers are naturally interested in Shakespeare the writer, and in his works; his finances would be at best a marginal consideration, relevant only insofar as questions of money and property might impinge on the author's professional and creative practice. If William Shakespeare of Stratford had written nothing, and had not become an actor, his biography would be of no particular national or international significance. He might have been remembered locally as a substantial citizen of a small provincial town. Is it not reasonable, then, that the historical data on Shakespeare's financial and property dealings should be relegated to an ancillary role in a biography?

There is another reason, however, for this marginalization of property and finance. Biographers of Shakespeare are academics or professional writers: they are not, by definition, themselves *per se* businessmen or financiers or dealers in property and goods, and so they tend to relegate to a subsidiary role the commercial transactions that dominate the factual basis of the Shakespeare life-story. But each biographer has to decide how to interrelate these different facets of the Shakespeare biography: to piece together the commercial transactions with the authorial *oeuvre*, to reconcile Shakespeare the businessman with Shakespeare the theatre poet.

Stanley Wells sees Shakespeare's wealth as an index of his artistic success, and regards his choice of investments as demonstrating his enduring adherence to Stratford as his real home. By the end of the sixteenth century

> Shakespeare was a rich man, a householder and a landowner, possessed of a grand mansion with barns and extensive gardens, the smaller but still substantial house in which he had been born, at least one cottage with garden, a large area of land which he leased for farming, and a major investment in tithes. All this centred on Stratford, the accumulated product of years of careful husbandry of income earned from the theatre. In London … he had no fixed base for any length of time, and he bought no property there until the end of his life.[19]

Here the writing and the involvement in theatre business came first, and generated wealth that was then used to furnish a comfortable life back in Shakespeare's Stratford 'home.' Like a tenured academic, fortunate enough to be paid for doing what he loves, Shakespeare made money by the exercise of his creative talents. Wells also believes, as we have seen, that the wealth generated from Shakespeare's theatrical endeavours was put to the service of providing an appropriate environment for intensive and concentrated writing, in the form of the comfortable 'study' in the big quiet house in tranquil Stratford-upon-Avon. Wells minimises the significance of Shakespeare's purchase of a London town house, though Shakespeare himself could hardly have known that 1614 was so close to 'the end of his life.'

Here then there is no sense of conflict between Shakespeare the author, actor and theatre professional, and Shakespeare the businessmen: the two are perfectly in harmony, their activities mutually supportive. Conscious that Shakespeare's role in the Welcombe enclosures has been criticized as both shabby and self-serving, and as inconsistent with the ethical views on wealth and poverty revealed in the plays, Wells admits that in this incident Shakespeare does not quite fulfil our ideal view of him:

> Although it would be nice to think that he was wholeheartedly a supporter of the poor, and so opposed to the enclosure, the indications are that he succeeded in sitting on the fence, safeguarding his own interests while not offending his rich friends (pp. 39–40).

But this is a minor discrepancy. Katherine Duncan-Jones on the other hand regards Shakespeare's behaviour here as completely reprehensible, and consistent with her view of him as a thoroughly unpleasant man:

> Shakespeare's was the selfish landowner's view. Such a position was all of a piece with his minimal bequest to the poor of Stratford in his will ... and with his failure to set up any kind of local charity.[20]

A similar view of Shakespeare's character is revealed by the purchase of the Blackfriars house. Duncan-Jones regards the cautious and calculating manner in which he acquired the house, and took measures to bar his wife from any claim to it, as evidence of a clear degradation in Shakespeare's character:

> 'Sweet master Shakespeare' was deteriorating into a bitter, wary, 'ungentle' man, no longer the 'open' and 'free' character praised by Jonson (p. 245).

Jonathan Bate adopts a more hospitable view of Shakespeare as a businessman. 'His fortune,' says Bate, 'was made not by a literary innovation but by a business decision.' Shakespeare could see that

> ... the serious money was made by manager Henslowe and lead actor Alleyn who ran the Rose Theatre as an entrepreneurial partnership. Shakespeare and his close associates came up with an alternative arrangement: the Lord

Chamberlain's Men was formed in 1594 as a joint-stock company, with the profits shared among the players.[21]

Shakespeare is credited here with more than shrewdness and 'careful husbandry' in the making and retaining of money. His business acumen seems here to be as innovative as his dramatic craftsmanship and linguistic creativity.[22]

But then Bate concurs with Wells that Shakespeare's main financial concern was to support his wife and family back in Stratford, and to invest in the infrastructure of a comfortable life there. Bate dispels what he calls the 'myth of Shakespeare's retirement' to Stratford, partly by showing that he remained active in London, but mainly by arguing that he was semi-retired long before: that he was, in Stanley Wells's phrase a 'literary commuter.' He lodged in London, and spent little money there. All his investments were in Stratford. The purchase of the Blackfriars house was 'the only occasion on which Shakespeare bought as opposed to rented a property in London' (p. 355).

According to Bate, Stratford was always his 'home,' London his place of work (p. 359). Thus Shakespeare always retained an affection for his home town, and a loyalty to his family, and his financial dealings can be read as expressions of that loyalty and affection:

Financially speaking, Shakespeare himself did very well by his wife and children, not least through his shrewd investments. In London he always remained in inexpensive lodgings; he was reputedly resistant to spending a lot of time and money out on the town. He saved his money and ploughed it back into property and land at home … making enough money to keep the family going and sustaining a marriage for well over thirty years: these are not the achievements of the romantic lover, but they are manifestations of love (p. 173).

Again the biographer finds only harmony in the reciprocal activities of businessman and author.

Two other biographers offer a contrasting view, finding much more substantive discrepancies between Shakespeare's commercial and artistic life-stories. Peter Ackroyd notes that there is a discontinuity between the gentleman who was so eager to possess land and the dramatic satirist who, in *Hamlet*, mocked any trust in such impermanent possessions. Shakespeare became, in his own words, merely 'spacious in the possession of dirt.' But 'it is doubtful,' comments Ackroyd, 'whether he took so ironical an attitude towards his own property.'[23] There is an incongruity here that has to be explained by recourse to a theory of dual personality, of a deep self-division:

His life as dramatist, and his life as townsman, were separate and not to be confused. (p. 386)

Looking at each of the problematical transactions listed above, Ackroyd sees no need to justify or condemn Shakespeare's role in any of them. He concurs with the consensus that Shakespeare purchased the Blackfriars house through trustees to keep his wife's hands off it: he 'made sure that the house reverted to his oldest daughter rather than his wife' (p. 468). Unlike Wells and Bate, Ackroyd broaches the possibility that Shakespeare might have planned to live in London permanently, perhaps completely severing his link with Anne. The house 'may have been an investment, or Shakespeare might have planned to live there permanently' (p. 467).

With respect to the Welcombe enclosures, Ackroyd observes that some historians have criticized Shakespeare's responses to the crisis of enclosures, and blamed him for not taking the side of the 'commons' in the dispute over land. Shakespeare may have genuinely favoured enclosure. Or more likely, in Ackroyd's view, he was indifferent:

> ... he may simply have believed that the process of enclosure would be ultimately beneficial. More likely than not, however, he 'believed' nothing whatever. He seems to have been incapable of taking sides in any controversy, and remained studiedly impartial in even those matters closest to him (p. 480).

In the Mountjoy-Bellott case (pp. 463–4) Shakespeare appears as at best 'cautious,' at worst evasive, since he was being asked to testify against his former landlord, possibly his friend, Mountjoy:

> He could not remember any details of any conversations. It might even be concluded that he was being deliberately vague or forgetful for the sake of his old friendship with Mountjoy (p. 464).

Ackroyd finds that the details of the case reveal much about how Shakespeare was regarded by other people. He seems to have impressed his friends and neighbours as honest, dependable, of a 'free and open nature.' But when it came to the crunch, and he was asked to testify to the truth or falsehood of the £50 dowry, he fell silent:

> The details of this ancient case are no longer of any consequence, except in so far as they help to illuminate Shakespeare's life in the ordinary world. He seems to have been willing to act as a 'go-between' in delicate marital negoti-ations, no doubt because he had a reputation for finesse in such matters. He was clearly not a forbidding or unapproachable man: quite the contrary. But when called to account for his actions he becomes non-committal or impartial, maintaining a studied neutrality. He withdraws; he becomes almost invisible (p. 464)

Stephen Greenblatt also sees Shakespeare's financial acumen as to some degree akin to his artistic capabilities: 'Imagination, entrepreneurial skill and unremitting labour had made him a wealthy man.'[24] But Greenblatt's explanation for what drove Shakespeare to become wealthy is quite different from the assumptions of Wells and Bate. As *King Lear* indicates, Shakespeare had a deep fear of dependence on his children:

> ... and from the surviving evidence he could scarcely be expected to find comfort in the enduring bond with his wife. His way of dealing with this fear was work – the enormous labours that enabled him to accumulate a small fortune – and then the investment of his capital in land and tithes (p. 361).

Greenblatt agrees with the other biographers that Shakespeare must have planned eventually to retire to Stratford:

> Shakespeare must have invested in Stratford with a view to leave London eventually and return 'home' (p. 377).

But whereas Wells and Bate see this homeward return in a wholly positive light, Greenblatt suggests that Shakespeare's descent from celebrity to domesticity, his embrace of the ordinary, was something that must have been accomplished with reluctance and distaste. To become 'a respected Stratford gentleman, no more' (p. 378) must have been experienced as a great falling off from the excitement and adulation of a life lived so close to the heart of the nation's cultural Renaissance.

Shakespeare's property dealings all partake of the rather sour mundanity of this grudging return to the provinces. The Welcombe enclosures show Shakespeare clearly behaving in ways not worthy of his genius and penetrating moral insight:

> Shakespeare stayed out of it, indifferent to its outcome, perhaps ... He did not stand to lose anything, and he did not choose to join his cousin Greene in a campaign on behalf of others who might be less fortunate. Perhaps, as some have said, Shakespeare believed in modernizing agriculture and thought that in the long run everyone would prosper; more likely, he simply did not care. It is not a terrible story, but it is not uplifting either. It is merely and disagreeably ordinary (p. 383).

For Greenblatt these different aspects of character cannot be harmonized, and Shakespeare must have been in some senses a multiple personality:

> Shakespeare was a master of double consciousness. He was a man who spent his money on a coat of arms but who mocked the pretentiousness of such a claim; a man who invested in real estate but who ridiculed in *Hamlet* precisely such an entrepreneur as he himself was; a man who spent his life

and his deepest energies on the theatre, but who laughed at the theatre and regretted making himself a show (p. 155).

†

It is often said that we know too little about Shakespeare's life, and that with more and better information we would be able to reach a fuller and clearer understanding of what made him the person he was. The implication here is that the more data we possess, the more solid and dependable will be our understanding of the life. When this assumption is tested against the evidence relating to Shakespeare the man of property, it immediately collapses. Although more is known about this aspect of Shakespeare's life than any other, this abundance of data leads to no certainty or assurance about the life circumscribed by the evidence, and generates if anything more extreme differences of opinion than any other aspect of this complex biography.

Thus, from this brief survey of recent biographical excursions, several entirely different Shakespeares emerge. There is the Shakespeare who was first and foremost a writer, dramatist and theatre professional, who cleverly adapted his commercial environment to maximize the profits from his work, and then used those profits to establish an infrastructure to support the work. For this character, financial transactions and property deals could never have featured very largely in a life devoted to cultural and imaginative activities. They were marginal to the mainstream of his life, and ancillary to the fulfilment of his artistic dreams. Or the evident business acumen that made Shakespeare a wealthy man can be seen as in some way an offshoot of the artistic capabilities, with commercial innovation and business enterprise coming as naturally to him as did poetic inspiration and imaginative creativity. This Shakespeare would be very welcome in a modern university.

In either case the position within this scenario of wife, family and adherence to the town of Stratford is of substantial importance. In achieving artistic success and making money in London, Shakespeare was not in any sense neglecting his domestic responsibilities, or betraying his loyalty to his native town, but rather protecting and safeguarding his position in both: keeping his family housed, fed and respectable, and preparing a comfortable domestic environment for his eventual return.

In these interpretations, exemplified here by the biographies of Wells and Bate, Shakespeare is not a divided man, but one who managed to harmonize his diverse activities into a successful synergy. The writing made money and generated business, the business made money to support the writing and safeguard the Stratford 'home.' There is no contradiction between the high moral values promoted in the plays and the life of the man who created them. Shakespeare the artist and Shakespeare the man of property are of one substance, indivisible.

In the other biographies cited here, the characters of Shakespeare the businessman and Shakespeare the artist sit together much more awkwardly. The worlds of culture and business are perceived as separate and in many ways inimical, espousing quite different values. The plays are read as promoting values of love and community and intellect and art, which are far more congenial to the academic or professional writer than the values of the business world. *The Merchant of Venice* could be regarded as a textbook instance of this distinct preference for the moral over the commercial in ethics, relationships and community. So the overwhelming evidence that the author of *The Merchant of Venice* was, in actuality and on occasion, himself a usurer and a property speculator cannot but create a sense of incongruity. In this field of interpretation, property and finance are anything but innocent accompaniments to the life of a successful author. Rather, they call into question Shakespeare's own moral integrity, his honesty and uprightness of dealing, even his fellow-feeling and concern for suffering humanity. In the three key commercial transactions detailed above, Shakespeare's actions can be seen as at best calculating and manipulative, at worst selfish and extortionate. Although he was obviously deeply involved in the contractual arrangements for the Bellott-Mountjoy marriage, he was prepared to say under oath that he could not remember the amount of the dowry. He could remember whole books and plays, but he could not remember that.

In the purchase of the Blackfriars property he seems to have acted in an underhand and manipulative way to keep his wife out of her lawful inheritance. And finally, in the affair of the Welcombe enclosures, Shakespeare either sided with the interests of land and capital, and against the interest of the common people, or deliberately avoided getting involved in a local dispute between the classes of Stratford. He seems to have possessed a remarkable memory for topographical detail about the fields round his own landed property (though he couldn't remember anything about someone's else's £50), but he seems to have forgotten his instincts of sympathy with the poor and oppressed, as expressed in the voice of his own creation, Lear:

> Poor naked wretches, whereso'er you are,
> That bide the pelting of this pitiless storm,
> How shall your houseless heads and unfed sides,
> Your loop'd and window'd raggedness, defend you
> From seasons such as these? O, I have ta'en
> Too little care of this! Take physic, pomp;
> Expose thyself to feel what wretches feel,
> That thou mayst shake the superflux to them,
> And show the heavens more just.[25]

Many commentators have suggested that in the case of the Welcombe enclosures it was Shakespeare himself who took 'too little care of this.' Dramatist

Edward Bond constructed a play *Bingo* out of this episode.[26] The problem presented to Bond by this history was that of understanding how a writer capable of voicing the immensely humane sympathy with the poor and dispossessed that we find in *King Lear* could subsequently play an oppressive or uncaring role in a real social crisis. Bond has Shakespeare, unable to bear the extremity of this contradiction, kill himself in despair.

For biographers such as Greenblatt, Ackroyd and Duncan-Jones this contradiction was certainly there in Shakespeare's life and character, but it is one he managed to live with, rather than one that drove him to suicidal despair. All three recognize something deeply unpleasant about the evidence characterizing Shakespeare the businessman. Duncan-Jones' view is that there was no contradiction, since Shakespeare himself really was the deeply unpleasant person suggested by the commercial record. Shakespeare the businessman and Shakespeare the writer were one and the same, equally unattractive, 'ungentle' personality.

Greenblatt recognises the contradiction, and acknowledges that it does Shakespeare no credit. But Shakespeare's commercial dealings were just 'ordinary,' the sort of thing everyone else did every day. It is only because we find so extraordinary a creature as Shakespeare doing such ordinary things, that we perceive a contradiction. For Greenblatt, this self-division was simply an inevitable downside for someone who had to reconcile so enormous a talent with the lineaments of an ordinary domestic life.

Ackroyd embraces the self-division, and finds no need to explain or atone for its abiding incongruity. Ultimately the true artist believes only in his art, and nothing else can ever equal its importance. The messiness of the artist's life is a more or less unfortunate, perhaps ultimately immaterial, consequence of the perfection of his art.

†

As we can see, the existence of more facts is in reality hardly conducive to surer certainty or clearer understanding. It might even be said that the opposite is the truth: the more information there is, the wider the liberty of interpretation that becomes possible. In the end, facts speak only through interpretation, and interpretation flourishes equally in an environment of knowledge, or in one of ignorance.

I suggested at the beginning of this chapter that since our professional biographers of Shakespeare are now mainly established and often very high-profile academics, some tension should be expected between their values and those of a sixteenth century entrepreneur. They might naturally prefer Shakespeare the writer to be a writer like themselves, erudite and intelligent, deeply serious and highly moral. They might find it more difficult to accept the other Shakespeare depicted in the documentary record: the man who obviously cared very deeply about money, and took every possible step to acquire it; who chased debtors for small sums, but was in no hurry to pay his own taxes; who possessed a remarkably selective memory that retained microscopic detail about his own land-holdings, but failed to recall the amount of poor young Bellott's dowry. It does not need Katherine Duncan-Jones' systematic attempts to blacken Shakespeare's character to see the unattractive side of the man who bought a London house, but disinherited his wife from any promise of it; and who seems to have cared more about his own commercial interests than about the plight of his poorer Stratford neighbours.

The biographers seek to reconcile the businessman with the poet in their different ways, producing their variant life-stories: the successful and affluent writer who invested wisely and lovingly in family and home; the skinflint landlord who thought more of his profits than of humanity; the inspired genius who was reluctantly obliged to come to terms with the ordinary. None of these biographers, except perhaps the one professional writer within the fold, Peter Ackroyd, consider the possibility that Shakespeare might have been as enthusiastic about money and property and land as he was about plays and poems; that his approach to commercial enterprise might have been just as imaginative and innovative as his attitude towards his art; and that the twin roles of artist and entrepreneur might in fact have constituted a complex symbiotic life-story.

LIFE FOUR

Story: 'Best for Winter'

'Best for Winter' is an attempt to imagine what might have gone on in Shakespeare's mind as he was writing *The Winter's Tale*, while simultaneously thinking about his property dealings, and reacting to his immediate physical surroundings. The 'stream-of-consciousness' method is reminiscent of James Joyce and Anthony Burgess. Quotations from *The Winter's Tale* and other plays are mingled with imagined memories of Shakespeare's rural childhood, extracts from the documents detailing his commercial transactions, and everyday detail from his London biography. The 'hybridity' explicitly discussed in the play is shown to be the very essence of both writing and life. William Wayte took out an injunction restraining Shakespeare and others from offering him physical violence. This strange detail of the life has never been satisfactorily explained. Shakespeare lodged in Silver Street between 1598 and 1604, while *The Winter's Tale* was probably written 1610–11.

Best for Winter

Let me see: every 'leven wether tods; every tod yields pound and odd shilling; fifteen hundred shorn. What comes the wool to? My father's voice, grumbling and spitting, everything to him was money, how much would it come to, whether wool or leather for the market price, his ewes and rams were gold and silver, he made them breed as fast. What more could he do, for his little flock of hungry sheep, mouths bleating for food, all shorn fleece and wincing withers in the winter's cold? So lean that blasts of January would blow us through and through. Hand-fast and hold was the watchword, hard to come by as it was, money, nothing to spare and all devoured in a twinkling, flesh and fell. Sheep or men, eat or be eaten, he kept us penned warm together and we lived, most of us, while the wolves prowled outside in the darkness. Every spring, woolly buttocks quiver, new lambs drop, wringing wet and wriggling, from the ewe's heaving loins, no sooner on the ground than up and kicking, twisting back to the mother for a taste of udder in the hungry sucking mouth. *Enter a Shepherd.* In trouble with the law of course, my father, over the wool-gathering, likewise the usury, his trade being otherwise, and none should meddle with another man's trade. But John first fed his family by any fair means, and let the law go hang. Anything could be turned to money, when the need arose: even the rubble of an old tumbled house. Pd to Mr. Shakespeare for one load of stone xd. They caught me too, holding ten quarters or forty bushels of malt or corn, I forget which, when women were dying in the hedgerows of hunger, and their babes mewled on the dry dead dug, but my babes never starved. A lawless family, then, we were, my own wild days no surprise to my father though a disappointment I have since redressed. I would there were no age between sixteen and three-and-twenty, or that youth would sleep out the rest; for there is nothing in the between but getting wenches with child, wronging the ancientry, stealing, fighting. Anne Hathaway, buxom and big-bellied at the altar in Worcester, her kinfolk standing close around me, she could testify to that, getting wenches with child. For she was the wench from Shottery o'er the dale, and with child, and there was none other nigh by whom the child in her womb might have been begotten. So I compassed a motion of the Prodigal Son, and married a tinker's wife within a mile. Young men will do't, if they come to't.

When daffodils begin to peer,
With heigh! the doxy over the dale,
Why, then comes in the sweet o' the year;
For the red blood reigns in the winter's pale.

There verily was some stair-work, some trunk-work, some behind-door-work. There was good smooth ploughing on that fair meadow ere the crop eared, but a goodly harvest it was to be sure, for she was fair and fertile as one of Laban's ewes. Mercy on 's, a barne, a very pretty barne! A boy or a child, I wonder? When she was delivered, a child she proved, Susanna, a pretty one. Some 'scape it was, but I took her up for pity. For wronging the ancientry and stealing, old Sir Thomas Lucy can speak of that, for it was his deer I stalked, in the shadows of his park, and it was his men who seized me, as I bore the deer home over my shoulder to Shottery. The pale moon shines by night. They had me up before him, that very morning, and if lousy justice had taken its course I should not have 'scaped whipping. But the fellows who were to carry me to the gaol were friends of my father's, and owed him a good turn. They were good stout fellows who held that God put all the earth's beasts at man's service, and cared nothing for the likes of Sir Thomas, who empaled his fields and kept food from the people's mouths, so they managed to lose me ere they reached the town, and I was away over the fields and bound for London before Sir Thomas brought me again to mind. And when I wander here and there, I then do most go right. And for fighting I had my share of that sport too, or would have, but that William Wayte being a coward who had wronged me and durst not stand like a man swore before the Judge of Queen's Bench that he stood in danger of death, or bodily hurt from William Shakespere. Money was at the root of that trouble too, but I would have given money to beat the perjured rogue about the head with one of his own cudgels. Yet I staid my hand and kept the peace: beating and hanging are terrors to me: for the life to come, I sleep out the thought of it. Money can make all safe; money is a warm fire, and bread on the table; money is quiet children and a contented wife. Money is a fence against the wolf, a safeguard against the grasping hand of the law. I penned my dreams, and spoke them on stage, and money fell around me in a shower like rain. Gold! all gold! It was told me I should be rich by the fairies. This is fairy gold, boy, and 'twill prove so. Keep it close: home, home, the next way. Away from London, take the road to Stratford. We are lucky, boy, good boy, the next way home. So home I went, not as a poacher escaped from justice, nor a prentice run away from his master, but a gentleman, known about the court, and a man of means with gold to lay out on what I chose. I chose New Place, Clopton's house, and nothing in my life ever pleased me so much as to walk through its rooms, and warm myself before its many fireplaces, and take my ease in its gardens and orchards. Sir Thomas Lucy would not send his men to attach me here, nor William Wayte pursue me from far-off London with his ruffians. New Place: my place. Paid for in cash, £60 of ready money. House and home. Let my sheep go. I staid not long in Stratford, true, for it was off back to London, to make more money, pen more dreams. Now they come to me, my Stratford neighbours, feeling from afar the warmth of my wealth. Here is Sturley, I hear, who calls me his countryman, and asks if I am willing to disburse some money upon some odd yardland or other at Shottrei or neare about. Haply I will, too, for it may suit me to secure land thereabout, but if I do, for me it will be, and not for them. Here is Quiney, comes cringing to me for £30, calls me his loving friend and countryman, tells me I shall friend him much in helping him out of all the debts he owes in London. A mind free from debt is a quiet mind. So it is, but he begs to be indebted to me! What of my mind's quiet? Not even in his own hand either, this letter, but a scrivener's copy. If they bargain with me, or recover money therefore, let them bring their money home as they may. I am no fool to be fleeced and shorn by their avaricious shears. They called me dog, when I was young and wild and running mad with lust and want, and now they would have monies. Hath a dog money? Is it possible a cur can lend £30? I am sick of them, and must to my work. *Revenir à mes moutons*, the French say: let us return to our sheep. The French. Bastard Normans. Norman bastards. Mountjoy's wife is screaming at him now, down below, another dalliance with some baggage come to light. Listen to them, ungh, ungh, ungh, eow, eow, eow, nobody can understand them, least of all themselves. Let me shut the door, though the evening is hot, and the room close. Shut it tight. Let me dream. Ne'er was dream so like a waking. Perdita: the lost one. The sea-coast of Bohemia: a child abandoned on a desolate shore, the father thinking it his friend's bastard, his wife an adulterous whore. Places remote enough are in Bohemia, to cast out an unwanted child. There weep and leave it crying; and, for the babe is counted lost for ever, Perdita, I prithee, call't. Come, poor babe. I did in time collect myself and thought this was so and no slumber. Dreams are toys. I have heard, but not believed, the spirits o' the dead may walk again: if such thing be, may not my little Hamnet play there with lost Perdita, on that desert shore, stolen from the dead? Weep I cannot, but my heart bleeds. Blossom, speed thee well! Go into the mountains, and seek that which is gone astray. My land is before you, to dwell where you please. A hundred and seven acres of land and 20 acres of pasture in Old Stratford bought for £320 from William and John Combe. From Ralph Hubaud a half-interest in a lease of Tythes of Corne grayne blade and heye. What is a player? a coney-catching rogue, a mountebank, a poor fool. I have given everything for show, and nothing is left. I have sold all my trumpery; not a ribbon, glass, pomander, brooch, table-book, ballad, knife, tape, glove, shoe-tie, bracelet, horn-ring, to keep my pack from fasting. They throng who should buy first, as if my trinkets had been hallowed and brought a benediction to the buyer. My verses, siren songs, so drew the herd to me that all their other senses stuck in ears: my sir's song, and admiring the nothing of it. So in this time of lethargy I picked and cut most of their festival purses. They flattered me like a dog, and showered me with gifts, but I was nothing to them, at the last, but a poor player, that struts and frets his hour upon the stage, and then is heard no more. Till I became a landlord, a householder, a lessee of tithes, an auncient freeholder in the fields of Old Stratford and Welcombe. Such a man is someone, a man of property, a gentleman of consequence. Combe and Mainwaring mean to enclose those fields, but I will lose nothing by it. I will be compensated for all such loss detriment and hindrance, by reason of any enclosure or decay of tillage, there meant and intended, by the same William Replingham, Attorney at Law. They are to fence round the smallholdings and common fields, the better to pasture the sheep. There is much profit thereby, and enrichment of the town. Yet Greene and his corporation oppose the enclosure, and call upon me to take their part. Greene comes to see me, hearing I am in town, asking how I did. I told him they assured me they meant to enclose no further than to Gospel Bush and so up straight (leaving out part of the dingles to the field) to the gate in Clopton hedge, and take in Salisbury's piece. And that they mean in April to survey the land and then to give satisfaction, and not before. And that I think, with Mr. Hall, that there will be nothing done at all. Was I lied to, or lying? For truthfully I told him what I heard, though truthfully I knew it was all lies, and the work would begin in January. I will protect my tithes, and secure against any loss reasonable satisfaction in yearly rent or a sum of money. Greene pleads for the poor, and their memorial rights to graze their beasts on the common land. What do I care? I was poor enough once, and my father laboured to feed us, as I laboured to feed my own. I am a true labourer. I earn that I eat, get that I wear, owe no man hate, envy no man's happiness, glad of other men's good, content with my harm, and the greatest of my pride is to see my ewes graze and my lambs suck. Let the sheep graze, and make some men rich, for they will need labourers in turn who will work for their food. Florizel and Perdita are to meet at the sheep-shearing. Mountjoy's wife is scolding in the back kitchen. A stink blows up from the river: plague breath. A pestilent gall to me. O Proserpin, for the flowers now, that frighted thou let'st fall from Dis's waggon! I must go. Leave this place. Their nightly brawling wearies me. I lied on oath for Mountjoy, hoping it would bring me some peace and quiet. Said I could not remember the amount of the dowry promised to Bellott. I remembered it well enough, but I cared little for the young man, and landlords' palms need greasing. Much good it did me, imperilling my immortal soul for £50. And still it goes on, the shouting and banging of doors and clattering of pots and pans. Owy, owy, owy; nong, nong, nong. I must fly. To Stratford? My garden will be bright and fresh with the spring. Daffodils, that come before the swallow dares, and take the winds of March with beauty. No: not there. If Silver Street is Purgatory, Stratford is very hell, with that scolding devil of a wife. Yet here I cannot entertain a friend, or bring home a wench for a long night's solace. I must take a house in London. What of Henry Walker's gate-house at Blackfriars? Black brows, they say, become some women best. If I buy it, Anne will have a third share for life in that part of my estate. I must keep it from her. Walker told me the house could be bought by trustees, and thereby become a joint tenancy. If I were to predecease the other trustees, Chancery would not recognize her privilege. That would serve: for I must not have her mingling in my London life, whether I am alive or dead. Knowing who I know, learning of who I lie with, turning o'er my things in a jealous rage … No, I'll none of it. I'll take the Blackfriars house, be less in Stratford, make my home here. And when the burden of age presses down upon me, and I am too sick to stay here by myself, then I'll trudge slowly home to Stratford, to die in my own bed. This thought cheers me. At least they are quiet again downstairs now. Mountjoy is back in the workshop, I can hear him angrily hammering. She will be sewing, jabbing her needle spitefully through the silk, wishing it were her husband's eyes. Venice gold in needlework. What a twisted skein is life: what a tangled web we weave. Gold and silver thread from Venice; silk from Damascus; pearls of the orient. Clattering pots in the kitchen; smell of frying onions. A man's anger; a woman's hate. My words too, precious jewels strung on cheap strings with counterfeit stones, to fool the senses, catch the breath, delight the eye. All is hybridity, promiscuity, miscegenation. For I have heard it said, there is an art which in its piedness shares with great creating nature. We marry a gentler scion to the wildest stock, and make conceive a bark of baser kind by bud of nobler race. This is an art which does mend nature, change it rather, but the art itself is nature. The play goes well. A melancholy piece, with a jealous king, a virtuous wife suspected, a son dead from grief, a daughter left to die on a distant shore, a man torn to pieces by a bear. So let me bring them all together at the end, and let reconciliation and forgiveness spring between them. A lost daughter returned; a wife back from the dead; a statue that moves and speaks. Nothing like life. Like an old tale still, which will have matter to rehearse, though credit be asleep, and not an ear open. It will do well though, the taste of the times being what it is, and make me some more money. A fleece against the coming cold. A sad tale's best for winter.

LIFE FIVE

Shakespeare in Love: 'Husband, I come'

Shakespeare is a great poet of love. Many of his verses and phrases on love embellish the language of popular romantic sentiment: 'Shall I compare thee to a summer's day?'; 'To me, fair friend, you never can be old'; 'Love is not love, that alters when it alteration finds.' His loving couples are archetypes of sexual relationship, whether happy or tragic in their fulfilment: Romeo and Juliet, Rosalind and Orlando, Othello and Desdemona. Some of his sonnets have replaced 1 Corinthians 13 as the essential reading for wedding ceremonies. Since Rowe collected stories about Shakespeare's youthful misdemeanours, there has been an inexhaustible public appetite for material dealing with his love life, culminating in the hugely successful and Oscar-winning film *Shakespeare in Love*. This, the most popular Shakespearean film to date, is a wholly fictional story about the erotic adventures of Shakespeare 'in love,' something we literally know nothing whatsover about.

The documentary record tells us nothing about Shakespeare's personal 'love life.' Notwithstanding, the biographical literature has much to say about it. But the many and varied lives of Shakespeare the lover pointedly illustrate the rule of 'less is more,' or more cynically, 'anything can be made out of nothing.' No aspect of Shakespeare's life is as sparsely documented as this one; and yet nothing has interested subsequent generations quite as much. The popular biographical literature makes a number of assumptions that most people would probably regard as well-known and self-evident fact. From this context the lay observer could be forgiven for assuming, as fact, that Shakespeare hated his wife, was gay lover to Henry Wriothsley, the Earl of Southampton, loved a 'Dark Lady' who was probably a prostitute, and died of syphilis. None of this colourful material has any firm basis in history (though some of it is implicit in the story told in Shakespeare's *Sonnets*), but all of it has achieved, as one writer put it, 'a hold on popular affection that no argument can weaken.'[1]

We know of course that he married Anne Hathaway, and had three children with her. We do not know that he loved her, or indeed that he didn't. We know that he dedicated a poem with protestations of love to the Earl of Southampton: 'The love I dedicate to your lordship is without end.'[2] But we do not know if that 'love' was more than the conventional sentiment liberally used in such promotional material, or whether the poet meant anything at all to the nobleman. Finally, we know that Shakespeare wrote prolifically and powerfully about love in his plays and poems, and we could naturally assume that he could not have done so without extensive experience of loving (and bitterly frustrating) sexual relationships with women, and perhaps with men. But this is mere assumption, not knowledge.

It is one thing to claim, inferring the author from the work, that the writer of the *Sonnets* and *Romeo and Juliet* knew enough about the pleasures and pains of love to create some of the most enduring love poetry in the language. But it is quite another thing to argue, placing the writer as cause and the writing as effect, that the poet Shakespeare derived this knowledge from specific relationships with theoretically identifiable people. In this case the overwhelming preponderance of writing over biography leaves the writing almost invariably speaking on behalf of the poet's life.

The next three chapters deal with Shakespeare as lover in three discrete guises: the husband, the gay lover of one or more men and the heterosexual lover of one or more mistresses. The first derives from fact, since Shakespeare was certainly a husband. The second involves some factual associations, but depends largely on inference from the *Sonnets* and the dedications to the narrative poems. The third is wholly fictional, drawn purely from the writings, though to some degree corroborated by tradition. We will begin with the only factual biographical record of Shakespeare as lover, his courtship of, and marriage to, Anne Hathaway.

Facts

These are the facts. We know that on November 28 1582 two husband-men of Stratford gave a bond of £40 (a large sum of money) 'to defend and save harm-less' the bishop of Worcester and his officers for licensing the marriage of 'William Shagspere' and 'Ann Hathwey of Stratford in the Dioces of Worcester maiden.' This tantalizing piece of information is to be found in the form of a marriage licence bond in the bishop's registry. Stratford was in the diocese of Worcester. There is no documentation of the marriage itself.[3]

This record indicates pretty clearly that the marriage of this couple was not conducted according to the appropriate forms, but was sponsored by people who really wanted it to take place without delay. A special licence was presumably acquired for the ceremony to take place without the customary reading of the banns. Anne's family were indemnifying the bishop against any legal consequences that might follow this irregularity.

We do not know for sure that this Anne was the daughter, known variously as Anne or Agnes, of Richard Hathaway from Shottery, who had died in the previous July, and had owned the house of which a part still survives, and is shown to visitors as 'Anne Hathaway's cottage.' But there is no reason to suspect they were not one and the same. The date on Anne's tombstone indicates that she was eight years older than William, which was again uncommon, as wives were normally younger than their husbands. But she was pregnant, a circumstance which is proved by the baptism on 28 May 1583 of daughter Susanna, and which explains the 'o'er hasty marriage' of six months earlier.[4]

There is another complication in the documentary record, in the fact that although the marriage license bond names Anne as 'Anne hathwey,' the marriage license record gives the name as 'Anna whately.' Most scholars have assumed that this was simply a mistake, that the clerk mis-spelt the name, forgot it, or confused two different people. Those who doubt Shakespeare's identity and authorship of the plays naturally make much of this anomaly, questioning the integrity of a record that shows one man marrying two different women on subsequent days.

More imaginative biographers have speculated much more freely about Anna Whately. Frank Harris, in *The Man Shakespeare* (1909), suggested that there were two women, and that Shakespeare dumped Anna Whately in favour of Anne Hathaway.[5] Anthony Burgess, in his 'conjectural' biography *Shakespeare*, followed suit, imagining that Shakespeare had 'copulated with Anne Hathway ... at least three months before he married her,' 'in a ryefield in high summer.'[6] He really wanted to marry another girl, the chaste Anna Whately of Temple Grafton, but with her there was no prospect of premarital sex. He was in love with Anna, but sexually obsessed with Anne Hathaway, and returned to Shottery for another 'bout of lust' with her. Burgess portrays Anne Hathaway as an older woman entrapping a young man into marriage by deliberately getting pregnant (p. 58), and thereby forcing Shakespeare to abandon his true love, Anna Whately.

Shakespeare must have continued to have sex with Anne Hathaway after marriage, as she bore two more children, the twins Hamnet and Judith, in February, 1585.[7] But in biographical literature it became a commonplace assumption that the marriage was unhappy. The story goes something like this: Shakespeare had to get married, as Anne was pregnant. Anne was considerably older than him. He spent most of his working life in London, at the very least living away from home for long periods, and possibly hardly visiting Stratford at all, so the couple could not have enjoyed a normal married life. It has often been observed that there is in the documentary record of Shakespeare's whole life, absolutely no trace of affection, loyalty or tenderness, 'no signs' in Stephen Greenblatt's words, 'of shared joy or grief,' subsisting between this husband and wife. In Shakespeare's will the only allusion to Anne is the notorious bequest of the 'second-best bed.' Instead of leaving her well-provided for, and with messages of tenderness addressed to a loving and faithful wife, as other dying men did, he left her only a piece of junk furniture.

So Shakespeare was sexually involved with Anne Hathaway, and served her as a husband, though the word 'love' has not attached to their relationship in the historical record. They may have promised to love one another in a betrothal rite, and in a marriage ceremony from the Book of Common Prayer, but any such declaration of commitment is lost.

Tradition

It is perhaps sobering to reflect that the documentary record has so little to tell us about Shakespeare as a husband: he got Anne Hathaway pregnant, and married her. Tradition has much more to report, and speculation about Shakespeare in love knows no end. And the early traditions are consistent in that they depict Shakespeare as a libertine who regularly enjoyed sex outside his marriage.

There is the story recorded by the lawyer John Manningham in his diary, 13 March 1602 (considered in Chapter 2 above) that Shakespeare overheard Burbage making an assignation with a lady in the audience, and made his way into her bed before his colleague could get there. The tale may be a legend, but it may also contain some element of truth. The London theatres occupied the same district as the brothels, and the contemporary theatre scene was undoubtedly a promiscuous culture. London was a long way from Stratford, and Shakespeare lived there in long absences from the marital home.

Another parallel source of traditional lore about Shakespeare's love life was dramatist Sir William D'Avenant, one of Rowe's key sources. D'Avenant's father John was landlord of the Crown Inn at Oxford. In the eighteenth century Sir William Oldys recorded that Shakespeare was a constant visitor to this theatre-loving host's tavern:

> Shakespeare often baited at the Crown Inn or Tavern in Oxford, in his journey to and from London. The landlady was a woman of great beauty and sprightly wit; and her husband, Mr. John Davenant … a grave melancholy man, who as well as his wife used much to delight in Shakespeare's company.[8]

What attracted him there seems to have been the landlady, described by John Aubrey as 'a very beautiful woman, and of a very good wit, and of conversation extremely agreeable.'[9]

The contribution of tradition to knowledge about Shakespeare's love life is that he was remembered or reinvented as a bit of a lad, who took full advantage of the sexual opportunities available to a theatrical celebrity. Manningham's anecdote shows him an afficionado of one-night stands; while the D'Avanent connection suggests that he had a long-term mistress, and even an illegitimate family in the country. All this material concurs in one emphasis: that Shakespeare's love life was adulterous.

Speculation

So the documentary record tells us that by the age of eighteen Shakespeare was having sex, or at least had had sex, with a local woman eight years his senior. This therefore is the only historical evidence we have about Shakespeare as a lover. Was he deeply in love with this woman, or just sowing wild oats? Was Anne his only sweetheart, or did he have a string of girls? Did he enjoy one brief night of passion with Anne, or were they 'going steady' for some time before she fell pregnant? All these possibilities have been raked over, again and again, in biographical speculation and in fiction. But of course we are no nearer to knowing the truth about any of them.

Shakespeare's family had money troubles, and Anne had in her own right a little property and some money. Was this marriage of a younger man to an older woman a marriage of convenience? We know that the Hathaway family actively sought the marriage, but we do not know whether the Shakespeare family wanted it. Shakespeare had to swear that he had his parents' consent to marry, as they were not there to agree formally to the bond. John Shakespeare may have viewed the prospect of alliance with a solid country family as something worth seeking. On the other hand he may have disapproved of the marriage, and the efforts of the Hathaway clan to ensure it happened may indicate that all the Shakespeares were unwilling partners in a misalliance. The young man's sexual passion and his seductive tongue perhaps got the better of him, and he found himself having got an older woman he had thought of only as a sexual partner 'into trouble.'

Thus even the act of sexual intercourse that placed William Shakespeare's seed into Anne Hathaway's body remains shrouded in mystery, since it may have been part of a calculated programme on the part of a family desperate to improve their circumstances; or an act of youthful rashness that produced unfortunate consequences that the young man then, with some reluctance, honourably faced up to. With his customary caution, Stanley Wells offers a glimpse of the young Shakespeare's emotional life: 'Shakespeare must have felt both the emotional turmoil and the physical demands of what was clearly a turbulent sexuality.'[10] Anne Hathaway may have been an element in his 'sexual education,' which bore fruit unusually early (p. 18).

When it comes to asserting opinions about Shakespeare as a husband, the biographers offer the customary wide range of diverse options. Re-examining the documentary records concerning Shakespeare's marriage, Jonathan Bate admits that 'It is, alas, almost impossible to unearth the significance of this information.'[11] What do these circumstances reveal, he asks, about Shakespeare's love-life?

Sexual precocity? Passionate ardour? A cunning way with seductive words? Carelessness when it came to the moment? ... Any, all or none of the above?

The marriage itself may then have been happy, or unhappy, or just fairly nondescript, a convenient arrangement from which neither spouse expected much in the way of romance.

Stephen Greenblatt represents a fairly strong example of the 'unhappy marriage' scenario. But he sees Anne Hathaway as initially an almost irresistible object of the young Shakespeare's emotional impulses. She was in every respect different. His family was Catholic, hers Protestant. His sexuality was ambivalent, hers normal. As Shakespeare's previous sexual interests, while he was at school, may well have been homosexual, Anne must have represented a straight antidote, 'a reassuringly conventional resolution to his sexual ambivalence and perplexity.'[12]

Anne was, however, Greenblatt continues, unusual in 'being her own woman' (p. 119), a woman of property: 'She was independent, in a way virtually ordained to excite a young man's sexual interest, and she was free to make her own decisions' (p. 119). In this scenario, Anne represented to the young Will one version of the freedom he clearly sought, though it was at best an 'imaginary resolution' of his aspirations. This puts a very positive spin on the relationship, restoring the romance to a courtship often suspected of lying somewhere between a marriage of convenience and a shotgun wedding. Greenblatt notes that often in Shakespeare's writings we find graphic portraits of sexually eager young men longing for the consummation of marriage: 'Shakespeare conveys, above all, a deep inward understanding of what it feels like to be young, desperate to wed, and tormented by delay' (p. 122).

But it all ends in tears. The romance that Greenblatt finds in their early relationship did not survive into marriage. Will may indeed have been a 'reluctant, perhaps highly reluctant' bridegroom. Again, the work supplies many examples of the miseries of enforced marriage. Greenblatt deduces from the circumstances of Shakespeare's life, and the reflections on love and marriage that fill his work, that Shakespeare's marriage was not happy. The marriage itself was a trap that caught a young man destined to play a much bigger role in the world. And he proceeded to embark on that career, which both required and conferred freedom, notwithstanding the ties of marriage and family. 'He could not get out of it … But he contrived, after three years time, not to live with his wife' (p. 143).

Shakespeare's marriage, Greenblatt affirms, was the scene of 'bitterness, sourness and cynicism' (p. 142). But his was not a life without love. He simply found love, as the traditions suggest, outside marriage. 'His imagination of love and in all likelihood his experiences of love flourished outside of the marriage bond' (p. 143). In London he was able to enjoy a separate and secluded private life, and there he found 'intimacy and lust and love' (p. 144).

For Greenblatt, Shakespeare's silence with regard to Anne, right up the very last, is decisive proof that their marriage was not one of love. Nowhere in the documentary record of the life is there any sign at all that Shakespeare loved Anne Hathaway:

Between his wedding licence and his last will and testament, Shakespeare left no direct, personal trace of his relationship with his wife – or none, in any case, that survives. From this supremely eloquent man, there have been found no love letters to Anne, no signs of shared joy or grief, no words of advice, not even any financial transactions (p. 125).

In the first draft of his will he mentioned everyone else, left something to everyone else, but, 'to his wife of thirty-four years, Anne, he left nothing, nothing at all' (p. 144). What Shakespeare felt toward his wife is defined by Greenblatt as a 'strange, ineradicable distaste' (p. 145). The epitaph on his grave was designed not merely as a general injunction to leave his remains be, but as a specific prophylactic against Anne's body being buried beside him. He did not want her near him, even in the long impersonal silence of the grave.

Clearly, in this analysis, Greenblatt is intentionally engaging in free-ranging speculation, extrapolating widely from the raw data. In its imaginative inventiveness this method is not that far away from the overtly fictional depictions offered by creative writers of Shakespeare's wedded life, showing the marriage to be unhappy and incapable of fulfilling Shakespeare's need for love and sexual excitement. Novelist Anthony Burgess, in his biography of Shakespeare, proposes that Anne was an ageing spinster, afraid of getting left on the shelf, when she and Shakespeare engaged in 'wanton fornication.'[13] The young man himself wanted to marry the chaste Anna Whately, but went back to Anne Hathaway for another 'bout of lust' (p. 59) from which she became pregnant. Will was thus forced into marriage. It was not long before Anne revealed herself as a shrew or 'virago,' who nagged Shakespeare mercilessly over money and houses and family status. Since, Burgess confidently assert, the marriage was based on sex alone, Will must soon have encountered 'transports of disgust,' the famous sexual revulsion expressed in some of the poems and plays, and 'had to get away from Anne' (p. 67).

Burgess's biography, published in 1970, abstracted this interpretation from his earlier novel *Nothing Like the Sun*, published in 1964. In the novel, a drunk young Shakespeare is caught by the older and sexually more experienced Anne, 'in a manner tricked, coney-caught, a court-dor to a cozening cotquean' (p. 31). He is then picked from among a number of young men by Anne's family as a likely candidate for press-ganging into marriage. Once wed, he suffers from Anne's domineering sexual aggression and continual nagging: Burgess makes Anne resemble both the Venus of *Venus and Adonis* and a shrew worthy of inclusion in Shakespeare's *Taming of the Shrew*. There are no illusions between them: 'You were out to catch,' he states flatly to his wife, 'and I was caught' (p. 41). Thus Shakespeare's departure for London is explained in terms of his being driven from home by the intolerable pressures of a forced marriage, and a sexually demanding and emasculating virago of a wife.

Jonathan Bate offers a much more optimistic view of the marriage. Many scholars have seen the story of Shakespeare's poem *Venus and Adonis*, 'in which an innocent boy is seduced by a sexually voracious older woman,'[14] as the story of Shakespeare's marriage to Anne Hathaway. And *The Taming of the Shrew* may be a commentary on the kind of married life that might well follow such a seduction: 'it has often been assumed that because Shakespeare wrote *The Taming of the Shrew*, his wife must have been one' (pp. 164–5).

But these extrapolations, Bate admits, are inconclusive: 'Like so much in Shakespeare's life and work, his marriage can be interpreted in diametrically opposed ways' (p. 165). Perhaps Shakespeare had a 'grand passion' for Anne that was 'prematurely consummated' (p. 165). Or perhaps the marriage was arranged between the families and lacked any element of romance. Ultimately, however, Bate is confident in asserting that Shakespeare loved his wife. How does he know this? Because he went though with the marriage, fathered several children and invested the proceeds of his work initially in a home for the family in Stratford. 'Making enough money to kept the family going and sustaining a marriage for well over thirty years: these are not the achievements of the romantic lover, but they are manifestations of love' (p. 173).

Peter Ackroyd favours an even more optimistic view of the marriage, though he sees it as ultimately too narrow a confine for Shakespeare's genius. It was not necessarily a compelled marriage at all, but a perfectly convenient and mutually agreeable domestic arrangement: 'Far from being a misalliance or forced marriage, as some have suggested, the partnership of William Shakespeare and Anne Hathaway could have been an eminently sensible arrangement.'[15] Throughout his life, Shakespeare revealed himself to be a cautious, practical, sensible and business-like man. Why should his approach to marriage have been any different? The fact that Anne was the older partner, often used to cast Shakespeare as the innocent and seduced party, suggests to Ackroyd quite the opposite: that the 18-year-old Shakespeare possessed a potent 'sexual self-confidence.' Why dally with the unpredictable promise of some young virgin, when you could enjoy the immediate pleasures of a mature sexual relationship?

Ackroyd thinks the couple were previously 'betrothed,' and therefore engaging in sexual relations recognised as legitimate, though premarital. He describes in painstaking detail their subsequent marriage ceremony, conducted in the old church at Temple Grafton, in Latin, and approximating to the traditional Catholic rite, by a priest with possibly Catholic leanings (pp. 88–9). Ackroyd is following here what became a popular view during the Victorian period. Scholars tried to argue that the couple may have been 'betrothed,' that is joined together by a 'troth-plight,' which would have legiti-mized sexual union as long as marriage followed. Such an arrangement might be made simply between two people promising themselves to one another, or as a public ceremony with witnesses. The church wedding would take place later, often to legitimize the union before the arrival of a child. If they were troth-plighted then they were lovers who intended to marry, not promiscuous and unfortunate sexual adventurers.

There is no evidence at all that this applied to Shakespeare, but this theory was naturally popular among Victorian scholars who were reluctant to regard Shakespeare as morally irresponsible. Such a view reassured prudish readers that the national poet was not a libertine. The betrothal hypothesis has, however, been revived in modern works such as Germaine Greer's *Shakespeare's Wife*, which goes to any lengths to rehabilitate Anne Hathaway's reputation. Greer's evidence about premarital betrothal is drawn from social history, and her argument is that what was common practice at the time must necessarily have been what happened to Shakespeare. But this need not be the case: not everyone adheres to common practice, and Shakespeare was a pretty unusual person in most respects. Moreover the efforts that were obviously made to get the marriage signed and sealed are not quite what we would expect from a wedding that had already in effect taken place, and lacked only the formal blessing of ecclesiastical ceremony. As Stanley Wells puts it, 'the urgency suggested by the terms of the marriage bond ... suggests that formalization of the union had not long been premeditated.'[16]

Modern biographers have observed that there is no factual evidence of any kind suggesting or implying such a prior contract. Ackroyd, however, mentions one piece of evidence that could conceivably prove the Shakespeare marriage to have been a love-match. On 16 March 1810, a labourer's wife found near Stratford churchyard a gold signet ring with the initials 'WS'. The letters are joined by an ornamental string and tassels, the upper bow or flourish of which forms the resemblance of a heart, known commonly as a 'true lover's knot.' In order for such an object to be found, it would first have to have been lost, but there is in fact a circumstantial context for exactly such a loss. In Shakespeare's will the words 'and seal' are crossed out, as if the signet with which to sign it was not available. The object, now in the Shakespeare Birthplace Trust Museum, raises the intriguing possibility that this was the very gold ring that Shakespeare exchanged with Anne Hathaway on the occasion of their betrothal. If so, it would represent the decisive proof of true love that is so singularly lacking from the historical record.[17]

When Shakespeare left Stratford for London, according to Ackroyd, there is no evidence that he was fleeing from a bad or forced marriage. It does seem improbable, he admits, that he would have left if the marriage had been an idyllically happy one. He was naturally 'restless and dissatisfied – some force greater than familial love drove him on' (p. 103). In other words the 'pull' factor of Shakespeare's burgeoning genius was much stronger than the 'push' factor of an unhappy marriage in precipitating his departure for London. The impression we get from Ackroyd is that Shakespeare's marriage was nothing out of the ordinary, neither happy nor unhappy. There was nothing particularly problematical about Anne as a wife, except that she had the misfortune to marry the greatest writer of all time, entering upon a union that could never have achieved 'the marriage of true minds.'

As the preceding discussion shows, there are as many possible 'lives' of Anne

Hathaway, or rather Anne Shakespeare, as there are of her famous husband. The entire biographical Hathaway construction rests on a few surviving facts: the age difference of the couple; the fact that she engaged in premarital sex; the fact that she had a 'cottage'; and the fact that Shakespeare in his will left her only the second-best bed. Nonetheless the paucity of evidence has never impeded the free play of imagination among those who have sought to give Anne an afterlife, whether as the castrating virago, or the long-suffering and misunderstood Mrs Shakespeare. The modern consensus used to be that Anne was an obstacle to the flowering of Shakespeare's genius, and that he had to get away from her, and from Stratford, before he could assume his true destiny. More recently the fashionable convention has been to restore Anne's reputation, making her into a good wife and mother, a capable female household manager, or even a partner to Shakespeare in more than just domestic matters – Germaine Greer has her initiating the publication of the First Folio. Neither consensus is any more or less convincing than the other. There are the facts, but the facts do not speak for themselves: they are continually disputed, and generate diverse contrasting scenarios. Traditions offer no help, since they restrict Shakespeare's experience of love to outside the marriage bond. Speculation produces equally plausible but utterly incompatible interpretations.

Which version approximates most closely to the truth? We will never know. But nothing will stop us from imagining ...

Memoir: 'Shakespeare's Ring: First Circle'

'Shakespeare's ring,' which forms a recurrent motif in the next three fictional pieces, can still be seen today in the Visitor's Centre at Shakespeare's Birthplace in Stratford. It was acquired in 1810 by Stratford solicitor and antiquarian Robert Bell Wheler (1785–1857), and given to the museum by his sister Anne after his death. The story of how he acquired the ring was found in an inter-leaved and annotated copy of Wheler's *Guide to Stratford-upon-Avon*, published in 1814. The text describes the discovery of the ring, and Wheler's subsequent efforts to legitimize its authenticity, including a consultation with the foremost Shakespeare scholar of the day, Edmond Malone. This reconstructive fiction begins with Wheler's own story, then goes on to incorporate passages from the work of several other Victorian Shakespeare scholars, quotations from *Measure for Measure, Two Gentlemen of Verona, The Merchant of Venice* and *King Richard the Third,* and some passages on the history of 'handfasting' from Germaine Greer's *Shakespeare's Wife*.

Shakespeare's Ring: First Circle

'Shakespeare's gold finger-ring, with the initials W. S., a true lovers knot intwined between them, beaded border, the face of the signet measuring f in. by J in. Presented by Miss ANNE WHELER, 1867.'

(From *Catalogue of the Manuscripts, Works of Art, Antiquities and Relics at present exhibited in Shakespeare's Birthplace Stratford-upon-Avon* [Printed for the Trustees and Guardians of Shakespeare's Birthplace Stratford-upon-Avon in the year 1910]).

Mr Robert Bell Wheler's Account of the Finding of Shakespeare's Ring
Upon Friday, the 16th day of March 1810, this ancient gold seal ring, weighing 12 penny-weights, and bearing the initials 'W. S.' engraved in Roman characters, was found by a labourer's wife, Mrs Martin, upon the surface of the mill close, adjoining Stratford Churchyard. It had undoubtedly been lost a great many years, being nearly black; and though it was purchased upon the same day for thirty-six shillings (the current value of the gold) the woman had sufficient time to destroy the precious patina by consenting to have it unnecessarily immersed in *aquafortis* to ascertain and prove the metal at a silver-smith's shop, which consequently restored its original colour. It is of tolerably large dimensions, and evidently a gentleman's ring of Elizabeth's age. The connection or union of the letters by the ornamental string and tassels, known commonly as a 'true lover's knot,' was then frequently used, and the crossing of the central lines of the W with the oblique direction of the lines of the S. exactly agree with the character of that day. The upper bow or flourish of this tracery forms the resemblance of a heart. Upon this seal ring being found, it immediately occurred to me that it might have belonged to our immortal poet.

Mr. Malone, in a conversation I had with him in London, the 20th of April 1812, about a month before his death, said that he had nothing to allege against the probability of my conjecture as to its owner, and that the seal-ring evidently belonged to a person in a very respectable class of society. After numerous researches into publick and private documents, I find no Stratfordian of that period so likely to own such a ring as Shakespeare. Upon retiring from the stage to his native town, our bard resided in the principal house here, which he had formerly purchased; had accumulated considerable property, and frequented the best company that Stratford and its neighbourhood afforded. To his will there is no seal affixed ; but it is a singular circumstance that in the concluding part of it where the Scrivener had written 'In witness whereof I have hereunto set my hand and Seal' the words 'and Seal' were struck out, and replaced by the word 'hand,' all of which more strongly and remarkably confirms my conjecture that the Poet had then lost this Signet Ring.

When, how and why he lost it, I have been unable to ascertain. Some gentlemen have suggested to me that the ring may have been one of those mentioned in his will and bequeathed to friends, but this is most improbable, else why would it have lain undiscovered so long in Stratford, so close to Shakespeare's home? Considering the beauty and value of the ring, the monogrammed initials on the ring, the true-lover's knot that decorates the ring, does it not seem more probable that such was the very ring with which Shakespeare espoused his lifetime love and true wedded wife, Anne Hathaway?

It has pleased some biographers of Shakespeare to allege against our immortal poet the character of a licentious libertine, a philanderer who was forced to wed the lady he had ruined, a poacher prosecuted for robbing the local gentry of their game. Such may be the moral character of some of our modern poets, as of the outlaws and banditti who plunder and ravish their way through our popular literature. Yet Shakespeare's poetical work throughout breathes such an accent of virtue, such purity of thought and feeling, that his life must surely have been coloured by the same high sentiments. Had William Shakespeare been the reprobate some of his biographers would have us believe, he would scarcely have made the journey from Stratford-on-Avon to Worcester, to bind himself to a woman whom he had dishonoured.

Furthermore, it is my belief that the poet and his bride were already man and wife when they met together in the pure embrace of wedded love. In those days a form of betrothal, known as 'handfasting,' was considered tantamount to a marriage, and it happened frequently that the ecclesiastical part of the ceremony was not completed till absolutely necessary for the legitimation of a child. The ceremony of wedlock was preceded by pre-contract, which according to the custom of the time and place, would have been looked on as having the validity of marriage. It was only from 1558, the year in which Queen Mary died, that the Catholic faith and the Catholic rites had been superseded by those of the Reformed religion. Religion was then in a state of transition, and people, especially those of the Midland counties, had a lingering affection for the old forms, and a covert dislike of the new. Moreover a public betrothal was then considered to be a binding ceremony, carrying with it conjugal rights, and barring the partners from entering into contract with any other. In Shakespeare's *Measure for Measure* Claudio says:

Upon a true contract
I got possession of Julietta's bed.
You know the lady. She is fast my wife,
Save that we do the denunciation lack
Of outward order.

Or witness the betrothal of Prince Florizel and the supposed shepherd's daughter Perdita, in the sheep-shearing scene in *The Winter's Tale,* where the young couple are betrothed in the presence of witnesses. The whole of this scene breathes the sweet fragrance of the Midland festivals, such as the Poet must have witnessed many times on the hills about his native town, or on the Cotswolds. What could be more likely than that the young Will Shakespeare, true son of Stratford's mayor, and in his own right a reigning prince of poetry, should have plighted his troth in just such a rustic habit to a lovely farmer's daughter, Anne Hathaway?

Now the seal ring lately discovered, is living and eternal proof of this sacred union, legally equivalent to marriage, and lacking only the final blessing of the church. Perhaps the ceremony took place at a family celebration attended by both their kin, since as one sixteenth century writer avers, often at a handfasting there took place great feasts and banquets, and the handfasted persons were that same night laid together, weeks before they went to church. Or perhaps the lovers stole away privily, as young couples do in Shakespeare's plays, and solemnly bound themselves to one another in some green secluded glade of the Forest of Arden.

However it was, one day in the summer of 1582, William Shakespeare took Anne Hathaway by the hand, and said to her the words of marriage, in the present tense: 'I take thee Anne to be my wife.' She responded in the same form: 'I take thee William to be my husband.' Once these words were exchanged, they were fast married. William kissed his bride, with all the tenderness of a pure and ardent young love, and then placed upon her finger a gold ring. 'Keep this remembrance for my sake,' he may have said to his young bride. She likewise performing the same action towards him, placed upon the third finger of Shakespeare's hand this very gold signet of which we speak. 'Why, then, we'll make exchange; she may have said: 'here, take you this.' The ring he gave to Anne is, alas, lost. But the ring she gave to him, bearing his initials W. S., we have through the blessings of providence now recovered. That which was lost is now found, and we trust that it will never be lost again.

The gold wedding ring symbolizes love, its high value the emblem of true love's worth. As a perfect circle, it stands for the completeness and fulfilment of married life. Encircling the groom's finger, it declares the fastness of the marriage bond. On its face, around the husband's name, engraved lines interlock, a true lovers' knot suggesting the increasing closeness of the couple, as they grow together in love. This was the ring Anne Hathaway gave to our immortal poet. This was the pledge he accepted from her, of undying and ever-deepening love.

How Shakespeare lost his ring, we can only surmise. That it should never have parted from his finger, is very plain from his own words in *The Merchant of Venice*. The ring was 'riveted with faith unto his flesh,' and he swore 'never to part with it.' He should not have left it, or plucked it from his finger, for all the wealth that the world masters. He should have worn it till his hour of death, and let it still lie with him in his grave.

But we cannot believe that Shakespeare held his wife's gift in such low esteem as to part with it so carelessly. He could not have easily mislaid it; nor cast it from his finger in some fit of trivial anger; nor thrown it aside following some rupture between husband and wife, he losing faith in her, or she in him. No: it was surely in those last days of the illness that ushered him to his eternal rest, before he signed his will and testament with that unsteady palsied hand, that Shakespeare and his betrothal ring were sundered. A dying man, he might have been wont to walk alone around the churchyard, visiting the grave of his lamented son and heir, mourning the loss of his departed mother and father, pondering on the great mystery of death so soon to be to him revealed.

I see him now, in my mind's eye. His tired flesh is wasted with sickness, his old bones wracked with pain. He limps along the churchyard wall, shivering from the winter's cold, furling his cloak about him, seeking the faint warmth of the thin February sun. His fingers are wasted almost to the bone, his ring is loose and slack around the swollen joints. He does not notice when his gold signet slips quietly from his hand, and drops with an inaudible splash into the flowing millrace. Tired and ill, he turns back home, and does not realise his loss until the evening, when he washes his hands for supper. With what solicitude and sorrowing remorse, respective of his vehement oaths, does our poet then turn to his wife, and tell her of its loss?

> ... my finger
> Hath not the ring upon it; it is gone.

But we cannot believe that Mistress Anne would have rounded on her husband with such harsh recrimination as does Portia in *The Merchant of Venice*. 'Even so void is your false heart of truth!' For the vow Shakespeare made of undying love resided not in the ring he accepted from Anne, but in the true heart that received her promise, and kept it throughout his life. To me these words from a play echo what must have been in Shakespeare's heart the day he took Anne Hathaway to wife:

> Look, how this ring encompasseth thy finger,
> Even so thy breast encloseth my poor heart;
> Wear both of them, for both of them are thine.

And so the ring that encompassed his finger merely stood for his heart that lay enfolded in his wife's bosom, as did hers in his. Though the token of their union be lost, from one another they were never to be parted, bliss or woe. They stayed together, fast married, from the day of their betrothal to that dark day of the poet's death. Anne never married again, but on her death went to join her husband in the crypt of Holy Trinity Church. Together throughout life, and eternally in death: fast bound in the eternal fellowship of this ring.

LIFE SIX

Shakespeare in Love: 'Fair Friend'

We do not know, therefore, whether or not Shakespeare loved his wife. We do know, on the other hand, that he did make a written declaration of 'love' to a beautiful and bisexual male aristocrat, Henry Wriothsley, the Earl of Southampton.

Facts

Shakespeare's *Venus and Adonis* was registered on 18 April 1593, and published with a respectful dedication:

To the Right Honourable Henrie Wriothsley, earl of Southampton

Right Honourable, I know not how I shall offend in dedicating my unpolished lines to your Lordship, nor how the world will censure me for choosing so strong a prop to support so weak a burthen, only if your Honour seem but pleased, I account myself highly praised, and vow to take advantage of all idle hours, till I have honoured you with some graver labour. But if the first heir of my invention prove deformed, I shall be sorry it had so noble a god-father : and never after ear so barren a land, for fear it yield me still so bad a harvest, I leave it to your Honourable survey, and your Honour to your heart's content, which I wish may always answer your own wish, and the worlds hopeful expectation.[1]

A year later the fruit of this 'graver labour' appeared. *Lucrece* was registered on 9 May1594, and published without a name on the title-page, but with a dedication, bearing Shakespeare's signature, to the same nobleman.

To the Right Honourable Henry Wriothesley, Earl of Southampton, and Baron of Tichfield.

The love I dedicate to your lordship is without end; whereof this pamphlet, without beginning, is but a superfluous moiety. The warrant I have of your honourable disposition, not the worth of my untutored lines, makes it assured of acceptance. Were my worth greater, my duty would show greater; meantime, as it is, it is bound to your lordship, to whom I wish long life, still lengthened with all happiness.[2]

The tone is much more direct, personal and intimate – 'What I have done is yours ... devoted yours' – than that of the dedication to *Venus and Adonis*. And this dedication protests love – 'The love I dedicate to your lordship is without end.' But of course these affirmations could mean anything from subservient loyalty to passionate homosexual admiration. These poems were clearly a hit: *Lucrece* was reprinted five times, and *Venus and Adonis* seven times, while the range of complimentary references appearing at the time indicates their striking popularity. The evidence would suggest that Shakespeare really made his name as a writer through these poems, so the initial growth of his reputation is potentially linked with that relationship of 'love' he appears to have had with the Earl of Southampton. The lives of writer and lover may here be closely intertwined.

Southampton must therefore have acted as a patron to Shakespeare, though we have no means of knowing what that entailed: funding Shakespeare's work, or putting in a good word with wealthy friends, or even just accepting the dedication, which would in itself have promoted the book. Nicholas Rowe recorded the story, transmitted to him by D'Avenant, that Southampton lent Shakespeare £1000. Most modern scholars do not believe this, as the sum is too great, and Southampton too poor to have afforded such a loan. But the anecdote implies at least some measure of generosity in patronage. The way Rowe recounts the story, however, suggests something rather more:

There is one Instance so singular in the Magnificence of this Patron of Shakespear's, that if I had not been assur'd that the Story was handed down by Sir William D'Avenant, who was probably very well acquainted with his Affairs, I should not have ventur'd to have inserted, that my Lord Southampton, at one time, gave him a thousand Pounds, to enable him to go through with a Purchase which he heard he had a mind to. A Bounty very great, and very rare at any time, and almost equal to that the present Age has shewn to French Dancers and italian Eunuchs.[3]

Rowe admits that the story is almost incredible, and that he would not have included it, had it not come from a reliable source. If it were true, he goes on, then the scale of generosity implies some form of personal intimacy, since it seems to match the sort of 'profuse Generosity' offered in his own time only to 'French Dancers and italian Eunuchs.' If there was a £1000 loan, Rowe is suggesting, then Shakespeare must have been to Southampton what a French dancer or Italian eunuch would be to a Restoration aristocrat – a favourite, plaything, pet, possibly a sex toy.

I have accorded Rowe's anecdote the status of 'fact' here, although much of his material is discussed under the heading of 'tradition.' This is because Rowe offers the story in the manner of a historian: he doesn't simply say 'this happened,' but cites the anecdote and provides its provenance. He even admits that he himself found it unbelievable, but he clearly thinks that something of substance must have lain behind it. The 'fact,' then, is not that this indubitably happened, or even that Rowe endorsed it, but that he thought it significant enough to be worth quoting.

Tradition

The dedication of *Lucrece* to Southampton would not in itself have led to the speculation that Shakespeare was close to the Earl, perhaps even involved in some kind of homosexual love affair. The basis of the imagined Shakespeare-Southampton liaison lies in Shakespeare's *Sonnets*, which seem to tell a story about the poet's tangled love relationships with a beautiful young man and a dark woman.[4] Here then we enter the game of reading Shakespeare's works as evidence of his life, treating the poetry as autobiographical. As I have frequently emphasized, to attempt this exercise with dramatic poetry is difficult and quite possibly pointless. But it is widely assumed that in the case of the *Sonnets*, which are of course lyric rather than dramatic poetry, the confessional mode of writing, in which the poet testifies to his own experience through his art, seems to be in operation.

The *Sonnets* begin with a sequence of poems persuading a beautiful and narcissistic young man to marry. This was exactly Southampton's situation, and it has been assumed that these poems were perhaps commissioned by some powerful figure who wanted to put every kind of pressure on the young man to get hitched. The poems than go on to express all the emotions of love, describe love relationships, narrate a kind of love story. The latter seems to centre around the poet himself, a beautiful man he is in love with (the 'fair friend'), a rival poet who competes with the author for the fair friend's favour, and a woman with whom he has a sexual relationship (the 'dark lady'). The fair friend and the dark lady both betray the poet by consummating their own relationship. This ménage is summed up in Sonnet 144:

Two loves I have of comfort and despair,
Which like two spirits do suggest me still:
The better angel is a man right fair,
The worser spirit a woman colour'd ill.
To win me soon to hell, my female evil
Tempteth my better angel from my side,
And would corrupt my saint to be a devil,
Wooing his purity with her foul pride.

And whether that my angel be turn'd fiend
Suspect I may, but not directly tell;
But being both from me, both to each friend,
I guess one angel in another's hell:
Yet this shall I ne'er know, but live in doubt,
Till my bad angel fire my good one out.

Here the male lover is the 'better angel,' the dark lady the 'worser spirit,' a 'female evil.' The poems are written in the first person, and many of the individual poems are tremendously powerful expressions of love in all its different moods and guises. The depiction of the 'fair friend' with his 'woman's face' clearly suggests the Earl of Southampton. In addition the opening sequence of sonnets constitutes a persuasive case for a narcissistic young man to marry, and this also perfectly fits Southampton's own biography. Some scholars have argued, for all or part of the sonnet sequence, that they also fit William Herbert, Earl of Pembroke; but there is no link between Shakespeare and Pembroke comparable to the factual connection embodied in those two dedications (the posthumous First Folio is dedicated to the Earls of Pembroke and Montgomery).[5] The sonnet collection was dedicated to a 'Mr W. H.,' a cryptic allusion and source of enormous historical interest, possibly alluding to 'Wriothsely, Henry' (or more naturally, though more speculatively, 'William Herbert').

But sonnets were written by many writers, conventionally as literary exercises; the 1609 collection was published without Shakespeare's name, and possibly without his approval; and the drama played out in their sequence may have as little to do with the circumstances of Shakespeare's life as the tragedy of Macbeth. As Stanley Wells puts it:

> The question of whether the Sonnets are autobiographical revelations of Shakespeare's inner self, or whether they are primarily literary exercises … has vexed readers for at least two centuries.[6]

But certainty is no closer; the poems still seduce and defy biographical extrapolation; and the vexation continues. The *Sonnets* may, in Wells' words, actually be quite impersonal, dramatic works, 'quasi-poetic fictions, speeches from an unwritten play' (p. 87).

There is however one piece of historical evidence, brought in here under the heading of 'tradition,' since it is a literary rather than a historical source, that suggests a more personal understanding of the Sonnets might be appropriate. In September 1594, a poem was published under the title *Willobie his Avisa, or the True Picture of a Modest Maid and of a Chaste and Constant Wife*.[7] The poem is imagined as a series of dialogues the virtuous heroine, Avisa, holds with a series of love-struck suitors. The book's supposed author, 'Henrico Willobago,' appears as one of these lovers, and in a passage of prose describing his experience appears a possible allusion to Shakespeare and the Earl of Southampton:

> H. W. being suddenly affected with the contagion of a fantastical wit at the first sight of Avisa, pineth a while in secret grief. At length, not able any longer to endure the burning heat of so fervent a humour, bewrayeth the secrecy of his disease unto his familiar friend *W. S.*, who not long before had tried the courtesy of the like passion and was now newly recovered of the like infection. Yet, finding his friend let blood in the same vein, took pleasure for a time to see him bleed, and instead of stopping the issue, he enlargeth the wound with the sharp razor of willing conceit.

W. S. encourages Willobie to believe that she will yield in the end. W.S. is described as a 'miserable comforter,' deluding his friend 'with an impossibility,' either so he would be able to laugh at him later, or 'he would see whether another could play his part better than himself,' and 'see whether it would sort to a happier end for this new actor than it did for *the old player*.' 'H. W.' may of course be 'Henry Wriothsely,' Earl of Southampton, and 'W. S.,' the 'old player,' 'William Shakespeare.' The poem does explicitly mention Shakespeare as the author of *Lucrece*. If so, then this source suggests that the poet and the nobleman shared the same woman, and in addition that they may have shared an infection of venereal disease. The significance of this piece of evidence is that it can be held to imply that the story told in Shakespeare's *Sonnets* was the true story of Shakespeare and Southampton, and that the *Sonnets* really are autobiographical.

If they are so, then there can be little doubt that Shakespeare was in love with the Earl of Southampton:

> A woman's face with nature's own hand painted,
> Hast thou, the master mistress of my passion;
> A woman's gentle heart, but not acquainted
> With shifting change, as is false women's fashion:
> An eye more bright than theirs, less false in rolling,
> Gilding the object whereupon it gazeth;
> A man in hue all hues in his controlling,
> Which steals men's eyes and women's souls amazeth.
> And for a woman wert thou first created;
> Till Nature, as she wrought thee, fell a-doting,
> And by addition me of thee defeated,
> By adding one thing to my purpose nothing.
> But since she prick'd thee out for women's pleasure,
> Mine be thy love and thy love's use their treasure. (Sonnet 20)

The addressee of the poem is a man, but in many ways effeminate: he has a woman's face, and a woman's gentle heart, and ought really to have been a woman. He is 'master mistress' of the poet's passion, a male lover filling the role normally supplied by a female mistress. The male lover is far superior to a woman, since women are generally false and fickle. Nature created him to be a woman, but then fell for her own production, and made him a man instead, 'prick'd him out' (supplied him with a penis) so he would become a sexual partner for women. The fact that the lover is a man is therefore an unfortunate accident, since the poet would rather he were a woman. The lover's prick comes between them.

If this poem is autobiographical, then it is an unashamed declaration of love from one man to another. It is not clear however whether the poem presupposes or invites a sexual relationship between the two men. If the lover's 'prick' can only be used on women, then that would suggest the contrary. The poet regretfully accepts that he can only possess the lover's 'love,' presumably of a Platonic kind, since only women can enjoy him sexually. This Platonic interpretation of the *Sonnets* is clearly a possible way of reading them. But as early as a 1640 reprint, the publisher John Benson was going out of his way to present the poems as heterosexual, by changing some pronouns and supplying misleading titles. This evidence indicates that some readers at least recognised some of the *Sonnets* as frankly homosexual, detected in their sexual orientation a certain impropriety, and sought to censor them so as to render them apparently heterosexual, to 'straighten them out' for the innocent contemporary reader.

Factually then we have only the dedications to the two narrative poems to persuade us that Shakespeare might have had some kind of relationship with the Earl of Southampton. In themselves the dedications could point to anything from a formal, perhaps quite impersonal connection of patronage, to an intimate friendship that could have entailed carnal homosexuality. The *Sonnets* can be read as providing literary evidence of such a relationship, suggesting more strongly that they were homosexual lovers. *Willobie his Avisa* partly corroborates the story of the *Sonnets,* though more in terms of the two men sharing one woman than in terms of their own homosexual attachment. Lastly, Rowe's £1000 anecdote suggests strongly that something unusually intimate was going on between the poet and the nobleman.

But if modern literary theory has taught us anything, it is that most truly valuable fictions rarely spell out with any transparency the life of their author. The autobiographical character of the *Sonnets* has been challenged, and the kind of masculine affection portrayed in them questioned. Once again, innumerable life stories may be inferred from Shakespeare's plays and poems, and some of these deductions could be accurate and true. There is simply no way of knowing that for certain.

Speculations

Biographers freely acknowledge the paucity of information underpinning this particular facet of the Shakespearean life-story. Stanley Wells displays character-istic caution in treating the dedications to the narrative poems and the *Sonnets* separately, and declining to link them together. Thus he acknowledges that the dedications indicate Shakespeare's rising status, though they might well have been formal expressions of the patronage relationship, while 'the relationship between poet and patron was not necessarily close.'[8] The deepened warmth of the second dedication implies that 'Southampton had become a friend as well as a patron' (p. 56). Wells dismisses Rowe's story of the £1000 loan as 'ridiculous' (p. 56). He then discusses the *Sonnets* separately, with no mention of Southampton. Thirty of these poems are indisputably addressed to a man, though some of them are often read out of context as heterosexual in orien-tation. The poems could be intensely personal, or primarily dramatic. Wells concedes that on balance they are probably personal; hence they suggest that Shakespeare was a lover of men. Some poems seem to deny that this was a sexual form of love, but the poems concerning male love, as Wells puts it, certainly 'use the language of love' (p. 90):

> If Shakespeare did not, in the fullest sense of the word, love a man, he certainly understood the feelings of those who do (p. 91).

But here the biographer does not pursue the identity of the beloved.

Stephen Greenblatt, by contrast, assumes that the relationship between Shakespeare and Southampton was much closer, and that the Earl is the subject of the *Sonnets*. Southampton was an enthusiastic theatre-goer; celebrated artists enjoyed some social ambiguity. Hence Southampton might have gone 'backstage' to meet Shakespeare.[9] Southampton fits exactly the portrait of the young man depicted in the *Sonnets*: indeed a contemporary miniature shows him to have been both narcissistic and effeminate, with 'long ringlets' and a 'rosebud mouth' (p. 231). And there was pressure on him to marry and beget an heir. Hence 'it is not unreasonable to speculate that the young man of the opening suite of the sonnets is Southampton,' because 'the earl's personal circumstances perfectly fit the situation that is sketched' (p. 240). The connection between the sonnets persuading the young man to marry, and those that are clearly expres-sions of love for the young man, is elusive but unmistakable:

> Something happened to the poet, the sonnets imply, when he undertook to persuade the beautiful youth to marry: he became aware that he was longing for the youth himself (p. 239).

We cannot know what actually happened – 'there is no direct access to whatever it was' (p. 246) – but the story told in the sonnets, of how 'admiration

ripens into adoration,' and 'passionate devotion slides towards abject subser-
vience' (p. 246), seems to be Shakespeare's own personal story. And why not?
'Elizabethans acknowledged the existence of same-sex desire' (p. 253), though
sodomy was certainly prohibited. Shakespeare and his young man may have
merely exchanged glances, or kissed and embraced, or gone to bed together.
Greenblatt's conclusion is that whatever the physical details, the story told
in the *Sonnets* of the Fair Friend and the Dark Lady seems to have been the
primary love interest of Shakespeare's life. There is no room in the *Sonnets*,
Greenblatt observes, for wife and children:

> About Anne Shakespeare he is silent; it is to his beautiful male friend that he
> writes his most celebrated words about love (p. 255).

A similar polarization can be found in the contrasting parallel accounts of
Jonathan Bate and Peter Ackroyd. Bate's interest in literary convention tends
to draw him towards love-poetry as 'an exercise in witty invention' rather
than a 'real-life story' from which one might try to deduce 'the identity of
the players.'[10] The 'fair youth' who seems to be the addressee of most of
Shakespeare's sonnets 'does not *have* to be a real person' (p. 209) and may
instead be a 'figuration,' an embodiment of some ideal. The *Sonnets*, according
to Bate, should be read as dramatic poems, in much the same way as the plays:

> Shakespeare's poems are more than anything else a drama of love's
> perplexity. We do not usually look for biographical originals for Viola/
> Cesario, Sebastian, Orsino, Olivia and Antonio, so we should not necessarily
> do so for the 'lovely boy' (p. 219).

Bate goes on to discuss what place Southampton might have had in this literary
drama. He considers the rival claims of Southampton and Pembroke to be the
'fair friend,' and suggests that both might be involved. But there are problems
in identifying the beloved friend of the *Sonnets* with either:

> How likely is it that so great a figure as an earl would have allowed a player
> and play-maker of lower middle-class origins … sufficient access to achieve
> the kind of intense intimacy that the sonnets purport to describe? (p. 222).

Bate's preference is to relate the poems not to a particular W.H., but rather to
'their historical moment. (p. 223). The poems are more concerned to explore
the contemporary 'perplexities of love' in a bisexualized court than to 'express
some urgent homosexual desire' on the part of the poet himself (p. 235).

Ackroyd on the other hand sees the Shakespeare-Southampton relationship
as much more substantial, personal and intimate. Like Greenblatt, he has
Southampton meeting Shakespeare backstage. There were many connections
between them, he argues – personal, family, religious – as well as the explicit

link visible in the two dedications. Ackroyd has no doubt that they were personally acquainted: 'That they did meet is certain.' The second dedication is 'sure evidence of greater intimacy.'[11] Shakespeare may even have worked for Southampton.

The story of the *Sonnets* is the story of Shakespeare's own love life. The plays may allude to chaste platonic love, but this was a poet who had a reputation for philandering in a notoriously promiscuous age (p. 294). The *Sonnets* show that Shakespeare 'had an understanding of devoted male friendship' (p. 295), and actors often have an ambiguous sexuality:

> This does not imply that he was in any sense homosexual but suggests, rather, an unfixed or floating sexual identity. He had the capacity for both female and male, and the scope of his art must have affected his life in the world. We may recall here the recently discovered portrait of the Earl of Southampton apparently dressed as a woman.

Shakespeare clearly therefore embraced homosexuality, though not necessarily of a physical kind: his may well have been 'a love not of the phallus, but of the mind' (p. 296). Sexual ambiguity was both a cultural norm and a professional qualification.

The biographers do not therefore come out and assert that Shakespeare had a sodomitical homosexual relationship with the Earl of Southampton, though some of them imply the possibility. It has been left to the novelists to follow these suggestions through to their logical conclusion, and to imagine a relationship consummated on that basis. In *Nothing Like the Sun* Anthony Burgess constructs a narrative that presupposes many of the biographers' speculations: that Southampton sought Shakespeare out through the mediation of John Florio; that Shakespeare and the Earl were close friends; and that the story of the *Sonnets* is a record of what passed between them and their mutual friend the Dark Lady. Burgess simply goes further with the same speculative apparatus, and imagines the two men involved in a physical homosexual passion.[12]

Burgess writes coyly of this consummation, avoiding any graphic representation of physical intimacy. No such discretion troubles Erica Jong, who in her novel *Serenissima* inflates the Shakespeare-Southampton embrace into a full-blown pornographic orgy. The novel's narrator indulges in a fantasy that during his so-called lost years, Shakespeare might have voyaged to Italy with Southampton: 'his patron and (some say) his lover.'[13] Southampton and Shakespeare are imagined arriving in Venice after a prolonged Grand Tour, and finding the city an appropriate locus for the earl's habitual licentiousness. Referred to ironically as 'Harry and Will,' the two men enact the story of the *Sonnets* in an orgy of troilism, sharing a prostitute, and engaging in sodomy at the same time. 'Harry' likes to share a woman in order to disguise his true sexual preference for men. Shakespeare is fellated, alternately by the whore and by Southampton; the latter sodomizes the woman, while Shakespeare takes her vaginally. The novel goes on to supply a new 'dark lady' in the form of Jessica, a Jewess of the Venetian Ghetto, who is also shared by the two men, loved by Shakespeare and raped by Southampton. Here the biographers' consensus that Shakespeare must have had a relationship of some sort with Southampton is imagined through to its logical conclusion in uninhibited homosexual and promiscuous sex. The story of the *Sonnets* is here graphically illustrated in the language of modern pornographic fiction.

†

Two dedications; a cryptic allusion in a contemporary poem; an anonymized sequence of sonnets; and a rumour of a colossal loan – little enough data on which to construct firm suppositions. As far as the facts go, Shakespeare and Southampton might not even have met. The dedications may have been purely professional and conventional; the sonnets may involve different people, or none at all; *Willobie his Avisa* may have been talking about someone else; and Rowe's tale of the loan might be as incredible as most modern scholars find it to be.

But the Shakespeare life-story has left enough traces, questions and tantalizing possibilities for biographers to construct imaginary scenarios of the Shakespeare-Southampton relationship. The novelists have only extrapolated the same speculations to a further remove, imaginatively penetrating deep into the most private of places.

Story: 'The Adventure of Shakespeare's Ring'

The paucity of evidence concerning Shakespeare's love life simply leaves a bigger hole to fill with speculative invention. The stories in the next two chapters, which address Shakespeare as straight and gay lover, depart from the context of historical biography and approach Shakespeare's life indirectly, via parallel and parody. 'The Adventure of Shakespeare's Ring' is of course an imitation of Sir Arthur Conan Doyle's Sherlock Holmes stories, beginning with the opening sentence of *The Hound of the Baskervilles*. The forensic analysis of Mr Harvey's cloak imitates that of Dr Mortimer's stick. There are naturally comparisons to be made between the methods of the famous fictional detective and those of the literary biographer, but I have left these implicit for the interested reader to disentangle. Sherlock Holmes often quotes Shakespeare in the original stories. One of his favourite tags is 'The game's afoot,' from *Henry V.* In 'The Adventure of Shakespeare's Ring,' I have given him some additional quotations, but his citations of *The Tempest* ('airy nothings') and of *Othello* ('[his] occupation's gone') can be found quoted in 'The Adventure of the Empty House' (1903). Most significantly for my purposes, in the same story Holmes quotes from *Twelfth Night:* '"journey's ending, lover's meeting", as the old play says.' Oscar Wilde appears as a character in 'The Adventure of Shakespeare's Ring,' and his dialogue contains quotations from his own works, and a speech he gave at his trial. The view of the *Sonnets* Wilde advances here is not that developed by the real Oscar Wilde in his famous essay 'The Portrait of Mr W.H.' Some description is imitated from Wilde's *The Picture of Dorian Gray*. Other quotations derive from Shakespeare's *Sonnets*.

The Adventure of Shakespeare's Ring

Mr Sherlock Holmes, who was usually very late in the mornings, save on those not infrequent occasions when he stayed awake all night, was up betimes when I presented myself at our breakfast table, in the pretty sitting room of the apartments we shared in Baker Street. Curiosity had obviously roused him early, for he was busy bestowing a searching scrutiny on an old evening cloak, which he had hung for the purpose from the central lamp fitting, to take advantage of the strong morning sunlight that streamed through the uncurtained window.

'Well, Watson, what do you make of it?'

'Other than that it was left here – I presume inadvertently – by the visitor who called last evening while we were at the opera, waited an hour and departed – very little. He left his cloak but not his visiting card, so we know nothing about him, or his business with you. Except that he will no doubt return, to retrieve his garment, if for no other reason.'

'But does the cloak itself tell you nothing about its wearer? Since we have been so unfortunate as to miss him, and have no notion of his errand, this accidental souvenir becomes of the highest importance. Let me hear you reconstruct the man by an examination of it.'

Piqued by Holmes's infectious curiosity, I came closer to look at the cloak. It was an undistinguished garment, made of dark cloth, of a discarded fashion, and very well worn in places. It was on the other hand lined with red silk, suggesting that both the cloak and the wearer had seen better days. Various stains around the overhanging cape sleeves conferred a rusty appearance on the cloth. There was a quantity of dried mud, of a brownish-yellow colour, encrusted around the hem. Otherwise the cloak seemed well-cared for, and regularly brushed about the shoulders.

The most interesting feature of the garment was its clasp. A simple chain to close the neck was ornamented with a curious badge or brooch, bearing what appeared to be a coat-of-arms. The heraldic device displayed a shield, crossed by a spear, and above it a falcon holding another spear. Beneath, a banner bore the motto, '*Non sans Drioct.*'

'I think,' said I, following so far as I could the methods of my companion, 'that our visitor is an elderly man of noble family who has fallen on hard times. He has known better circumstances, and has been obliged to descend into obscurity: perhaps a quarrel with his family, or some scandal that forced him to forsake his accustomed manner of living. He keeps but one old man-servant in his house. He lives, I suggest, in the East End of London, and walked all the way here. He is of a retiring character, and absent-minded by nature. As to what he wants with you, I can only guess. The cloak tells me nothing on that point, and we will have to wait for the return of the man himself for enlightenment.'

'Explain to me how you arrived at these conclusions.'

Flattered by Holmes's apparent admiration for my forensic capacities, I went on. 'The cloak is well-made, and was at one time an expensive garment. But it is of an old fashion, and has not been replaced. So its owner is less well-off than he was. The clasp has a coat-of-arms, which I assume to be a crest of nobility to which he has some right or title. He is perhaps a lesser scion of a great family, some younger brother perhaps, who has inherited the escutcheon of aristocracy but no fortune.'

'Yes, go on.'

'From the mud round the hem I infer that he has walked through dirty, unswept streets, from some insalubrious part of town. I guess that he cannot afford the cab fare, which evidence of impecuniosity is consistent with the antiquity of his cloak. Such a man would have good reason for the cultivation of anonymity, so he left no indication as to his identity. And he is absent-minded, or he would not have departed without his cape.'

'Excellent, Watson, excellent. You do me honour as a most apt and ready pupil. I must confess I am very much in your debt.'

He had never said as much before, and I must admit that his words gave me keen pleasure, for I had often been piqued by his indifference to my admiration. I was proud to think that I had so far mastered his system as to apply it in a way that earned his approval. He returned to his own scrutiny of the cloak, examined it for a few minutes with his naked eyes, then looked it over again with a convex lens.

'Interesting, though elementary,' he said, returning to his favourite corner of the settee. 'It gives a basis for several deductions.'

'Has anything escaped me?' I asked with some self-importance. 'I trust there is nothing of consequence which I have overlooked.'

'I am afraid, my dear Watson, that most of your conclusions were incorrect. But in noting your fallacies, I have been guided towards the truth. The man is certainly a walker, and he is not rich. Beyond that, your sketch of him is in all particulars entirely erroneous.'

Deflated, I settled once more into my customary position of Plato to Holmes' Socrates, listening and recording, rather than originating knowledge and wisdom.

'Let me hear your theories, then, Holmes.'

'Certainly, my dear fellow. The cloak is old and out of fashion, true. But it was not purchased new by the present owner from some gentleman's outfitters in Saville Row. Look carefully inside the collar: you will see broken stitches where a name or monogram has been removed. The cloak was bought second-hand.'

I peered at the lining, and indeed it was so.

'The cloak is certainly well-kept, but not by a servant. Observe, if you will, the nap around the shoulders. The brush has been dragged repeatedly across the cloth, but in several different directions. A trained servant would always brush one way. He brushes it himself. Furthermore, a decent servant would surely have made some attempt to remove the stains around the cape sleeves. Look at them closely Watson. Use the glass. Stains of ink, and traces of candle-wax. A man of letters, then, who has sat up writing by candle-light in a room cold enough to require the wearing of a cloak. A dedicated scholar, as well as a poor one.'

'And the mud?'

'Not East End mud, Watson, not the filth of some unswept pavement in Whitechapel. London mud is immediately recognisable under cursory forensic examination, for it consists of a specific recipe of ingredients: soil, sand, brick-dust, soot, straw, horse-dung and the excrement of humans and dogs. This is a pure loam picked up from the edge of a ploughed field. Our visitor walks and collects mud on his cloak because he is a countryman. The colour of the mud is consistent with the native soil of the English Midlands, most likely Warwickshire.'

'Can you really be so precise?' I asked incredulously, beginning to suspect my friend was playing with me.

'In this case with tolerable certainty. There are two other clues that point me in that direction. One is the clasp. It is not the existing coat of arms of any noble family, but it does bear the device of a very distinguished man, one with whom you claim familiarity. Have you not seen it before?'

'It does look vaguely familiar. I am no expert in these matters.'

'Clearly,' said Holmes drily, and reaching behind him, drew from the little bookshelf that held my small library, a green leather-bound volume. He placed it before me, and pointed to a crest that was embossed in gold leaf on the cover.

'Why it is exactly the same!' I exclaimed. 'But this is a volume of ... Shakespeare's *Sonnets!*'

'Which you seem to have perused with little attention. The crest is that granted by the College of Arms to the Shakespeare family in 1596. Now assuming that our visitor is not William Shakespeare come back from the dead to assert his authorship of his works, the badge must be worn as a mark of his interest in Shakespeare. In any case our mystery will soon be solved. No doubt he will be at the door within the next five minutes.'

'Is that a guess?'

'I said "no doubt", Watson. Did you observe when we left the opera yesterday that it had rained? Our man would not have gone far in the rain without returning for his cloak. I doubt if he is truly absent-minded; scholars pretend to be so, to avoid involvement in anything but their work. So he stayed near here. Most of the small commercial hotels serve breakfast from 7 a.m., so giving him half an hour for a hurried breakfast, he should shortly be with us. Before he arrives, let us sum up what we know of him. We know he is a writer. If he were a professional academic, he would surely be able to afford a fire to write by. He is some amateur enthusiast, some incurable lifelong student. In summary, I believe we will find our man to be an elderly retired assistant professor at the University of Birmingham, who devotes his life to the study of Shakespeare.'

'Because of the Warwickshire mud?' I said, finding this conclusion hugely far-fetched, and with some asperity at the way in which Holmes had dismissed my stumbling attempts at deduction.

'Partly,' said Holmes coolly, lighting a cigarette. 'There is the mud. There is the connection with Shakespeare of Warwickshire. And if you look in the inside pocket of the cloak, you will find the stub of railway ticket, indicating that our man came down yesterday on the Birmingham train.'

Before I could protest at this blatant piece of trickery, we heard the doorbell ring, as Holmes had predicted.

'Now is the dramatic moment of fate, Watson, when you hear a step upon the stair that is walking into your life, and you know not whether for good or ill.'

Mrs. Hudson ushered in a small man, dressed respectably in a tweed suit. He was considerably younger than either of us had estimated. His hair was cropped unusually close, his jaw clean-shaven, and a heavy moustache covered his upper lip. He looked from one to the other of us with cold, confident eyes. He extended a small hand to Holmes, who had stood to greet him, and bowed courteously to me.

'I am sorry to have missed you last night, Mr. Holmes,' he said, with a trace of Midlands accent, and taking a seat. 'And I would not be disturbing you now, if it were not that I need your help, and that the case is in the public interest. I should say that I can pay you only a modest fee.'

Holmes waved the apology aside. 'If the case is interesting, that will be payment enough.'

The little man's eyes flickered observantly around the room as he introduced himself, noting the cloak hung from the lamp, and the volume of *Sonnets* on the table. 'I see you have already begun your inquiries. My name is William Harvey.'

'Mr W. H.?,' said Holmes quietly, indicating the book on the table.

'A fortuitous coincidence,' replied the visitor, smiling. 'I was a schoolteacher at Stratford Grammar School, but retired from that work to devote my life to the study of Shakespeare.'

'Oh that's bad, bad,' murmured Holmes.

'Why is it bad?'

'Nothing, nothing. Only that you have disarranged some of our little deductions. Pray proceed.'

'I am a member of the Shakespeare Birthplace Trust, and have some responsibility for the collection of artefacts we exhibit at the Birthplace in Stratford-upon-Avon. One week ago, a crime was committed, and I am seeking your confidential assistance in solving it.'

He drew from an inside pocket of his jacket a sheet of newspaper from the *Warwickshire Herald,* and handed it to Holmes, pointing him to an article marked up on the page.

Break-in at Shakespeare's Birthplace Foiled

Only the presence of mind of our local constable, Officer Sadler, has prevented a serious loss of Shakespeare treasures from the Birthplace in Henley Street. Constable Sadler, making his usual night round, noticed a light showing inside the locked and empty house, and proceeded to investigate. Going round the side of the house, he heard a commotion at the rear, and was just in time to see the culprit making off through the garden and across the fields. He gave chase, but lost the burglar in the dark. Returning to the house, he found the rear door prised open, and raised the alarm. On examination of the house's contents, it was discovered that nothing had been stolen. It is assumed that the burglar's intentions were thwarted by the appearance of the police. The house is closed to visitors while repairs can be made to the broken door.

'Interesting,' said Holmes, dropping the paper on the table. 'But not the whole story. You would not seek to interest me in a failed burglary in a small provincial town. "Serious loss prevented." "Nothing stolen." My redoubtable colleagues in the county police can surely deal with the dangers consequent on a broken back door.'

'You are correct, sir, of course. But the newspaper report is inaccurate. Something was stolen.'

Holmes leaned forward in his chair with an expression of intense interest. 'Go on,' he said.

'You understand that any investigation of this crime must be conducted with the utmost secrecy.'

'I have already inferred such a conclusion from the fact that you appear to have kept this information from the press, and presumably from the police.'

'You are correct, sir. Once I have confided this secret to you gentleman, there will be only two people in the world – I beg your pardon, Dr. Watson, three – who know of it. Except of course the thief and his associates.'

'We accept your confidence, sir,' said Holmes. 'Please continue.'

Mr. Harvey reached slowly into his pocket and drew out a small jewellery box of blue morocco leather, which he opened and placed on the table. It contained a gold signet ring, apparently of some antiquity. The face bore the inverted letters WS. The initials were joined by a tracery of ornamental string and tassels, the upper flourish of which formed the resemblance of a heart.

'Shakespeare's ring,' murmured Holmes.

'You know of this?,' I asked, surprised at my companion's prior knowledge.

'Yes, it was much talked of some years ago, when it was given to the Birthplace, where it is on permanent exhibition. So it has not been stolen?'

'Oh yes it has, Mr. Holmes. The ring you are holding is an exact copy. It was left in place of the true ring by the burglar.'

Holmes was studying the ring through his magnifying glass, turning it round and scrutinizing it intently from every angle. 'A copy,' he said thoughtfully. 'How do you know?'

'Because the original bears an inscription on the inside. This, as you see, is blank. The ring lay in a display case, slipped over a ferrule so the inside was not visible to external observation.'

Carefully Holmes replaced the ring in its case. 'So you want the true ring back?'

'Yes,' said Harvey, 'I want it back. I care nothing as to the perpetrator's being brought to justice, and indeed would prefer the whole matter to remain secret. But Shakespeare's ring should be back where it belongs, in Shakespeare's family home, the house where he was born.'

Holmes looked up from the ring to our visitor, who coolly returned his somewhat unmannerly stare. 'What does the inscription say?,' he asked.

"*Pences pour moye.*"

Holmes nodded. "Think on me." Suddenly he looked at me, and with an expression I had never seen before on his face, a strange mixture of curiosity, apprehension and concern, asked: 'Should we take this case, Watson?'

I was nonplussed, since he had never asked such a question of me before. 'It is certainly an intriguing case. And its solution would, one might say, be in the public interest.'

'But who knows where it might lead?' said Holmes softly, almost to himself. "Think on me." Then with his more customary brusqueness, he said: 'I will take the case. May I keep the ring and the paper? Both will be returned to you. We will join you in Stratford tomorrow, if that is convenient, to examine the scene of the crime and begin our search.'

'Thank you, Mr. Holmes. Your services will be greatly valued.' Harvey stood up to leave, and Holmes busied himself taking down the cloak. As the little man was approaching the door, Holmes said suddenly, 'One question, please, before you go. Does the police officer patrol regularly?.'

'Yes. At the same time every night.'

'Thank you,' said Holmes, 'most interesting.' Then as Harvey's hand was on the door knob, Holmes suddenly asked him: 'Why did you open the display cabinet?'

There was a slight, almost imperceptible hesitation, before our visitor replied. 'The ring was the most valuable piece we have on display. It could be easily transported and hidden. I thought it the burglar's most likely target.'

'Thank you, Mr. Harvey. That will be all for now. We will see you tomorrow in Stratford.'

I followed Mr. Harvey down the stairs to see him out. At the front door he turned and spoke to me, looking down at the floor as if in some embarrassment.

'Dr. Watson, your friend is by reputation a man of almost superhuman ability, is he not?.'

'It is no exaggeration to describe him thus.'

'You are a man more like myself, a competent professional without any remarkable gifts. Is it not so?'

'Why yes,' I said in some amusement, 'that is a fair assessment.'

'And your admiration for your friend knows no bounds, is that correct?'

I was strangely stirred by the little man's curious catechism. 'I would follow him,' I said solemnly, 'to the very ends of the earth.'

'Thank you,' said Harvey, looking up at me at last. 'That is all I wished to know.'

As I mounted the stair again, I thought I heard the sitting-room door closing. But Holmes was still on the settee examining the paper and the ring. 'Come, Watson, come,' he said, rubbing his hands. 'This morning I can say, with more than usual propriety, that "the game's afoot".'

'Then we are for Stratford in the morning?' I asked.

'No, Watson. You will go to Stratford, and perform a forensic examination of the scene. I believe there is nothing to be found there, but we cannot afford to neglect any possible clue. I will be here in London, since I am certain both the ring and the thief are here. For the rest of today, my dear fellow, please make yourself busy preparing for your journey. I have numerous hypotheses to test, and you will not find me companionable. Let us meet at dinner and review our position.'

†

'Well, Watson,' said Holmes to me that night, 'what are your opinions so far?'

'That this burglary was a clever as well as a knavish piece of work. The criminal acquired a copy of the ring, some cheap souvenir no doubt, and took it with him to substitute for the real one. He presumably hoped to steal other items as well, but was disturbed by the police constable. He will already have fenced the ring to his underworld associates for a fraction of its true value. Clearly he hoped that the ring's disappearance would not be noticed for a time at least, long enough for the trail to grow cold.'

'Accurate as far as it goes, Watson,' said Holmes. 'You are on the right track. But this was more than a clever piece of skulduggery performed by a smart local cracksman. Much, much more.'

'What are your thoughts?' I asked, intrigued by his dissatisfaction with what seemed the obvious explanation.

'Let us review the evidence. We have three pieces: the ring, the newspaper article and Mr Harvey's story.'

'All solid evidence. All consistent. All mutually corroborating.'

'No, Watson. All three counterfeit. The ring is a fake, of course, we know. The newspaper article is a cover-up, and our visitor's story is at least partly a lie.'

'You amaze me. Show me your reasoning.'

'First the ring. It is not a cheap imitation designed only to distract attention until someone – a cleaner perhaps – looked a bit more closely. I have shown it to an expert jeweller: it is a precise copy, made by an accomplished craftsman, and fashioned of the purest gold. The copy would have cost more to make than your estimate of what the cracksman would get from his fence. Someone would have had to study the ring minutely in its display case, in order to supply the goldsmith with precise directions as to how to reproduce it. The ruse would have worked, had it not been for the inscription, invisible from the outside, and for our friend's surprising alacrity in realizing the ring's disappearance. Second, the account of the burglary in the paper. What sort of local man would time his break-in to coincide with the regular patrol of the reliable village officer? What sort of burglar uses a light to do his work, and risks alerting the whole street? Where would such a man seek to dispose of such a notorious piece of loot? No; our friends of the *Warwickshire Herald* have been too easily satisfied with this most implausible account. Last, our visitor. Everything he told us is true except for one significant omission.'

'And that is ...?'

'He knew that the removal of the ring was the thief's objective. He checked immediately, though there was no sign that the case had been tampered with, and the ring appeared to be undisturbed. And he knew exactly how to satisfy himself that it had gone.'

'So what in general do you conclude from all this?'

'At this stage, everything and nothing. The ring has a meaning beyond its value. Someone wanted it badly enough to pay a professional criminal to acquire it by these means, and to make the crime look like a failed burglary. Such expertise is expensive: the cost of the crime must have far exceeded the value that could be obtained from the ring. Who in any case would buy such a famous stolen jewel? No, Watson, there is much more here than meets the eye.'

'What are your instructions?'

'Go to Stratford. Take the ring back to Harvey. Tell him to put it back on display, so there will be no public alarm. Investigate the scene of the burglary. It will be of interest to me to know how the criminal gained entry; how he got access to the ring; and how he made his escape. Talk to Harvey again, and glean what you can from the conversation.'

'And you ...?'

I have a number of leads to follow here. Let us say goodnight, for we both have a long day tomorrow.'

†

I did as Holmes bade, and took the train to Birmingham. Reaching Stratford at midday, I lunched with Harvey at the Falcon, and in the afternoon examined the crime scene at the Birthplace in Henley Street. I found the door at the rear roughly jemmied open. This was where the burglar had gained entry, and through the same means had made his escape. I looked at the ground alongside the path, as I had seen Holmes do, and could see only two distinct sets of footprints: the boots of the constable, and the smaller shoes of the burglar himself. It was clear he had made an easy escape across the fields in the dark, probably laying up in some barn or hayrick before taking the road to London, as Holmes was sure he had, at first light. Inside the house there was little sign of disturbance. I made a careful examination of the display cabinet, the glass top of which seemed securely jointed into the heavy wooden base. But looking underneath I could see that a simple lever released a panel that gave easy access to the contents.

I conversed again with Harvey, who lived in a pretty cottage not far from the Birthplace. He was evidently a bachelor, his only servant being a fresh-faced and athletic-looking young man who admitted me. Harvey was if anything more guarded with me than he had been with Holmes the day before, though my presence should scarcely have inspired any corresponding intimidation. He restated the facts as he had initially disclosed them, reiterating that the ring was highly prized, and its restoration much desired. Thinking about what Holmes had said, I pressed him a little more about the significance of the ring. With a scholar's hesitancy he explained that although the ownership of the ring, with its corroboration by the detail in Shakespeare's will, was not in doubt, what it meant to Shakespeare was a matter of conjecture. It may have been simply his own signet, acquired to stamp legal documents. It may have been a gift from his father. When I asked if it might have had some connection with his wife, as I had read somewhere, a wedding or betrothal ring, he showed surprisingly little interest. He had heard, he said, of the theory that it was a betrothal ring given to Shakespeare by Anne Hathaway. But he knew of no evidence to support this hypothesis.

I found this conversation frustrating, since it led me no further in understanding what the meaning of the ring, which Holmes had said exceeded its value, might be. The perception grew upon me that Harvey was withholding something. I sent a telegram to Holmes in London summing up my findings, and confiding my instinct that there was some aspect of this affair that remained unrevealed, some evidence that dare not show itself, some truth that dare not speak its name.

†

It was nigh on dinner-time by the time I got back to London, and Holmes was already dressed. I noticed that he had dressed more fastidiously than usual, adding to his ordinary evening suit a white silk cravat, and a shirt front with elaborate frills. His fingers were decorated with rings, and in place of his usual meerschaum pipe, he was gripping between his teeth a large gold and amber cigarette-holder. 'Hurry, Watson,' he said, 'we have little time. We dine at Mancini's, and I have tickets for the opera. We will need to pay particular attention tonight, since the opera bears indirectly on our case – it is Wagner's *Rheingold*. Afterwards we will be undertaking a little excursion to further our inquiries, so expect to be up late. And take your sword-stick with you.'

When we emerged from the theatre into Covent Garden, Holmes signalled to a waiting cab which drew up beside us as if by appointment. He said nothing to the driver, who quickly steered the carriage out of the crowded streets and headed towards the river. The public houses were just closing, and men and women clustering in broken groups around their doors. The sound of drunken singing drifted fragmentarily on the evening breeze. As we drove on, the gas lamps became fewer, and the streets more narrow and gloomy. A mist from the river gathered around. Steam rose from the horse as it splashed through the puddles.

Suddenly the driver drew up with a jerk at the top of a dark lane. Over the low roofs and jagged chimney stacks of the houses rose the black masts of ships. We alighted and walked in the direction of the quay, till we reached a small shabby house that was wedged in between two factories. Holmes stopped at the door, and gave a peculiar knock. Shortly after I heard steps in the passage, and the chain being unhooked. A squat misshapen figure flattened itself into the shadows as we passed along the hall. At the end of the passage we entered a long, low room, lit by flaring gas jets. Some Malays were crouching round a charcoal stove, playing with bone counters. From behind the bar a woman came to meet Holmes, and led us up some stairs to a back room. In this shabby, smoke-filled den, a number of occupants rested on grubby beds, or mattresses spread on the floor. They all displayed the twisted limbs and gaping mouths of opium smokers.

Holmes was directed by the woman towards an alcove screened off from the room by a dirty hanging curtain of red beaded strings. We went through into the recess, and there, sitting up on the bed, was a young man of extraordinary personal beauty, dressed in elaborate evening clothes rather like those Holmes had assumed. On a little table beside him lay some long thin pipes, bits of some green waxy paste, and a half-empty tumbler of brandy. He struck me as familiar, though I could not place him; perhaps I had seen his picture somewhere, in a gallery, or a newspaper.

With his crisp gold hair and finely curved scarlet lips, he seemed out of place. It seemed to me a paradox that such pure beauty should be found in so foul a den as this. But as I looked closer I could see that his pupils were dilated with the effects of the drug, and from lustreless eyes he looked back at us with the slow detachment and indifference of the opium smoker. Holmes sat beside him on the bed, and took his hand, which was extraordinarily white and limp. The young man put up no resistance.

'Watson, this is Lord Alfred Douglas,' Holmes said to me. 'I believe he has some information of relevance to our inquiries.'

One side of Douglas' mouth crooked up in a half-smile, like a man who has had a stroke. 'Mr. Sherlock Holmes, the famous detective. I was expecting you.'

'Oh,' said Holmes non-committally.

'Yes,' said Douglas. 'You have entered my world now, Mr Holmes, and in my world no informant is to be trusted. Each one is a double agent. Everyone you paid for information immediately reported back to my associates. I know all about your errand.'

'But you have made no effort to avoid being found in what I understand to be one of your usual haunts?' said Holmes.

Douglas looked at him with an expression I could not read. 'I thought we might reach some kind of understanding.'

There was a long pause in which they looked at one another, Holmes still holding the young man's hand. Then Holmes said 'Watson, I would like to speak with Lord Alfred privately. Would you please go back downstairs to the bar, and amuse yourself for half an hour?'

I did as he bade, my trust in my friend being absolute, though I understood nothing of what was going on. I went and stood nervously at the seedy bar, and without being asked, the woman who had showed us upstairs placed before me a bottle of brandy and a dirty glass. Further along the bar two dandified and effeminate-looking youths whispered and giggled together. I took some of the brandy, though it tasted of the river, and its raw fiery warmth took some of the chill from my soul.

I wondered what Holmes was up to, and how he planned to get the information he wanted from Lord Alfred Douglas. I knew that in the course of his vocation Holmes associated closely with many deviant characters, and often concealed his identity in some bizarre disguise. But in this case he seemed to have entered much more deeply into his role, and *in propria persona*. It may have been the influence of the dark and mysterious quest we followed, or the depressing environment surrounding me, but I could not dispel the feeling of melancholy that clung about me, as the river's mist curled round the masts of the ships I could see through the window, as they lay moored by the dark silent wharves. The grand, sad rhythms of Wagner's music pulsed gently through my mind. How much longer would Holmes be? And what were these strange emotions stirring within me: feelings of doubt and anxiety; fears and forebodings; and even an odd kind of jealousy that my friend had left me here to tend upon the hours and times of his desires. Had I no precious time of my own to spend, no services to do, till he required?

At last Holmes came down the stairs, and signalled to me that we were to leave. In the short walk up the dark lane to meet our cab he said nothing, and once in the hansom remained for a while taciturn and subdued. Soon however he began to talk, though, as he often did, not about the affair at hand, but about Wagner's music, of which he had the crudest ideas. I remained silent, still under the spell of my melancholy mood. One of Sherlock Holmes' defects was that he was exceedingly loath to communicate his full plans to any other person until the instant of their fulfilment; partly it came no doubt from his own masterful nature, which loved to dominate and surprise those close to him. Partly also from his professional caution, which urged him never to take any chances. The result, however, was very trying to one acting as his agent and assistant. I had often suffered from it, but never so much as on that long drive in the darkness. Holmes had said nothing, and I could only surmise what his course of action would be.

Back in Baker Street, the hour being so late, we went straight to bed.

'Goodnight, Watson. Tomorrow I hope to solve the crime, so there will be no more mystery.'

'Can you tell me nothing more?.'

He shook his head. 'I fear not. Except that tomorrow we will be paying a visit to Mr. Oscar Wilde.'

†

Next evening, as Holmes had promised, we drew up outside a pretty red-brick house in Tite Street, Chelsea. We were admitted, and shown into an extraordinary sitting-room, decorated entirely in white, walls, furniture, even carpets. A red lampshade hung from the ceiling, casting a pool of light onto a terra cotta statue which stood on the table on a red diamond-shaped cloth. We were not kept waiting long, when Wilde himself, wearing his astrakhan evening coat, yellow kid gloves and extravagant yellow shoes, came in and greeted us. I had seen him about town, of course, but had never met him. Though he affected the languorous elegance of the dandy, removing one glove and extending to us a soft white hand, his long droll face and vivacious eyes sparkled with the wit and intelligence for which he was famous.

'You are going out, I perceive, Mr Wilde, 'said Holmes. 'We will not detain you long.'

'It is only to the opera, Mr Holmes,' replied Wilde in his slow, musical voice, as he fitted a cigarette into a jade cigarette-holder. '*Das Rheingold.* It is hardly worth my entering before the interval, for in the dark no-one can see me.'

'But do you not enjoy the music?'

'Oh yes of course. Dear Wagner's music is so loud one can talk all the way through without being overheard. Some hock and seltzer? I always take hock and seltzer. Do help yourselves; my servant is French, and always has something more important to do than to tend to my needs. His name is *Cretin*, or at least that is what I call him. But how can I assist you gentlemen?'

'Mr Wilde,' Holmes began, 'We come to you on a matter of some delicacy. A crime has been committed, and though I am sure you yourself have no knowledge of it, you are an unwitting beneficiary.'

Wilde drew on his cigarette, and looked from one to the other of us with an expression of perplexity. He seemed genuinely at a loss for words, a condition of which he had little experience.

'Mr Wilde,' said Holmes. 'This a matter of great confidence. You know my reputation as I know yours. I offer you the word of a gentlemen that anything spoken here will stay within these walls.'

Wilde bowed his assent.

'May I ask you, then,' said Holmes, 'to remove your other glove?'

Wilde hesitated, but then stripped the glove off his left hand, revealing to my astonishment that he wore what appeared to be Shakespeare's ring on the third finger of his left hand.

'A beautiful thing,' said Holmes, indicating the ring. 'A copy of Shakespeare's signet. Will you tell me how you came by it?'

'It was a gift from a friend.'

'From Lord Alfred Douglas. And will you tell me, Mr Wilde, what the ring means to you, and why you wear it on that particular finger?'

Wilde turned the ring on his finger and held it up to the light. 'What it signifies, Mr Holmes, is "The Love that dare not speak its name".'

'Please elaborate.'

'Throughout history there have been many examples of great affection between an elder and a younger man. In the Bible there is David and Jonathan. Plato made it the very basis of his philosophy. You will find it in the sonnets of Michelangelo and Shakespeare. It is a deep, spiritual affection that is as pure as it is perfect. It dictates and pervades great works of art like those of Shakespeare and Michelangelo. It is in this century misunderstood, so much misunderstood that it may be described as the "Love that dare not speak its name". It is beautiful, it is fine, it is the noblest form of affection. There is nothing unnatural about it. It is intellectual, and it repeatedly exists between an elder and a younger man, when the elder man has intellect, and the younger man has all the joy, hope and glamour of life before him. That it should be so the world does not understand. The world mocks at it and sometimes puts one in the pillory for it. The common herd like to think that the original of this ring sat on Shakespeare's finger merely to stamp legal documents. As if a true poet would really concern himself with such trivialities! Or they will tell you that it was given him by his wife, a woman to whom he clearly had no abiding attachment. No, Mr Holmes; the ring of which this is a copy was given to Shakespeare by the Earl of Southampton. Between the two, the noble and the poet, there existed just such a common bond as the one I have described. Shakespeare was the elder man – he describes himself as in the "twilight" of his day – and Southampton the younger – the "fair friend" who never could grow old. Shakespeare was the bearer of a remarkable talent, and Southampton admired and loved him for it. They loved one another as a man loves a woman. They loved, and quarrelled, and parted, as lovers do. But not before Shakespeare had expressed his love in that beautiful sequence of poems; and not before Southampton had given him the original of this ring, as a token of their mutual affection. '"W" and "S", William and Southampton, joined in mutual affection, the one to the other. You will know, Mr Holmes, as who does not, that I too have a love, as Shakespeare did; that he also is an aristocrat, with a noble admiration for the beautiful and true; and that he is young, younger than I. Nothing could be more natural, then, than that he should present to me this facsimile of the token representing the love between Shakespeare and Southampton. If there has been something reprehensible in his acquisition of this token, I know nothing of it. The gift itself was as innocent as childhood.'

'Indeed,' said Holmes. 'Your friend Lord Alfred is in many ways a child. But surely a very experienced innocent. What do those initials "W. S." mean to you, Mr Wilde, appearing as they do on your own hand?'

'"Wilde and Shakespeare" was Bosie's suggestion.'

'Very apt. But I have heard of another possibility, of a more esoteric nature.'

'Ah yes,' returned Wilde returning Holmes' level stare. 'So have I. "Wilde and Salome", I think you mean? The old prophet and the beautiful young temptress by whom he lost his head?'

'But Salome was a woman.'

'With a man's desire, a man's will, and a man's lust for revenge. A true master-mistress of passion. It is all in my play, Mr. Holmes.'

'Which I look forward to seeing,' said Holmes, rising to his feet and holding out his hand. Wilde took and held it for what seemed to me a long time, as if the two men were exchanging some kind of recognition. Then Holmes broke the pause, moved to stand before the fire-place, and assumed his more 'official' manner.

'I have to inform you, Mr Wilde, that the ring upon your finger is not, as you believe, a copy of Shakespeare's ring, but the very ring itself. Stolen from Shakespeare's birthplace by a young man of your acquaintance, and at the behest of Lord Alfred himself. This exact copy,' and he produced what seemed to me to be the very ring Mr Harvey had shown to us, 'was left in place of the original to ward off suspicion.'

Wilde looked at the copy with an expression of surprise and concern. 'How do you know which is which, Mr Holmes?'

'The ring you wear has an inscription on the inside: "*Pences pour moye*", does it not?.'

'Indeed it does.'

'This copy does not. I assure you Mr Wilde, there is no doubt as to which ring is which.'

There was a long pause in which Wilde stared intently at the ring on his finger. Then he spoke, his voice tremulous with disappointment. 'Foolish, foolish boy. Has he learned nothing from what I have tried to teach him? Does he not know that artifice is more true than reality? That the copy is more valuable than the original? Nothing that actually occurs is of the smallest importance. He is like one of those silly boys who, after reading the adventures of Jack Shepherd or Dick Turpin, pillage the stalls of unfortunate applewomen, break into sweet-shops at night, and alarm old gentleman returning from the city by leaping out on them in suburban lanes, with black masks and unloaded revolvers. What do I want with Shakespeare's own ring, bearing as it does the curse of betrayal? The ring that binds only to separate? Is that how Bosie and I are to end?'

He slipped the ring from his finger and held it out to Holmes. 'Please, Mr Holmes, take it back. Restore it to Stratford. I want nothing to do with it. But

I beg you to withhold any proceedings you may be planning against Bosie. He is far too innocent and foolish to have done this with true criminal intent. He did it only for love of me.'

'I have no such intentions, Mr Wilde,' said Holmes. 'To recover the ring was our only quest. Please accept this copy as a substitute. It is in all respects identical, save for the inscription. And let the matter end there. You will hear no more of it.'

As we left Wilde's house the evening was closing in. Without speaking we walked together around the corner to the Embankment, and watched the sun set in inexplicable splendour over the red sails and blackened hulls of boats riding softly on the shining Thames.

'Well, Watson,' began Holmes, in an unusually gentle tone of voice. 'Do you remember my asking you if we should take this case?'

'Yes indeed, I remember it well.'

'And my wondering where it would lead us?'

'That too.'

Holmes was silent for a moment. 'You said once that you would follow me to the ends of the earth, did you not?'

So he had been listening when I made that declaration to Harvey! 'Yes I did, and meant it.'

'I would not ask you to go so far. But that makes it easier to propose that you should come away with me to the Continent.'

'Where?'

'Oh anywhere. It's all the same to me. To where the end of this affair awaits us. There is a train from Victoria at a quarter after midnight. Will you come, as you are, without sending any word, without taking any luggage? Just the two of us, now, tonight?'

'What of the ring? Should we not return it?'

'All in good time. For now, "sits the wind fair" for France.'

And so we left, that very night, on the boat-train for Paris. Holmes was too well-known a character to be able to board such a train without being observed by policemen, informants, criminals, special agents. But when he wanted to elude pursuit, no man was more cunning and resourceful. When the train stopped at Canterbury, we slipped off it and made our way cross-country to Newhaven, where we boarded a ferry to Dieppe. From there we travelled on to Brussels and Strasbourg, with Holmes always watching for any sign of recognition. Having satisfied himself that we were not being followed, and could proceed on our journey with the protection of anonymity, we drifted on at greater leisure towards Switzerland, via Luxembourg and Basle.

For a charming week we wandered up the valley of the Rhone and then, branching off at Leuk, made our way over the Gemmi pass, still deep in snow, and so by way of Interlaken to Meiringen. In the course of our journey, he explained to me every detail of the case he had so brilliantly solved, so that gradually I realized its full meaning, for Wilde and Bosie, for Shakespeare and

Southampton, and even at last, though this recognition was long in coming, for the two of us. Holmes had suspected from the beginning that there was more to Harvey's story than met the eye, and my report from Stratford had confirmed him in that opinion. From the outset he had been convinced, as he had said, that the ring possessed a meaning that exceeded its value, though it had taken him some time to deduce what that meaning might be. He had initiated his inquiries with the goldsmith to whom he had taken the counterfeit ring. From his workshop in a little courtyard off Hatton Garden this craftsman kept himself informed of all the news and gossip relating to the movement of jewellery and precious metals, including underworld intelligence on stolen goods. Holmes had intervened to save this man's reputation in the course of the scandal involving the theft of the Empress of Austria's diamonds. The goldsmith was able to tell immediately who had fashioned the fake ring, and through his network of informants soon established that the true ring had been stolen to order by a gifted amateur, who was not part of any criminal network, but had known association with a secret society of aristocratic homosexuals known as 'The Circle.'

Knowing that such a freemasonry would be impenetrable, Holmes had instead delved into a seedy underworld of 'rent boys' and male prostitutes that was familiar to him, but that I barely knew existed. Heavily disguised, and extravagantly generous in what he would pay for information, Holmes soon made headway with this unscrupulous set, characters devoid of all decency and honour, and acquired the identity of the thief. He tracked the man down and watched his lodgings, and was able by bribery to intercept messages intended for him. He was able to establish that the man was in contact with Lord Alfred Douglas. Tracking Douglas down was easy, and thus the trail led straight to Wilde.

I asked Holmes how he had contrived to retain possession of the counterfeit ring. He explained that he had taken the precaution of commissioning a second copy from his Hatton Garden connections, so the same ring would seem simultaneously to be safe on display in Stratford, gleaming on Oscar Wilde's finger, and hidden in Holmes' pocket.

I admitted that I would never have suspected the true state of affairs in this case, as I had never thought of Shakespeare as a lover of men.

'You see, Watson,' observed Holmes, 'how often you have complained that I keep my suspicions secret from you, and keep you in the dark till the last page is turned? Yes, I have read such sentiments in your fanciful little accounts of my cases. But in this instance, it was not my secrecy, but your innocence, that prevented you from seeing the truth. You think Shakespeare was a "normal" man, though he wrote poems of passionate love to a homosexual aristocrat. You made nothing of our friend Harvey's unusual interest in the ring, combined with his peculiar domestic arrangements. Indeed it was not until I drew you into the company of notorious sodomites that the truth began to dawn on you!'

It was all true, and I was at a loss to understand what it was that had blocked my vision. 'Yes, I begin to see it now.'

'But do you see it all? Do you see it clearly? Watson, why have you never married?'

'Never found the right girl, I suppose.'

'No, Watson, you have never found *any* girl. You care nothing for women. You live with another man. Has it never occurred to you that as far as appearances go, we might ourselves be taken for homosexuals?'

I blushed to the roots of my hair, not so much at the impropriety of what he had said, as at the fact that I felt somehow exposed, unmasked, detected.

'Now I beg you to stop pondering and frowning, for as our new friend Oscar Wilde would say, intellect destroys the harmony of any face. "Our occupation's gone", as Shakespeare says somewhere. Let us enjoy the pleasures of idleness.'

It was not difficult to follow his advice, as we sat side by side in the sunny garden of a little Alpine hotel, sipping an excellent local wine, surrounded by immense green peaks that framed a perfect blue sky. It was then that Holmes took my left hand in his, and before I could remonstrate, slipped Shakespeare's ring onto my empty wedding finger.

'"Journey's end in lovers' meeting", as the old play says. Let these initials signify the names of a new couple,' he said. '"W. S": Watson and Sherlock. Till death us do part.'

It was also in this charming spot, as we sat at breakfast, that we hit upon a stratagem for covering our disappearance. The reader familiar with my published accounts of his cases will be aware that it was in this wild and beautiful region Holmes is supposed to have vanished, falling to his death into the abyss of the Reichenbach Falls, while grappling with his arch-enemy Professor Moriarty. Everything I describe in that story is true: the footprints leading to the edge of the chasm; the abandoned alpenstock and cigarette case; the complete disappearance of the world's most famous detective. It pains me to relate, however, having always tried to be honest with my readers, that there was no struggle with Professor Moriarty, and that the clues left at the scene were planted as an elaborate hoax aimed at convincing the public we had both plunged to our deaths. Holmes and I staged the whole crime scene, and jointly wrote the account published as 'The Adventure of the Final Problem' in the *Strand Magazine*. Bidding farewell to the ghosts of our former selves, we set off on the next stage of our journey towards Italy.

Via Milan we reached Rome, and there settled into a new life of relative anonymity and unaccustomed idleness. We rented a small apartment, and spent the days in the cafes, or sauntering around the ruins, or visiting the art collections. Our neighbours accepted us for what we were, two English gentlemen seeking some privacy among the discreet anonymity of the great Roman *populus*. It was here I found myself intoxicated by the ruinous splendour of the ancient world. In that hard bright sunlight, the beauty of the human body, exposed in ostentatious nudity, everywhere collided with the eye.

In particular, I was aware of the unashamed evidence of love between men, which flourished as much in the dark passages of modern Rome as it had when Hadrian was besotted with his lovely Antinous.

We heard the news of Oscar Wilde's arrest and imprisonment, and sorrowed for him. After his release, he found his way to Rome, and we were able to offer the poor and broken man the comfort of our society. Together we visited the galleries and museums, and gazed at some of Rome's most exquisite works of art, the Capitoline Faun, the Belvedere Apollo. I still remember watching Wilde standing in front of that wonderful statue of the 'Dying Gaul' in the Capitoline Museum. He seemed astounded by the beauty of its form, yet wounded to the soul by its attitude of tragic defeat. The expression on his face, of unappeasable yearning, was unforgettable. And so he soon discarded our company in favour of his 'boys,' Arnoldo and Dario, handsome but disreputable characters who sponged on him and robbed him of what little he had.

We knew he had not long to live, and when we heard of his death in Paris, Holmes and I both instinctively knew that our holiday from society would soon be over. Nothing was said; all was understood. One day as we crossed the Ponte San'Angelo, walking away from St Peter's, where I had offered a prayer for Oscar's soul, Holmes said simply 'Back to "normality"', Watson.' And I knew exactly what he meant.

†

And so we set off to retrace our steps, back to England. As the train was slowing down to enter the outskirts of Milan, I took Shakespeare's ring from my finger and returned it to Holmes.

'Yes, Watson, we have no need of it now. It has served its purpose, for us as it did for Oscar and Bosie, and for William and Henry, all those years ago.'

Then to my surprise Holmes pulled down the carriage window, drew back his arm and flung the ring from the moving train. I saw it flash through the air, a glint of gold against green, then fall into the thick clustering bushes of the railway siding.

'Holmes!' I cried. 'Shakespeare's ring!'

'Is no longer our concern. Just remember the message, Watson. "*Pences pour moye*". "Think on me". That is all we know, and all we need to know.'

As the train thundered into a tunnel through the Alps, he turned the conversation to other topics, and the subject of this strange narrative was never mentioned again.

Shakespeare in Love: 'A female evil'

We now come to an episode in the Shakespeare biography for which there is no historical or documentary evidence whatsoever. This concerns his relationship, if there was any, with the notorious 'Dark Lady of the *Sonnets.*' 'She' exists only as the addressee of a series of poems contained in Shakespeare's *Sonnets*, specifically *Sonnets* 127–154. In this literary context, she is as fully created as any person in a play. We know about her appearance, her character, her morals, her behaviour towards the poet. What we do not know, on the other hand, is whether this fictional person corresponds to any actual living person, and whether or not such a person was involved in a love relationship with the poet. In short, we do not know if the *Sonnets* of Shakespeare represent Shakespeare's own autobiography.

The *Sonnets* do seem to tell some kind of story, in which the 'characters' of the 'fair friend,' the 'rival poet' and the Dark Lady all have a role to play. Most of *Sonnets* 127–154 clearly involve a female addressee (many of the poems are sexually ambiguous, and could involve a man or a woman). She is notoriously dark, dark-haired, dark-eyed and dark-skinned. The poet sees her as beautiful, but only in her transgression of the conventional standards of beauty:

In the old age black was not counted fair,
Or if it were, it bore not beauty's name;
But now is black beauty's successive heir,
And beauty slander'd with a bastard shame:
For since each hand hath put on nature's power,
Fairing the foul with art's false borrow'd face,
Sweet beauty hath no name, no holy bower,
But is profaned, if not lives in disgrace.
Therefore my mistress' brows are raven black,
Her eyes so suited, and they mourners seem
At such who, not born fair, no beauty lack,
Slandering creation with a false esteem:
Yet so they mourn, becoming of their woe,
That every tongue says beauty should look so. (Sonnet 127)

Since 'fairness' – which combines the concepts of 'blond' and 'beautiful' – can now be acquired by cosmetic art, false hair and concealing make-up, only the kind of dark unadorned beauty possessed by his mistress can be admired as true beauty. The affair is adulterous on both sides, breaking each lover's 'bed-vow'[1] to his and her respective spouses. The mistress then has a relationship with the 'fair friend,' so the poet is doubly betrayed. He goes on loving her, or is unable to rid himself of his compulsive lust for her, but hates himself for it:

> My love is as a fever, longing still
> For that which longer nurseth the disease,
> Feeding on that which doth preserve the ill,
> The uncertain sickly appetite to please.
> My reason, the physician to my love,
> Angry that his prescriptions are not kept,
> Hath left me, and I desperate now approve
> Desire is death, which physic did except.
> Past cure I am, now reason is past care,
> And frantic-mad with evermore unrest;
> My thoughts and my discourse as madmen's are,
> At random from the truth vainly express'd;
> For I have sworn thee fair and thought thee bright,
> Who art as black as hell, as dark as night. (Sonnet 147)

Here the 'uncertain sickly appetite' of lust is interwoven with metaphors of illness, implying metaphorically that the relationship is self-destructive, and perhaps, more literally, that sexual contact with the mistress puts him in danger of contracting venereal disease. The powerful assertion that 'Desire is death' may operate on a number of levels: sexual desire is conventionally treated, in love poetry of this time, as a fatal attraction; the relationship is destroying him; or to persist in sexual intimacy may bring about his death from syphilis. The famous Sonnet 129 – 'The expense of spirit in a waste of shame' – is a powerful expression of this sexual compulsion, violently damaging to the lover, evacu-ating the sexual relationship of any real pleasure or true satisfaction, providing no hope of any solution to a self-destructive obsession:

> The expense of spirit in a waste of shame
> Is lust in action: and till action, lust
> Is perjured, murderous, bloody, full of blame,
> Savage, extreme, rude, cruel, not to trust;
> Enjoyed no sooner but despised straight;
> Past reason hunted; and no sooner had,
> Past reason hated, as a swallowed bait,
> On purpose laid to make the taker mad.
> Mad in pursuit and in possession so;

Had, having, and in quest to have extreme;
A bliss in proof, and proved, a very woe;
Before, a joy proposed; behind a dream.
All this the world well knows; yet none knows well
To shun the heaven that leads men to this hell.

Here lust is portrayed, in wholly negative terms, as an appetite which is psychologically damaging, futile and unsatisfying. At no point in the repetitive cycle of desire, fulfilment and aftermath is there any genuine pleasure or resolution: yet the sexual compulsion persists, and no-one knows how to put an end to it.

At least two of the poems explicitly play with the author's name 'Will':

Whoever hath her wish, thou hast thy 'Will,'
And 'Will' to boot, and 'Will' in overplus;
More than enough am I that vex thee still,
To thy sweet will making addition thus. (Sonnet 135)

It could be argued that to put one's own forename at the centre of the poetic action in this way amounts to a signing of the literary document as in some way autobiographical. But this is still literature, not life. The drama is real enough, but drama is not biography. To speculate about the identity of the Dark Lady presupposes a number of highly questionable assumptions: that the *Sonnets* are autobiographical; that they narrate the story of actual life-events; that the Dark Lady was Shakespeare's mistress, and that he had an adulterous affair with her. None of this is inherently impossible or even improbable. But because there is no corroboration at all in the factual record, nothing to link the character in the poems with an identifiable person, the Dark Lady remains to all intents and purposes a fictional character, as authentic and as unreal as Portia or Rosaline or Desdemona.

Facts

The documentary facts can be disposed of quickly and simply. There are none. The only certain existence of the Dark Lady is as a fictional character.

Tradition

The emphasis of tradition in respect of Shakespeare's love life is that it was mainly adulterous. I have already mentioned in more than one context the story recorded by the lawyer John Manningham in his diary, March 13 1602, that Shakespeare overheard Burbage, who had been playing Richard III, making an assignation with a lady in the audience, and made his way into her bed before his colleague could get there. 'William the Conqueror was before Richard the Third' bears all the hallmarks of an urban legend about the sexual charisma of celebrities. But it may contain some element of truth. Shakespeare the actor and writer may have enjoyed on the London theatre scene a sexual liberty that would have been much more difficult for a respectable Stratford gentleman to sustain. If so, then his apparent preference for life in London, and his long absences from the marital home in Stratford, become easily intelligible.

A parallel source of traditional lore about Shakespeare's love-life was dramatist Sir William D'Avenant, whose father John was landlord of the Crown Inn at Oxford. John Aubrey reported that:

> Mr William Shakespeare was wont to goe into Warwickshire once a yeare, and did commonly in his journey lye at this house in Oxon. where he was exceedingly respected.[2]

The attraction there seems however to have been not the sufficiency of the vintner's provender, but the landlady, 'a very beautifull woman, and of a very good witt, and of conversation extremely agreable.'[3] Aubrey also recorded that Shakespeare seemed very fond of Mrs Davenant's children, as recalled by William's brother Robert: 'I have heard parson Robert say that Mr. W. Shakespeare haz given him a hundred kisses.'

William D'Avenant was reputed to be Shakespeare's godson, and Aubrey says that D'Avenant was not averse to being taken as his actual (illegitimate) son.

> Now Sir William would sometimes, when he was pleasant over a glasse of wine with his most intimate friends – e.g. Sam. Butler (author of Hudibras), &c. – say, that it seemed to him that he writt with the very spirit of Shakespeare, and scemd contented enough to be thought his son. He would tell them the story as above, in which way his mother had a very light report.

What D'Avanant is quoted as having said here could be construed simply as a metaphor: he wished to be thought Shakespeare's *literary* descendant. But Aubrey clearly took the allusion *literally*, suggesting that such a claim cast on D'Avenant's mother 'a very light report,' that is 'portrayed her as a very loose woman.'

Speculation

John Manningham's anecdote, with its portrayal of a lustful and sexually promiscuous Shakespeare, provides for some biographers a way into the real-life drama of the *Sonnets*. Thus Katherine Duncan-Jones comments: 'Though the Manningham story sounds in some ways too good to be true, its basic components conform remarkably well to the poetic analysis of the lustful 'Will' of Sonnets 127–52.'[4] In the story, Shakespeare appears as a sexual opportunist, hungrily competitive, and possibly more attached to the male rival than to the woman he tricks into sex. In the *Sonnets*, 'Will' is lustful, attached to 'a promiscuous woman of little beauty and no breeding' (p. 132), artistically competitive with the 'rival poet,' and in reality much more firmly wedded to his male friend than to the woman who comes between them. For Duncan-Jones, then, the *Sonnets* map readily onto the contours of Shakespeare's own life. Sex was more to do with professional advancement than with abiding affection, so the handsome male lover is preferred, while the woman he uses as a 'sexual convenience' is treated with 'resentment and dislike' (p. 133). Duncan-Jones proceeds on the firm assumption that the Sonnets are autobiographical, but does not venture to find or identify any real-life candidates for the Dark Lady.

Plenty of other scholars have however ridden forth in the name of that quest. 'Enormous effort has been expended to identify the principal rival poet and the "Dark Lady",' writes Stephen Greenblatt, naming the three most favoured candidates. 'Was the Dark Lady the poet Emilia Lanier, former mistress of the Lord Chamberlain, or the courtier Mary Fitton, or the prostitute known as Lucy Negro?'[5] For Greenblatt however such identifications are pointless.

> If even the identity of the young man of the first seventeen sonnets as Southampton is rash, to attempt to name the other figures is beyond rashness (p. 233).

This is not, however, because there was no Dark Lady, but has to do with the nature of such collections of love poetry, and with the context in which they were circulated:

> The whole enterprise of writing a sonnet sequence precisely involved drawing a translucent curtain … over the scene, so that only shadowy figures are visible to the public (p. 233–4).

The *Sonnets*, in other words, deliberately operate to intensify the shared experience of reading within a small coterie of people who are in effect reading about themselves. Those who read them are also in them, but the poems personalize without publicizing what went on between the members of the group.

> Sonnets … were at once private and social; that is, they characteristically took the form of a personal, intimate address, and at the same time they circulated within a small group whose values and desires they reflected, articulated and reinforced (p. 235).

The narrative of the sequence seems to consist of 'specific events' (p. 246), and biographers have naturally been drawn into the attempt to identify their real-life equivalents:

> Biographers have often succumbed to the temptation to turn these intimations of events into a full-blown romantic plot, but to do so requires pulling against the strong gravitational force of the individual poems (p. 247).

Greenblatt clearly acknowledges that the drama narrated in the *Sonnets*, or something very like it, really happened. But the quest to discover the actual participants in that drama is – perhaps always was – a hopeless quest.

Michael Wood also admits that 'the so-called Dark Lady has proved a tempting pitfall to biographers,' but enters a cautionary note: 'and some would think it unwise to read the Sonnets so literally.'[6] But he then proceeds to dive head first into very same pit: 'If we take them as a mainly private record of real events and emotions,' then 'Shakespeare's mistress must have been a real woman ...' (p. 203). The autobiographical premise points to an apparently self-evident assertion that then raises the inevitable question, 'who was she?' (p. 203). For Wood she was Emilia Lanier, a remarkable woman who was the first female author in England to publish a volume of poetry (in 1610). She was dark, of a Venetian family; one of her relatives was described as a 'Moor'; she was a musician (the lady of the *Sonnets* is shown playing a keyboard instrument);[7] she was the mistress of noblemen. 'If the Sonnets are autobiographical and she was a real person' (p. 210) then she fits the bill. Wood presents a case, previously assembled by others scholars, that proposes to link Shakespeare with Emilia by a web of circumstantial evidence. She was born Emilia Bassano, into a family of Venetian musicians that may have had a Jewish past; she was dark-skinned; she was mistress of Shakespeare's patron Lord Hunsden.

As is often the case with circumstantial evidence, the attempt to link Shakespeare with Emilia throws up remarkably compelling parallels. There are personal contiguities and potential links into the plays, especially the Venetian plays, where we can find characters called both Emilia and Bassanio; and of course a beautiful Jewess, and a serious interest in Jewishness (though there is no certainty that the Bassanos were Jews). Yet what is missing from the record is one single piece of evidence establishing that there was some personal connection between Shakespeare and Emilia Lanier. Without that, the parallels, however persuasive, could be merely accidental, in that they inhabited contingent worlds, but did not actually know one another; or genuine, in the sense that that they demonstrate the possibility of a personal connection, without proving that Emilia was Shakespeare's mistress and the Dark Lady of the Sonnets.

In his biography *Shakespeare*, Anthony Burgess also names the main candidates for the identity of the dark lady as Emilia Lanier, Mary Fitton and Lucy Negro. If the 'fair friend' was William Herbert, Earl of Pembroke, as Burgess suspects, then Mary Fitton, known as 'Mall,' could well be the Dark Lady, since she was his mistress, and bore him a son. There is a cryptic reference to 'Mistress Mall's picture' in *Twelfth Night*. Burgess's obvious preference however is for the Dark Lady to have been a black prostitute. If she was really black, and as promiscuous as the *Sonnets* suggest (she is alluded to as 'the bay where all men ride')[8], then she could have been one of the dark-skinned whores of the London brothels, and even one in particular, known as 'Lucy Negro, Abbess de Clerkenwell,' who appeared in a show at Gray's Inn in 1594. The satirical revel presented her as an abbess in charge of a convent of nuns with 'burning lamps.' In fact, she ran a brothel in Clerkenwell and her 'sisters' were whores capable of infecting their clients with the 'burning' pox. For Burgess the sexual disgust of the *Sonnets* points to a whore/client relationship, where the woman was 'anonymous, an instrument of elemental pleasure' inevitably followed on the part of the client by 'remorse' (p. 148).

Lucy Negro is mentioned as a possible candidate by other biographers: she was a real woman, had been at court, and she was a prostitute. She must have been dark, like the lady of the *Sonnets*, though not necessarily an actual 'negro.' The Dark Lady of the *Sonnets* is promiscuous, though there is no reference to her being paid for sex. In his novel *Nothing Like the Sun*, Burgess take this hypothesis to its logical conclusion, and constructs a whole narrative around the premise that Shakespeare's mistress was a black Muslim African woman. The young Shakespeare has his first encounter with a Dark Lady in the form of a black prostitute in Bristol. He is overcome with lust for her, but does not have enough money, so does not enjoy her. Suffused with the glamour of an exotic orientalism, this Dark Lady with her golden skin, black hair, thick lips and flat, wide nose proves irresistibly attractive to him. Later when Shakespeare is established in London as a successful poet and playwright, he encounters another black woman who reminds him of this earlier fantasy. From the East Indies, of a family of noble Moors, taken to Bristol and educated as an English gentlewoman, her name is Lucy, but she is not a whore.[9] Eventually Shakespeare realizes she is Lucy Negro, and in the course of the novel she has sexual relations with both Southampton (who in the novel is the 'fair friend') and Richard Burbage. Towards the end, Shakespeare sees her again, pitiably decrepit and stricken with the venereal disease she has already transmitted to him.

Other biographers either recognise that the *Sonnets* contain some autobiographical drama which is not accessible to scholarly inquiry, or question the autobiographical hypothesis altogether. For Jonathan Bate there was, and is, no 'Dark Lady' in the living, concrete, identifiable sense that compels some other biographers. The circulation and publication of sonnet sequences, following the fashion inaugurated by Sidney's *Astrophil and Stella*, was a professional prerequisite for ambitious writers. Such collections inevitably 'tantalized' the reader with the question of autobiography, 'whether love poetry was an exercise in witty invention ... or whether there was a real-life story behind a sonnet sequence and, if there was, what was the identity of the players.'[10] Bate's own preference is for the former hypothesis: the 'Dark Lady' may be a dark allegorical conceit, rather than an identifiable individual: 'We cannot rule out the possibility that she is not so much a real person as an embodiment of Venus' (p. 209). If there was an autobiographical story behind the *Sonnets*, it is in any case now no longer accessible:

> The very lack of names – even of a mythological-allegorical kind – suggests that attempting to 'unshadow' the origin of the Sonnets is to read them against the grain. Shakespeare's original intention was to circulate them among his private friends, so perhaps we should be content to let them remain private (p. 220).

Bate's commentary on the *Sonnets* emphasizes their innovative quality with regard to established conventions. They are quite unlike other examples of contemporary love poetry. Shakespeare's sonnets adore not one true love, but two; not an angel or goddess, but a 'female evil.' The love triangle is a miniature drama rather than a lyrical confession of devotion like most other sonnet sequences of the time; the *Sonnets* are as much a play as is *Twelfth Night*. Here the biographical quest peters out, since 'we do not usually look for biographical originals for Viola/Cesario, Sebastian, Orsino, Olivia and Antonio, so we should not necessarily do so for the "lovely boy" or the "dark lady".' The *Sonnets* speak, as do other similar poems of the time, of immortalizing the beloved in verse. But because the identity of the beloved is never revealed, and the only name explicitly put forward is that of the poet, 'Shakespeare's *Sonnets* do not immortalize anyone except Shakespeare' (p. 219).

Stanley Wells also respects this 'privacy' of the sonnets, and admits that they may have been written 'on the basis of imagined rather than actual experience,'[11] though he is less inclined than Bate to see them as a literary exercise. At a push, he would guess that they are 'private poems, personal and almost confessional in nature' (p. 88). This is particularly the case with the Dark Lady sonnets, which 'read like intensely private utterances' (p. 87). If the poems are autobiographical, then the 'two loves' described in them involve very different forms of sexual attachment. The sonnets to the 'fair friend' represent a 'far happier' (p. 88) relationship than those to the woman, which would be a 'reflection of an adulterous affair which gave the poet as much shame as pleasure' (p. 88). No real-life autobiographical drama emerges clearly from the poems, though Wells clearly feels there may have been one. Far from commemorating identifiable people, the poems anonymize all partic-ipants except the poet himself: 'the only name that emerges is Shakespeare's own Will' (p. 86). This is also Peter Ackroyd's conclusion: reviewing the same circumstantial evidence, he prefers to detach Shakespeare 'as poet' from the contextual detail. Stories about Shakespeare and various dark ladies are 'very dramatic … but not art.'[12] The poems are an interior, not an exterior drama: 'His subject as his own self' (p. 292).

> In the only sense that matters, Shakespeare addresses the *Sonnets* to himself (p. 291).

The fact that Shakespeare's own personal name is to be found inside the Sonnets may well of course be regarded as a significant piece of evidence. It links the outside of the work, and the milieu in which it was written, with the inside, connects text, paratext and context. It moves the poet's signature from the front of the book to its centre. On the face of it, this seems to represent irrefutable evidence that the 'Will' of the poems is the William Shakespeare who wrote them, and that the Sonnets are indeed an autobiographical work.

Looking more closely at the 'Will' poems, Sonnets 135–6, these assumptions become more questionable:

> Whoever hath her wish, thou hast thy 'Will,'
> And 'Will' to boot, and 'Will' in overplus;
> More than enough am I that vex thee still,
> To thy sweet will making addition thus.
> Wilt thou, whose will is large and spacious,
> Not once vouchsafe to hide my will in thine?
> Shall will in others seem right gracious,
> And in my will no fair acceptance shine?
> The sea all water, yet receives rain still
> And in abundance addeth to his store;
> So thou, being rich in 'Will,' add to thy 'Will'
> One will of mine, to make thy large 'Will' more.
> Let no unkind, no fair beseechers kill;
> Think all but one, and me in that one 'Will.'

In the poem, the name 'Will' becomes a sliding signifier alluding to a range of different signifieds. It means the sexual appetites of both lovers, and by extension their genital organs, 'willy' and vagina. It means a preference as well as a person, desire for the loved object as well as the object itself. Thus in effect the name, taken as a personal identifier, means far more, and far less, once located within the complex semiotic interplay of the poem. It no longer designates a specific individual, but rather describes a state or process in which two individuals are locked in a frustrating and intolerable standoff. She seems 'willing' to have sex with other men, but not with him. Her sexual organ is 'large and spacious' enough to swallow the 'wills' of others, but she denies access to 'Will' himself. Just as the sea can absorb an infinite volume of rainwater, she is capable of adding any number of male sexual organs to her 'store.' So why not his?

In every dimension, the name 'Will' is losing rather than gaining meaning from this impasse. His name becomes washed out as it stands for the generic and anonymous male penis. Because she won't have him, he is left undefined and anonymized. If she were to accept him, and give him access to her body, he would become lost in it, as other men have done, becoming just one more drop of rain absorbed by a great sea. It is tempting to the biographer to think that 'Will in overplus' here means 'excess of Shakespeare,' or as it were 'more than enough information from which to construct the Shakespearean life-story.' But in fact it means nothing more informative than 'excess' of anonymous sexual partners, whose attributes become reduced to the lowest common denominator, the sexual urge, the sexual organ, the 'will.'

The other 'Will' poem, Sonnet 136, makes this even more explicit:

> If thy soul check thee that I come so near,
> Swear to thy blind soul that I was thy Will,
> And will, thy soul knows, is admitted there;
> Thus far for love, my love-suit, sweet, fulfil.
> Will, will fulfil the treasure of thy love,
> Ay, fill it full with wills, and my will one.
> In things of great receipt with ease we prove
> Among a number one is reckoned none:
> Then in the number let me pass untold,
> Though in thy store's account I one must be;
> For nothing hold me, so it please thee hold
> That nothing me, a something sweet to thee:
> Make but my name thy love, and love that still,
> And then thou lovest me for my name is 'Will.'

Again the woman takes in any number of 'wills,' so the addition of his should be an insignificant increment. 'Among a number one is reckoned none': one more will make little difference, even though that one is him: 'Then in the number let me pass untold.' 'For nothing hold me,' he says: just let me lose myself among the crowd of her other lovers. 'So it please thee,' he says, 'hold/That nothing me.' This is loss of identity, not the formation of autobiographical discourse; the life is lost in the relationship, while the authorial identity is lost in the work. To juxtapose 'nothing' and 'me' tells its own sad story, but it cannot be the whole story of the poet's life. The voice that speaks in the poems, counselling the reader to regard the authorial life as 'nothing,' seems to deny the very possibility of autobiography.

Story: 'Shakespeare's Ring: Full Circle'

This fictional story echoes Ernest Hemingway's novel *A Farewell to Arms* (1929), and imitates Hemingway's prose style. It transfers the story of Shakespeare's *Sonnets* to a First World War setting. A few details derive from other sources such as Hemingway's own description of his wounding, and the *Sonnets* are quoted extensively.

Shakespeare's Ring: Full Circle
Northern Italy, June 1915

The Italian lines stretched along the contours of the river, eastwards as far as the eye could see. All along the line, men in grey uniforms and steel helmets leaned on the parapets of the trenches, rifles and fixed bayonets pointing across the river towards an unseen enemy. The river flowed fast but wide here, pale green from the snows of the mountains and ruffled with small white waves, flowing faster in deep channels that ran between grey and white boulders. Up here they called such a stream '*torrente*,' and if you followed its course with your eye you could see where it fell from a broad crease in the pale grey mountain, and up above patches of snow that slipped and melted into the channel of a small *fiume* that smoked and tumbled down the slopes and gathered depth and pace until it reached the valley and rushed along a few yards from our trenches.

Across the river was an alpine meadow that snaked smoothly upwards to break into fringes of pine-forest on the slopes of the mountain that protected our lines from the Austrian positions, except at this end where an observation post was left deliberately exposed. A tour of duty here was seldom a pleasure, since the Austrians shelled it daily, though always in a desultory way that suggested no strong inclination to attack. But the observation trench was dug deeply and well, and covered with wooden planks with a thick shield of earth, and tunnels dug into the walls of the trench where we crouched during a serious bombardment. It was a good dugout and safe, and so far no one had died in it or even been wounded.

From here we could see around the side of the mountain to where in the thick pinewoods we knew the Austrians had their artillery concealed. Through this gap in the mountains we could see more and higher peaks, green to the snowline and above at this time of the year, pale grey, and beyond more and more mountains and higher, to where peaks snow-capped even in mid-summer hung like a vision in the distance, and then only when the weather was clear and the sky a hard alpine blue.

I focused my field glasses on the woods beyond the sloping flank of the mountain, hoping to spot flashes from their artillery so we could advise our own batteries where they should target the Austrian guns. But the enemy artillery was too well concealed, and we usually received no warning of a bombardment until the shells were already over our heads.

'Can you see anything, Guilelmo?' asked Genio, who leaned on the parapet next to me.

'No,' I replied, panning the glasses across the far country, 'and don't call me Guilelmo.'

'*Prego*, Signior Tenente,' he replied. 'You are so kind to us, you see, we think of you not so much as an officer, but as a friend.'

The men had some difficulty in taking me seriously as an officer, since I was American, though American-Italian, and spoke with what they regarded as an accent, and had what they considered a non-Italian – even partly a German – name, Guilelmo Sciacchi. My family had left Italy for New York when I was a baby, but I was raised an Italian patriot, and as soon as my military training was completed at West Point I was shipped to Italy to command a platoon.

'Just remember,' I said, 'if you run away from the Austrians, I will still shoot you. Though only in the friendliest way.'

'Run away?' put in Basso, another joker. 'Let those Austrians come over the river right now, and I'll kill a hundred of them.' We had been expecting an Austrian offensive for some time now, and the men were nervous.

'You see, Tenente,' said Genio, in a mock-serious voice, 'we are here to ensure that no enemy sets foot on the sacred soil of our fatherland.'

The others sniggered at this recruiting, poster language. 'You are too lenient, Tenente' interposed Guzzi, a socialist from Torino. 'You should impose a more vigorous military discipline.'

'The Austrians will soon teach you discipline,' I said, then suddenly saw what looked like a yellow flash from across the river, and shouted 'Down!,' and the men disappeared like rats into the dugout, and sure enough there came the shrill whistle and scream of a shell that fell short, throwing up a cloud of dirt just across the stream only twenty yards from the trench. Then came another, but by now I had joined the men under cover so I could hear only the bump of the burst and the singing sounds of fragments flying away. Then I heard a noise like an engine starting up and then there was a flash that blinded and a roar like an oncoming train and everything was black like a train rushing through a tunnel and ahead the bright light at the end. Then I felt the train reverse and slide backwards and I was in the trench and there was earth churned up and splintered wood and the spilled contents of sandbags and someone cursing in pain.

My legs were buried, and when I tried to pull them out I knew they were injured and I hoped if I lived I would not lose a leg. There was firing all along the line, machine gun and rifle-fire across the river, so at last the Austrians were attacking. Next to me Genio lay awkwardly across the trench and I knew he was dead. Then I felt someone grab my arms and somebody else lifted my legs and we were out of the trench and running while the machine gun bullets zipped around us like a swarm of angry wasps. Basso and Guzzi had taken a few splinters of shrapnel from the detonation of the trench mortar but were otherwise unhurt. They ran with me all the way to the dressing station and I felt nothing except the fear of losing my legs. They laid me as gently as they could on the ground outside the tent where the wounded received first aid before being transported to the field hospital. All around me men were lying unconscious, or moaning softly, or dying, or already dead. Two other men took me inside and the medical sergeant bandaged both my legs and gave me a drink of brandy. By the time they had loaded me into a car to take me to the field hospital the shock had diminished and the pain had started and I had lost interest in everything. At the field hospital they removed the larger fragments of shrapnel and rebound the wounds and packed me into a transport convoy that was going somewhere, though I had no idea where and cared even less, as long as I was not to be crippled, as long as I could keep my legs.

My wounds were not deep, and my left knee was smashed, but there was nothing life-threatening. The danger in the hot weather was from infection, and sure enough the wounds became septic, and within a day or two of being hit I was fast in the grip of a high fever, and lost in the fog of a delirium where everything seemed unreal but inescapable, and I was aware only of pain and fear and nausea and the sensation that I could not understand what was happening to my own body. All light seemed to fall on my eyes like stones, and my hands and fingers were so big there was not room in the bed for them. Once I was convinced my legs had been amputated and my feeling of them only a memory, and I hauled myself conscious to see them still there in bandages and to know I had not lost them.

It was only afterwards that I learned what had happened to me during all this period of fevered semi-consciousness, which was that I had been so quickly transported back from the lines all the way to the American hospital in Milan only through the influence and authority of my friend and fellow-officer Captain Henry Rothleigh, who was with the Third Army, and who heard I had been wounded and got himself over to my section of the front to ensure my safe passage and proper treatment. Henry was from an old southern family, whereas I was the son of immigrants from Little Italy. His grandfather had fought with General Johnstone at Shiloh, while mine had ridden with Garibaldi when he crossed the Straits of Messina and marched north towards Naples. At West Point we had become firm friends, in spite of the class difference, shared a room together, and were even referred to as 'The Inseparables.' It was true we were unusually close even for military comrades, perhaps too close for our commanding officer, who when the time came for us to join the war dispatched us to different units so we did not serve together. Henry had stayed with me for a few days during my fever, then once I was past the worst rejoined his unit. Thanks to his good offices I enjoyed the isolation of a separate room, while most of the wounded lay together in crowded wards.

All the time in my delirium there were people all round me who did things to me that were painful or comforting but I did not know what they were doing or who did them. There were faces and hands of doctors and nurses and orderlies, and they were all the same, but one face that came to me seemed a face out of nightmares, since all these other faces were white and this one was black, black with white eyes and white teeth, and it was a face from childhood dreams or stories to scare children of a black person who would do you harm if you were bad. Whenever the face appeared I tried to flinch away, but could not move, and tried to cry out but could only mumble sounds without meaning.

Then one day when I finally woke as to an ordinary morning, my fever gone and my head clear, the creature of my nightmares walked into the room. She was dressed in the white and blue of a nurse's uniform, she was a woman of a most extraordinary physical presence, and she was black. A starched white cap perched on her black hair, that was not tightly curled, but long and pulled up into a knot at the back, and her skin was golden-brown rather than black, her eyes big and dark, her nose slightly splayed but not broad, her lips full and shapely but not thick like the cartoons of negroes I had seen in the funny papers back home. Her breasts pushed out the bib of her uniform, and she was black, and she seemed to me beautiful, and when I saw her something happened to me.

'Good morning, Sleeping Beauty!' she said as she checked my chart. 'We thought you were never going to wake up.'

Her voice was the voice of the Deep South, musical and low. Her manner was brisk and businesslike as she examined my bandages and took my temperature. I on the other hand was fascinated by her and could not take my eyes off her face, her breasts, her shapely legs in their black stockings. I had never known a black person, though of course there were many in New York, but they kept to their own territory north of the park, and the colour bar segregated us so you could live your life in the city without ever having anything to do with a negro. There were one or two black cadets at West Point, but they were considered unreliable as soldiers, and most of them seemed to fail the course for one reason or another. But here was a negro, who was so obviously and ostentatiously an attractive woman, whose duties as a nurse brought her into such close physical contact with me that I could not begin to master the turbulence of emotions and sensations I felt in her presence. I would have expected to feel revulsion at the touch of a black person, but instead I felt only excitement.

Being stared at, either for her colour or for her attractiveness, must have been an occupational hazard for her, and she seemed to treat me impersonally, as if I was nothing to her but a patient. Or was there something more? 'The doctor will see you later,' she said, but putting her hand on my shoulder and leaving it there surely a little longer than necessary?

I could not stop thinking about her, though she did not appear again on the ward that day. I lay awake most of the night, but there was no sign of her. Then again it was morning and she was there and I was sleepy from my vigil and as she pulled back the covers to check my bandages her hand encountered my erection which sprang hopelessly and uncontrollably upwards towards her. I had not seen a woman for weeks, had not been with a girl for months, and then only a brief drunken encounter in the regimental whorehouse. She merely raised an eyebrow and said, 'You can put him away. You won't be needing him for a while.' But again, I was sure that as her hand brushed the shaft of my penis, her lips had parted a little.

Days passed, and with each morning she seemed to stay a little longer, as if she liked my company and was in no hurry to leave. I learned that she was from Savannah, Georgia, and had moved north away from the slave-lands to train as a nurse in a hospital in Pittsburgh. Her name was Wilhelmina, and everyone called her Willie. She had always dreamed of putting her skills as a nurse to the service of some great humanitarian effort, and so volunteered when the war broke out to work with the Red Cross in Italy. She was clearly a first-class nurse, and had she been white would have been a matron. This she knew, but would not let it sour her love for the work. Her grandparents had been slaves: how could her life not be better than theirs? I asked her surname, and gathered from her reticence on the subject that her family had emerged from slavery bearing only their master's name, so she had chosen her own, which was Seacole. She told me it was the name of famous black nurse who had served in the Crimea at the same time as Florence Nightingale. I had heard of Florence Nightingale, of course, but never of Mary Seacole.

Morning after morning I had to endure the torment of her touching me in the most intimate manner, and one day the ache of desire became too much for me, and I tried to kiss her. She pushed me firmly back on the pillow with a 'Be a good boy.' The moment felt conventional, a wounded soldier falling for his nurse, an embarrassing *faux pas*. I said I was sorry, but she did not speak and left the room. I thought her offended, but suddenly she came back in, sat on the side of the bed and kissed me on the lips. Her mouth felt like no woman's mouth I had ever touched for sweetness, though her breath smelt of garlic, and her teeth as she parted her lips seemed to me huge, but the soft touch of her pink tongue against mine drew me down into an unfathomable darkness.

'Wait for me,' she said, and was gone. That was all. I waited for the next morning, but she did not come on duty. I waited all day, and there was no sign of her. I was deeply anxious, thinking that our kiss might have been observed, that she was perhaps in trouble, not just for breaching the ethics of her duty, but for breaking some unwritten colour bar forbidding any intimacy between races. I felt distressed that I was the occasion of her getting into trouble, if trouble there was, and that she might be dismissed, and that I would never see her again. I could have asked the other staff for news of her, but feared that such inquiry might only make things worse for her. So I lay helpless until night came, then, tired with anxiety and longing, fell asleep.

Something woke me. The room was in darkness, but the blinds had not been drawn, and a white moonlight spilled across the floor. I knew that someone was there, though I could not see who, and all I could hear was the rustling of clothes, and then she slid into the bed and was astride me, and kissing me with that bright red fruit of a mouth. She had stripped down to her chemise and stockings, and as she knelt over me my erection rose to meet her, and she pressed herself down onto me, inch by agonizing inch, till I thought I would cry out, but she had her hand over my mouth to stifle the shout. I thought I would come straight away, but she used her muscles to grip the base of my shaft and to hold back the dammed-up torrent of want. She held me like that, while she stroked herself to a shivering little spasm, then let me go to thrust into her, to let everything go, to lose myself in that dark urgent flood, while she had tightened her hand over my mouth to reduce my cries to the kind of snorting moan that could easily have come from any uneasy sleeper. Then she kissed me again and drew away as to rise. I tried to hold her, my hands cupped over her buttocks to glue her to me in a sealant of semen and sweat, the skin under my hands smooth and sinuous as the pelt of a young deer. But she pulled away, with a 'Too dangerous!,' and was back into her clothes and gone.

She had taken on regular night duty so she and I could be together. From then on while I stayed in the hospital I saw her only in the night, and she was my lady of darkness, who I saw only in moonlight that silvered the contours of her black skin. She was always in control, since I was literally a patient, passive and prostrate, crucified on the rood of my passion. She was a much more experienced lover, knowing how to bring both of us to fulfilment without ever betraying, by any noise or disturbance, the violence of our nightly convergence. We spoke little, only a few whispers, so she seemed to me less and less a person, more as some dark goddess who kept me in her thrall, or as some exotic wild beast who had chosen to lie with the prey she could easily devour. I began to wonder why she had chosen me, or if indeed she had. Was I her only conquest, or was this how she did her rounds, passing from one bed to another, serving all the young men in her care, one by one? A woman could do that, where a man was spent in one session. Was she a receptacle for all that youthful virility, dammed up by the forced abstinence of war? Was my lady of darkness a lady of the night? Was that dark maelstrom into which I plunged again and again, careless whether I surfaced again or sank to my dissolution, nothing more than a bay where all men ride?

Sometimes I lay dreaming the day away, waiting for the advent of dusk as a sentry waits for the first breath of morning, I would watch the other nurses, and wonder how it was that with so many pretty girls of my own colour and kind, I should have fallen for a negress? The white nurses were attentive and excitable, but they meant nothing to me. I had found a new language of beauty, and the words of the old dialect seemed empty of meaning. If a man could think of black as fair, then whiteness must have lost its synonymity with beauty. Of course the white girls wore make-up, dyed their hair, plucked their eyebrows and made themselves pretty with art's false borrowed face. Willy's raven black eyes seemed in mourning for this loss of honesty and innocence, for they expressed a true beauty unadorned by artifice. Perhaps black would one day become the new beautiful.

Henry came to see me, heading for a few days leave in Rome. I was glad to see him, as she had been obliged to take a break from night duty, since no nurse would endure night shifts indefinitely without some ulterior motive. She would work for a few days, she said, then volunteer again for the nights. As Henry sat by my bed, looking tanned and handsome in his captain's uniform, Willy came in to do my chart. Henry was clearly surprised to see her, but kept his rather aristocratic insouciance. I introduced him to her as my friend, and he shook her hand politely. She appraised him coolly, and smiled at him in a way I did not like, though it was true I did not like her smiling at any other man.

'How novel!' he remarked when she had left. 'Don't you mind having a little nigger round your bed?'

'She's a good nurse,' I said, 'and pretty.' I was unable to tell him the truth. 'I don't mind her colour.'

'Interesting,' he said, looking after her. 'Never thought of a black as pretty. My family used to own slaves. They took very good care of them, treated them as family. But they say the old slave-owners used to lie with the pretty slave women to get strong young half-breeds to work in their fields. Would you credit it?' He said nothing more of her before leaving to catch his train for Rome.

My wounds had all but healed, and I was to be discharged. I was granted two weeks convalescent leave. I begged Willy to apply for leave herself, so we could go away together. She said it was impossible, they would never grant it. But when, worn down by my importunities, she asked, the leave was given her without demur. We were to go separately to Torino, the nearest big town where no one would know either of us.

On the way to the station I passed the window of an antique jeweller's, and paused to see if there was any little trinket I could buy to please her. There in the centre of the display was a gold signet ring, bearing by some incredible coincidence her initials, 'W. S.' I went in and haggled with the proprieter, who had clearly had the ring for some time and had been unable to sell it, presumably because no-one with those initials had passed by. He asked an absurd price, but accepted a reasonable one. I slipped it into my pocket and went on to the station.

I took the train for Torino and waited for her outside the lovely art nouveau facade of Porta Nuova. Her train was delayed, and I did not believe she would come. Then a flood of people rushed out of the station, and porters with bags, and a jabber of Italian, and towards the end she was there, walking alone, looking cool in the stifling heat, wearing a white cotton dress and white shoes. I had never seen her in civilian clothes, and she seemed to me like the most beautiful thing I had ever looked at.

We checked into a hotel next door to the station. I gave the ring I had bought for her in Milan, and she wore it on her wedding finger so we could pass as a married couple. The staff seemed unperturbed by her colour, which I put down to their tolerance. We were shown to a room of faded luxury reminiscent of the belle époque: striped wallpaper, ornate art nouveau wall lights, a huge chandelier and a grotesque but inviting four-poster bed. It was a corner room and had two sets of French doors and two balconies, one overlooking the station and the other the Corso. We threw open both sets of doors, so the strong August light poured in from two directions and turned the bed into a pool of gold.

The situation was strange and uncomfortable. Though we had been so close, it had always been in darkness. I had had lovers enough, but I had never made love to a woman in daylight, indeed never seen a naked woman lying in the sunshine, and never encountered this intolerable ostentation of black skin. I was almost afraid, but she held her arms out to me and drew me down towards her. I tried to bury myself into the sweetness of her body, kissing and licking every inch of her skin, pressing my head between her breasts. In the bright daylight, everything seemed to speak loudly of her blackness: long dark hair spread on the pillow; the dark aureoles round her breasts; and above all, what lay between her legs, the thick tight matted curls of her pubic hair, like a spaniel's fur, bisected by a bright pink slash that opened like a wound. I pressed my face into it so I could hardly breathe, and she had to push me away, and show me how to touch her gently and with sensitivity. The inside of her was like the lining of a seashell, iridescent with orient pearl, and the taste of it like the salt lick and tang of the sour sea-spray. Then she did what I had never seen any woman do, put her hand down to part her bright pink lips, caressed her own clitoris with her fingers, and brought herself to a shivering orgasm. A cloud of abandonment and oblivion fogged my eyes, my mind went black, and I lost myself in the dark labyrinth of her body. For what seemed like an infinity I rocked on the pulsing wave of that inexhaustible ocean, until at last my own desire burst its banks and poured its full current into her ever-receiving sea.

When we awoke it was already evening, the sky was a dusky pink, and swallows were diving and swooping around the balcony. We got up and went out to eat, and arm-in-arm like a real couple strolled around the long colonnaded walks of the city. Along the pillared porticos, the prostitutes stood and offered themselves without shame or inhibition. Some were young and pretty, others old and worn-looking, but all seemed to have their clientele. Furtive little men ducked round corners and exchanged shrill coded whistles. Willy walked with her eyes downcast, while some bold girl slipped out her tongue and fluttered it at me. Has Willy ever done this, I wondered, driven perhaps by poverty and want, to sell herself for a few dollars? These women were as attractive and well dressed as she was: she could easily have been one of them. I glanced from the roguish eyes of the whores to her downcast lids. Was there some secret knowledge shared between them, my lady of darkness, and these ladies of the night? Was this the solution of the dark impenetrable mystery she was more and more becoming to me?

When we got back to the hotel I could tell from the way the concierge looked at us that he believed she too was a prostitute, and I her client. Back in the room I made love to her again, this time with furious violence, as if that way I might reach her inner being, pluck out the heart of her mystery. She responded with equal force, bucking and rolling in a shameless frenzy of passion. She sat on my face and pressed the wet wound of her pink vagina down onto my mouth. She took my penis in her mouth and slid that bright pink tongue up and down the shaft. She offered her anus to me, as if knowing that this was a route I had travelled before, with men if not with women. She gave me everything, and I followed her into a nameless obscene darkness where everything was possible, and nothing forbidden.

The next morning I woke before her as the first light of the sun slipped between the shutters. I lay regarding her features as she slept on the pillow next to me, and wondered if perhaps they were not a little coarser than I had initially thought. Her hair grew like black wires. Her nose seemed broader, her mouth disproportionately big, the lips a bluish colour in the morning light. Her breath was sour. She woke when the light touched her cheek, smiled at me and held out her arms. She seemed extraordinarily black against the white sheets. Her skin smelt of sweat, with an acridity that obscured the musky scent of her perfume. I noticed that there was black hair under her arms. She pushed my head down between her legs, and there in that rank and fetid jungle, I was overwhelmed by a zoo smell of animal excretions, the sour taste of my own seed and the faint smell of urine.

I felt we had to get out of this city with its foul drains, its heavy heat, its whores and pimps and complaisant citizens who watched impassively as the great game of sexual exchange went on around them. We took a train north, towards Aosta and the mountains. I felt I needed fresh air, an unimpeded landscape, a bigger sky. We stayed in an alberge in Courmayeur near the foot of the Mont Blanc massif. From the Italian side it is Monte Bianco, and quite a different mountain, thrusting upwards with sharp peaks veined in snow, not the smooth round dome you see from Chamonix. We took a room with a view of Monte Bianco, and here you could sit on the bed with the French doors open and the sky was full of mountains. I took her up the funicular to the great glacier that stretches from Punta Hellbronner to Aiguille du Midi. I wanted to trek across the glacier, but there were no guides as they had all gone to the war. She was apprehensive, feeling the snow and ice under her feet, and would only venture a few steps towards that great white trackless blankness that lay dazzling in the sun. As I stood and watched her standing alone, silhouetted against that white immensity, she seemed again beautiful in her blackness, and I was half in love with her. But I knew then, as clearly as I have ever known since, that there was no future for us, that this was all there was. I belonged to the people of Monte Bianco, to the race of the white mountains, and to us blackness would always be a blot against the white landscape, a strange compulsion, but also a source of fear, and mistrust, and ultimately of repulsion.

She began to speak of this as we stood under the mountain, as if it had all been said rather than merely felt between us. I cannot reproduce her words exactly, perhaps because the recollection is too painful, but this is the gist of what she said.

'You are like all young men: you want too much. If you could just seize the moment as it passes, you would be happy for a while. But you feel already the disappointment that lies at the end of pleasure. You know already the loss that lies at the heart of possession. After the war, you will go home to the States, marry a pure young Italian girl, and have children. You will be happy. And yet you will feel always a something lacking. At night when you embrace your beautiful white virgin bride, you will invite the memory of my shadow back into your bed, and I will lie between you. You will preserve your love for her, and keep your lust for me. That is all I will ever have of you. But it is all I expect. And for me it is enough.'

She took my face between her hands, and spoke to me earnestly and with immense sincerity. 'Just try to be happy, here, now.'

But I could not. We went back to Milan, where the autumn was setting in. The roads were wet and the trees were shedding their leaves. She returned to her duties at the hospital, and I was kept busy with strategic and planning work at a base nearby. We continued to meet, hiding ourselves in the shabby suburbs of the city, trying to rekindle a dying flame. I still wanted her, and the want could still make me feel sick and faint when I thought of it, but there was no pleasure in it. Through long days of dark skies and sudden showers and glimpses of watery sunshine, my yearning for her would irritate and exacerbate my temper to madness. I felt myself becoming a seething cauldron of extreme emotions, savage and cruel. I trusted no-one, and lied to everyone, even to Henry who had previously held all my confidence. Towards her I felt violence and cruelty, not love. Sometimes it crossed my mind that I might murder her, in some sordid room that we rented by the hour, so I would be free of guilt and shame. How long would it be before her corpse was discovered?

When we came together it was as if my spirit was merely expending itself in a waste of shame. As soon as I had had her, as much in hate as in love, I wanted her again, as if I drank along with her bodily fluids some subtle poison capable of driving the victim to a frenzy of further desire. I looked forward to joy with an aching of desire that once got, became a long forgotten dream. Looking at the pale, drawn faces of the men who moved around me in the city, I was convinced that they were in the grip of the same dark obsession. But not one of them could tell me how to avoid it; not one of them knew.

I saw Henry intermittently, as he also had duties in Milan. But he was often absent, and when present preoccupied. We never spoke of Willy. Then one day as I was walking up the marble steps of the hospital, to my astonishment I met him coming out. He made light of the chance encounter, saying something about a wounded comrade. I went in and found Willy, talking to some of the other nurses. As I walked through the door they all looked up at me and I knew, as positively as I had ever known anything, that they had been together. I turned on my heel and walked out. I was done with the lot of them.

It did not finish there, though that is where it truly ended. I will not waste your time by narrating the subsequent meetings, the accusations, the tears and recriminations, the lies and equivocations. At the time they were difficult and painful, but they did not carry into the future any abiding suffering. I asked her to return the ring, and she told me she had lost it. She had given it to Henry, since I saw it glinting on his hand when he removed his glove during a briefing. Though he had so much more than I ever did, he still wanted everything of mine. Some time later, I found the ring in my locker, and guessed that he had discarded both gem and woman with the same cruel insouciance.

I was wounded three times in that summer of 1915. The first wound, inflicted by an Austrian trench mortar, healed quickly and left no lasting damage except a slight limp in my left leg. The second wound was the laceration of my affair with Willy, which struck deep and left an enduring scar. She also left me a dose of gonorrhoea, which was painful but cleared up quickly enough with treatment. The third was my betrayal by Henry, which proved in the end the unkindest cut of all.

If my war-wound was a Gethsemane, and my liaison with the dark lady a nailing on the cross, then my betrayal by Henry was the spear though the side of all my hopes. At one fell swoop I was bereft of friend and lover. My two angels fell together, clasping one another as they tumbled on ragged, tattered wings down through airy space, a summer's day, plummeting together into their own common hell. I saw out the rest of the war and returned home to the States, never seeing or hearing from either of them again, and fulfilled Willy's predictions by marrying a sweet Italian girl and starting a family. I left the army and went to work in my father's wine business.

I kept the ring with my personal things, and occasionally came across it when looking for something else. It carried intact the memory of that summer, as clearly recorded in the gold as the letters engraved on its surface. They were her initials of course, but ironically mine too when I allowed my Italian name to lapse naturally into its English equivalent, William. So the ring linked us indissolubly together, my own younger self, and the black woman who had branded me with an ineradicable scar, burned me with a vestigial flame.

I would put the ring away with a shrug; it was all so long ago, and seemed almost another existence. But that night, in bed, when I turned to my wife and began to entice her to love, a dark shadow fell between us, some lascivious succubus from the past that intercepted my passion and kindled between us an unusual flame. My wife knew nothing of it, and by the morning the other was gone. But she had lain there in superfluous presence, between our two white sweating bodies, the uneasy memory of a long-lost love. My black Madonna; my dear, dolorous, delightful, diseased dark lady.

Shakespeare the Catholic

†

In some manuscript notes, jotted down in the later seventeenth century, Richard Davies, chaplain of Corpus Christi College, Oxford, wrote of William Shakespeare:

> Aetat 53. He dyed Apr. 23 1616 probably at Stratford, for there he is buryed, and hath a Monument on which lays a Heavy curse upon anyone who shal remove his bones. He dyed a papist.[1]

'He dyed a papist,' a Roman Catholic. We have no idea what kind of evidence lay behind this claim, or how Davies acquired it. It seems most likely that he heard it from someone, who heard it from someone else, who heard it from someone who was maybe there. Call it oral history, received tradition, hearsay, rumour or gossip: we cannot know how close Davies' annotation was to what actually happened around Shakespeare's deathbed on the 23 April 1616.

What did it mean, to 'die a papist'? Perhaps Davies meant that Shakespeare was born a papist, and never left off being one to his dying day. Once a Catholic, always a Catholic, as the old saying goes. Davies was a successful career Anglican, and may have viewed Shakespeare critically as a stubborn recusant, who lived and died incorrigibly in the Old Faith. He may have been saying something like: 'A great man of letters he may have been, but he lived and died a papist.'

This part of his notes is not concerned however with Shakespeare's youth or maturity, but with 'Last Things': burial, monuments, funerary inscriptions, bones – 'graves, and worms, and epitaphs.' He documents the curse inscribed over Shakespeare's tomb in Holy Trinity Church, Stratford:

GOOD FREND FOR IESVS SAKE FORBEARE,
TO DIGG THE DVST ENCLOASED HEARE:
BLESTE BE Ye MAN Yt SPARES THES STONES,
AND CVRST BE HE Yt MOVES MY BONES.

His mind was focused on Shakespeare *in articulo mortis,* not in the flower of his achievement; rather on things dying, than on things new-born.

Perhaps when Davies wrote that Shakespeare 'died a papist' he meant exactly that: at the very end of his life Shakespeare formally accepted the rites of the Church of Rome, received extreme unction from a Catholic priest, and died in the faith of the church. Perhaps these were the last words he heard in this world:

Per istam sanctam unctiónem et suam piisimam misericórdiam, indúlgeat tibi Dóminus quidquid per (visum, audtiotum, odorátum, gustum et locutiónem, tactum, gressum deliquisti.)[2]

(By this holy unction and His own most gracious mercy, may the Lord pardon you whatever sin you have committed by your sight, hearing, smell, taste, speech, touch and walk).

Very few scholars have considered that this might have occurred, or speculated about how such a ritual might have been performed. The absence of evidence encourages us to preserve a respectful distance from what, at the time, would have been a supremely important family and community event, quite unlike the non-event death has often become in a secular modern world. Davies's curious note also intriguingly directs the inquirer into that other literary biographer's no-go area, Shakespeare's own heart and soul. What was the nature of his spiritual life, his beliefs, his faith? How did he approach the terrible mystery of death?

'He dyed a papist.' Did Shakespeare live the kind of life that might naturally have led to the crowning glory of such a death? Did he die in the love of Christ, in the arms of the Church, and in sure and certain hope of the resurrection to eternal life? Did he live, as well as die, a papist?

†

Facts

Shakespeare's parents were born into the seismic aftershocks of Henry VIII's Reformation. His father, born in 1530, lived through the brief and zealous reign of Protestant Edward (1547–1553), and the even briefer and equally fundamentalist regime of Catholic Mary Tudor (1553–1558). By the time of Shakespeare's birth in 1564, Elizabeth had restored the Protestant faith to the Church of England. Attendance at Protestant services was obligatory, and absence punishable by fine. Those who, like Shakespeare's father John, held civic office, had to swear an oath of allegiance to the Queen as supreme head of the Church: so Shakespeare's father must have done so.

He had to prove his loyalty in other ways too. In 1559 an iconoclastic royal injunction demanded the removal of all signs of 'superstition' and 'idolatry' from places of worship.[3] A series of paintings on the walls of Stratford's Guild Chapel, including a magnificent 'Doom' or depiction of the Last Judgement, was defaced, covered over with whitewash. The job was supervised by Shakespeare's father, who was Chamberlain of Stratford in 1563–4. It is listed in his accounts: 'Item payd for defasyng ymages in ye chappell ij^s.'[4]

It was possible in this environment to remain openly a Roman Catholic, and many did. But it was very difficult, and even dangerous, to live, to hold public office, and to profess and practise religion as a Catholic. Later, Catholicism would be identified with political dissidence, and considered *prima facie* evidence of potential or actual treason. Catholics were not only fined, but arrested, interrogated, imprisoned, tortured and executed in most cruel and barbaric fashion.

Shakespeare's mother Mary Arden was probably related to a family that remained fiercely loyal to the Old Faith. Edward Arden, who may have been kin, was executed by hanging, drawing and quartering in 1583 for plotting against the queen. His severed head was impaled and displayed, a grisly trophy, on London Bridge. William Shakespeare might thus have had a direct and close family connection to Catholic conspiracy and to bloody government reprisal.

In 1592, Shakespeare's father John was identified in a government report as a 'recusant,' that is a Catholic who refused to attend the services of the Church of England.[5] He pleaded, as others also did, that his absences were to avoid being arrested for debt. He was always in debt, but never apparently arrested: he was certainly appearing at public functions around the same time. Perhaps he preferred to stay in bed on Sundays. Or perhaps he was, in reality, a recusant Catholic. If so, the defacing of the images in the Guild Chapel must have been, for him, a very painful duty.

In 1757 a bricklayer working on what had been John Shakespeare's house (now 'Shakespeare's Birthplace') found hidden between the rafters and the roof an extraordinary document. It was a six-page, hand-written testament of Catholic faith, in fourteen articles, each page signed in the name of John Shakespeare. The document was suspected as a forgery, until later discoveries corroborated its authenticity. It was composed by Carlo Borromeo, Cardinal Archbishop of Milan, and used as a propaganda tool in the spiritual campaigns of the Counter-Reformation. Thousands of copies had obviously been distributed to Catholics by travelling Jesuits, with the intention of reinforcing, and encouraging them to make public profession of, their faith.[6]

The document signed by John Shakespeare was most likely brought to England by the Jesuit missionaries Edmund Campion and Robert Persons, who travelled from Rome via Milan, where they met with Cardinal Borromeo. Campion stayed with Sir William Catesby only twelve miles from Stratford; the house of the Catholic magnate, father of Robert Catesby the Gunpowder

Plotter, must have served as headquarters for the Jesuit's evangelical mission. The pamphlets would have been distributed to Catholic believers, including John Shakespeare, at secret masses or meetings or even clandestine home visits. Signing such a document clearly makes Shakespeare's father not only a recusant, but a devout and dedicated, Roman Catholic.

John Shakespeare's 'Spiritual Testament' was an illegal and comprehensively heretical declaration of faith in Catholic doctrine, in the sacraments and in Purgatory, together with prayers to the Blessed Virgin and the saints:

IV.

I, John Shakespeare, do protest that I will also pass out of this life, armed with the last sacrament of extreme unction: the which if through any let or hindrance I should not then be able to have, I do now also for that time demand and crave the same; beseeching his divine majesty that He will be pleased to anoint my senses both internal and external; with the sacred oil of His infinite mercy, and to pardon me all my sins committed by seeing, speaking, feeling, smelling, hearing, touching, or by any other way whatsoever.[7]

According to this document Shakespeare's father certainly intended to 'dye a papist,' comforted at the end by the sacrament of anointing that had been outlawed by the Protestant Church of England.

This was William Shakespeare's home life. What sort of religious and cultural influences did he encounter at school? It is not known whether Shakespeare attended Stratford Grammar School, though the plays and poems could not have been written without a good school education, or the equivalent in expensive private tuition. Rowe's biography states that Shakespeare's father had to withdraw him from school to help in the shop, but that implies that at least for some time he was there. Of the six masters presiding at the Stratford Grammar School during the period in which Shakespeare may have attended, four were Roman Catholics. Two came from Oxford colleges with strong Catholic connections, St John's (Jesuit martyr Campion's college) and Brasenose. John Cottam was brother to Thomas Cottam, a Jesuit associate of Campion who was tortured in the Tower, and executed in 1582. Simon Hunt retired in 1575 to the seminary at Douai, and became a Jesuit.[8]

There is little doubt that a strong network of kinship, acquaintance and proximity linked the Shakespeares with the Catholic community in Warwickshire, a county where government commissioners found that 'most of the common people are still papist at heart.'[9] Along with the Ardens, local families like the Treshams, the Winters, the Catesbys, kept the Old Faith alive. Arden was executed for sheltering John Somerville, convicted of conspiracy against the Queen's life: John Shakespeare's testament was probably hidden at that time from government officers who were searching local houses for incriminating evidence against Catholics. The other family names mentioned are also those of the conspirators – Thomas Tresham, Thomas and Robert Winter, Robert Catesby – who, after the failed Gunpowder Plot, retreated to the Midlands, and died or were captured fighting for their lost cause.

There is little doubt that Shakespeare's father and mother were both Catholics, probably 'church papists' who outwardly conformed, concealing their true faith, but nonetheless kept getting into trouble with the authorities. Catholicism seems to have persisted to the next generation, since William's own daughter Susanna was cited in May 1606 as a recusant who failed to appear at Easter Communion. The twins Hamnet and Judith were clearly named after their godparents, Stratford neighbours Hamnet and Judith Sadler, who were definitely Catholics. If Shakespeare did 'retire' to Stratford in his later years (he certainly spent more time there, though still active in London, and of course died there) then he can only have found this papistical atmosphere congenial.

Shakespeare's literary career also kept him in close association with Catholics. His patron, and possibly close friend, the Earl of Southampton, came from a prominent Catholic family. Southampton's father assisted Campion, and Catholics were sheltered in his mother's house in Holborn. Southampton's tutor and confessor was Jesuit poet and martyr Robert Southwell. There may have been a link between Shakespeare and Southwell, who was put to death in 1595.[10] Southwell may have alluded to Shakespeare in a tract as 'my loving cousin W. S.,' and Shakespeare certainly used an image from his poem 'The Burning Babe' in *Macbeth*. Early modern historian John Speed, in some remarks on the character assassination of Sir John Oldcastle (original of Falstaff) seems to have linked Shakespeare with Jesuit Robert Persons, referring to 'the papist and his poet.'[11]

†

Speculations

Despite the weight of this evidence, it all remains circumstantial, and neither proves nor disproves William Shakespeare's Catholicism. There is no doubt that Shakespeare was closely hemmed in by Catholicism, but that does not in itself make him a Catholic. At the very centre of this whirlwind of conspiracy, recusancy, resistance and rebellion, Shakespeare keeps his silence. Most of the effort engaged in proving Shakespeare's Catholic connections has, perhaps significantly, focused on the 'Lost Years,' during which period he virtually disappears from the biographer's view. Between the record of his marriage in 1582, and the first mention of him in the London theatre in 1592, nothing is known of where he was, or what he was doing. He fathered children, the twins who were baptized in 1584; and he may have been personally involved in a Stratford family property case brought to court in 1587.

Proponents of the 'Catholic Shakespeare' theory believe they may have found this lost Shakespeare, in the shape of a William Shakeshafte who served Catholic gentleman Alexander Hoghton at his seat of Hoghton Hall in Lancashire. This idea was first suggested as far back as 1937, and has recently gained a new lease of life. In his will, Alexander Hoghton recommended for employment as players Shakeshafte and Fulk Gillom to Sir Thomas Hesketh, a patron of the drama. Many scholars believe that this Shakeshafte was the seventeen-year-old Shakespeare, and indeed that this is how he found his way into the theatrical profession. Stratford schoolmaster John Cottam was from Hoghton, and could have recommended young Shakespeare to the Hoghtons as a private tutor (John Aubrey stated that Shakespeare had been 'a schole-master in the country'). Campion and his Jesuit mission certainly travelled to Lancashire, so it is possible that Shakespeare was recruited by them into some kind of Catholic service.[12] The theory depends however on a combination of circumstantial evidence and on the identification of Shakespeare with Shakeshafte. It all remains at the level of speculation rather than of fact.

†

Was Shakespeare a Catholic? And what did it mean at that time to be one? He certainly had every opportunity to participate in the Catholic faith in any one of a number of different ways.

He might, like his parents, have lived as a church papist, outwardly conforming to the Church of England, hiding his true feelings. And yet, although both his father and his daughter were cited as recusants, he was not. He may have been more successful at concealing his true religion; but since of course he lived a much more public life than these other members of his family, he also had much more opportunity of being observed and reported.

He might have been a full member of the Catholic underground that was clearly so busy all round him, attending secret masses, communicating with Catholic priests, maybe signing his own copy of Cardinal Borromeo's testament. He might have been drawn even deeper into that clandestine world, approaching close to the borders of conspiracy. Could he have done this without ever getting into trouble with the authorities? If his patron Southampton could play a leading role in the failed Essex rebellion and yet survive, it is not impossible that a very popular poet and royal servant might have been afforded unusual latitude in such matters.

It is possible that he was deeply immersed in that underground Catholic culture, deep enough to acquire significant and dangerous knowledge of networks and conspiracies, and that he owed his extraordinarily innocent career, untouched by any imputation of heresy, to the kind of official protection given to government informers. He may, in other words, have been a double agent, a spy, as Christopher Marlowe probably was. Although there is not a shred of evidence to support this suggestion, Shakespeare would not have been the first – or the last – man of letters to dabble in intelligence work; and it may be that his dramatist's impartiality enabled him to play for both teams.

Or he might have been simply an impressionable young man, brought up in secretive loyalty to the faith, evangelized by brilliant and charismatic missionaries like Campion, who went along with the cause until he realized some of its terrible consequences, and then swiftly disengaged himself and had nothing more to do with it. He might have sat through secret masses, said the Latin prayers, taken the Eucharist, without any of those grave and ancient observances ever really touching his heart. He might even have left Stratford partly to get away from these influences, rather than to deepen his Catholic engagement in faraway papist Lancashire. And he might then finally, only when death stared him in the face, have felt a faint yearning for the assurances of the old religion, confessed his sins to a priest, and died a papist.

Although Shakespeare had clearly been hugely successful in 'a world that had lost the comfort of religion,' he might, as Michael Wood suggests, have 'turned back to such comfort at the end':

> Like many people who had lived through the Elizabethan age, he probably eschewed certainties and no longer held any deep sectarian conviction. But … it may be, as Davies records, that he was drawn to his childhood certainties at the end. And if he did go through that last ancient rite of passage on his deathbed, was it perhaps as much in loyalty to the past, to his parents and ancestors, and to the spirits of England?[13]

If, on the other hand, Shakespeare really did live, as well as die, a Catholic, then the evidence for his faith lies beyond the reach of history, scholarship or literary analysis. He kept his secrets to himself, and took them with him to the grave, ensuring, like Hamlet, that none should pluck out the heart of his mystery. Richard Wilson sees a connection between Davies' statement that Shakespeare died a Catholic, and the adjoining reference to the malediction placed on Shakespeare's tomb against anyone who would think to open his grave.

> The paradox of a secret both open and concealed tempts us to guess that what lies in the grave beside the body of the Bard, 'full seventeen foot deep' according to one account, is in fact his own copy of the Borromeo Testament of faith brought by Campion from Milan, with its vow made 'in presence of the Blessed Virgin Mary, my Angel Guardian, and all the Celestial Court.'[14]

Thus, according to this unprovable implication, the open confession of William Shakespeare's faith lies buried seventeen feet down, in a tomb no one dares to open. The secret of Catholic Shakespeare, literally encrypted, is preserved in death, as it was maintained in life. 'The fact' Wilson goes on, 'that we could not prove it, unless we broke the taboo and desecrated the tomb, is the ultimate guarantee of Shakespeare's secrecy and so sets the seal upon his work' (p. 297).

Story: 'He dyed a papist'

This story puts together some of the historical material about Shakespeare's Catholic background, and from it conjectures a possible death-bed scene to account for the Tradition that he 'died a papist.' Shakespeare's ramblings here are taken from Ben Jonson's *The Devil is an Ass* (1616), 5.8, which according to Katherine Duncan-Jones (*Ungentle*, pp. 266–7) may have preserved 'eyewitness impressions' of Shakespeare's death-bed; and from Shakespeare's own *King Lear*.

He dyed a papist

'*Gi' me some garlic, garlic, garlic, garlic!*'

Words flowed from him, as they always had, but now no longer measured, musical and sweet, but thickly mired with nonsense, blasphemy and phlegm. As the madness collared him, and shook his wasted body as a terrier shakes a rat, he heard them running to his bedside.

When he opened his eyes, there they all were, like characters arranged round a theatrical death-bed. Anne, rough face seamed and swollen; Judith, eyes red from weeping, or her husband's wine; Susanna, cool and candle-pale in the lamplight; and standing close behind her, the long lean shadow of her husband, Dr. Hall.

He stared at them, his head bobbing, waiting to see what they would do. Talk about him as if he wasn't there? Discuss some new remedy from Dr. Hall's inexhaustible cornucopia of physic? Or just stand there, like people bored with waiting for someone who's taking too long to die?

Again the rage racked him: madness flowed from his mouth.

'*My wife's a whore,*' he rasped, '*I'll kiss her no more!*'

Down, *hysterica passio*. Down, thou climbing sorrow.

'Heed him not,' said the Doctor. 'Tis the Devil speaks in him.'

'*The devil is good company,*' said Will slyly. '*Yes, wis.*'

'How he is changed,' said Susanna. 'His Voice!'

Ay, his voice. How it had rung and piped across the boards and round the galleries, plangent as a bronze bell, or still as the note of a hautbois heard on a summer evening. Now filed down to a rough and ragged croak, floundering for breath, a tired nag hacking hard past the foul mire of a cough. The traces loose, a voice not his, words he could no longer master.

An unperfect actor, for fear beside his part? No, but thinking how that bastard Ben would write this scene into a play, getting his revenge at last, so all would know this was the manner of Will Shakespeare's end. Perished by an impertinent pustule of pox. Bald, mad, paralysed, his ribs aflame with agony like some poor soul's in hell. His heart swelled to the size of a cow's, the blood beating backwards in his veins.

The Doctor came forward and took his wrist, cool professional fingers testing his pulse. Will tried to shake him off.

'*Thoult come with a needle and thrust it in,*
Pull out that, and put in a pin!
Kill the physician, and the fee bestow
Upon the foul disease!'

'Do you not know us, father?' pleaded Susanna.

'Aye, I know you well enough,' he muttered. 'All four of you. Whore, baggage, nun and quack. Knight, shite, owl, foul. *Quebremos el ojo de burlas.* I know you all; but have much ado to know myself. Leave me to die in peace.'

Susanna held him by the shoulders, while the Doctor administered a potion. Give me to drink Mandragora. The familiar sweetness flowed through him, and he sank down again, full fathom five, down through the clear green swell to where, on the sandy seabed, his father's bones flowered amongst the coral.

†

The room was full of smoke. The air smelt sweet. The figures at the foot of his bed seemed unchanged, standing in exactly the same position, as if they really were actors resuming their places for another run-through of the scene. But something was different.

There was his wife, God damn her long-suffering patience. There was his younger daughter, the one who could have died instead of her twin brother, but instead lived to shame him by her marriage to that fat, red-faced oaf, Quiney. There was Susanna, always beautiful in her luminous pallor. But the figure standing behind her was not the Doctor, but someone else. Someone shorter, stouter, round faced and genial. Who? He struggled to focus his eyes. The room was filled with burning incense. A surplice; a stole; a rosary.

He tried to speak but the words failed him. He tried to tell them that he had no need of a Catholic priest, having many years of life left to him. That he had no use for a Catholic priest, being a communicant member of the Church of England. That they were mad to risk such danger as to harbour a Catholic priest, and for the sake of one who would willingly accept eternal oblivion rather than the probing interrogations of final judgement.

He had had the worst of all worlds, communing with saintly Jesuits whose flawless innocence easily reconciled them to martyrdom, and obdurate sinners who took freely of all the world, the flesh and the devil had to offer, confident in ultimate absolution, even if necessary at the point of death. He thought of Southampton, that demon with the face of an angel. Though they shared together equally in the abominations of mortal sin, they were most unequal in terms of the penalties to be paid. There in the Tower, Southampton had his crucifix, and his rosary beads, and the companionship of the Blessed Virgin; while he stood on the verge of a great precipice, an abyss through which blew the angry tempest of divine displeasure.

Susanna stood aside, and the priest approached the bed. Will could neither speak nor move, and lay inert under the clergyman's ministrations. Gently he took a phial of oil, dabbed it on a bit of cloth, and softly wiped the oil into the palms of Will's hands, the soles of his feet, the lids of his eyes, his nostrils, his lips, all the while muttering Latin prayers.

'Per sacrosáncta humánae reparatiónis mystéria remittat tibi omnipotens Deus omnes praeséntis et futúrae vitae paenas, Paradísi portas apériat, et ad gáudia sempitérna perdúcat.'

The dying man did not know which was more fearful, the certainty of death, confirmed by this black-robed harbinger, or the fear all that horror from the past, sweeping over him again, now when he could put up no resistance. It all came back, the chanting, the beautiful old prayers, the taste of bread and body, *corpus Christi*, lying on the tongue. The piety and the pain; the rack and the scavenger's daughter. Thumbscrew and manacles, brazier and gallows. A burning, all-consuming love, inseparable from a crippling fear. If he could but speak! If he could only move!

He lifted a hand to his forehead, as if to wipe away the sacramental oil. The three women flinched, the priest stood back as if to permit the sinner his last moment of choice. Susanna clasped her rosary between her palms, and raised her hands in prayer. He turned his face to the wall.

†

A little, little grave. Poor Hamnet. He had shuddered, he remembered, as he stood by the tiny plot in Holy Trinity churchyard. The small pile of earth, thick black loam and yellow clods of clay overturned to the air, seemed obscene, as if the exhumation were exposing the flesh under the earth's skin. He shuddered, not from cold, though there was a small chill in the September evening, but to imagine those frail bones, respectfully composed now and tightly sheathed in their winding sheet, but so soon to disunite, as the fragile flesh corrupted and dissolved. My son.

He had not been there to nurse the boy in his illness; had not lain a cool hand of ineffectual blessing on the febrile forehead; had not seen the little limbs folded together, or paced behind the bier as it was borne to the churchyard. He had taken for granted Hamnet Shakespeare as his son and heir; but he had scarcely been any kind of father to the boy.

What indeed was he doing here now, paying unnecessary respects, enduring his wife's bitter and majestic silence, condemned by the reproachful incomprehension on the faces of the little girls, as they stared at him with their mother's eyes? Looking down he saw that mud was caked onto his patent leather pumps, and he fastidiously stepped back from the grave. Many miles from here, he wrote and acted death every day. But nothing had prepared him for the climbing sorrow induced by this modest little exit from the world's great stage.

Beside him stood his father, whose copious tears shamed the flinty self-command of his dry-eyed son. John had been the first to rush out when Will stumbled wearily from his horse outside the house in Henley Street. The old man was crying when he flung his arms around his son's neck, and clung to him in a passion of grief, and a smell of stale beer and old age. He was crying as they walked though the High Street, accepting commiserations from friends and neighbours. He was crying as they stood by the grave, tears running down the white stubble of his face. Inconsolably he wept for his little grandson, gone inexplicably before him into that great void dark.

And all the while, Will knew, there was something the old man wanted to say, something that must out and be spoken, though the father was as unwilling to utter it as the son reluctant to hear. Gently he took his father's arm, and turned him from the grave, an open wound in the torn earth, and towards the church.

'What was it like? The funeral?'

'Oh beautiful, beautiful,' said the old man, his sobs subsiding. 'He looked so peaceful you know, all his pain washed away. Poor little lad. "For He shall wipe away every tear from their eyes". He said that, the Vicar. Beautiful it was. Beautiful service. But Will ....'

'Go on.'

John Shakespeare glanced behind him and came close, confiding, pleading, hanging on William's arm.

'*What ceremony else*, Will? Is that all, for your only son? A few words from Cranmer's prayer book; a handful of dust scattered over his little face?.'

Will tried to draw his arm away. 'What could I do? You ask too much.'

'You could pray for him, Will, as our Saviour taught us. You could find a priest to say Mass for his little soul. You could cheer him on his way with bell, book and candle. You could give him the words of intercession. He's out there now, lost in some great grey limbo, alone and crying for his mother. We can speak to him, Will. Through the church. We can send him our prayers. Through a priest. We can help him ...'

Will was walking away, thinking of Tyburn and the Tower. Of his cousin Edward, nothing left of him but a blackened skull, grinning at the crowds on London Bridge. Of Southwell, left hanging by his hands while his tormentor casually went about his business. Of Campion at his trial, his broken hands wrapped in a linen cloth, too enfeebled by torture to lift a cup of drink to his own lips.

The old man called after him as he strode quickly back towards the house, away from Stratford, back in the direction of London and safety.

'What will you do for me, when my time comes?' he shouted after his son, indifferent to whoever might hear. 'Will you leave me burning in Purgatory, without a drop of mercy to cool my tongue?'

†

Whitewash. By its very blankness the wall next to him gestured at something unsaid, mute witness to an invisible meaning. Just a bare surface, creamy off-white, rough-textured in patches where the lime had run, a piece flaked off and yellow underneath, strands of hair from the plaster tangled with hog's bristles from the workman's brush.

Why did it seem to speak to him, that wall that never held meaning before? Was it an invitation, a blank canvas waiting to be coated with all the colours of his fancy? Or was there some picture lying concealed beneath, some defaced image slackly slubbered over with whitewash, some pigment of palimpsest, latent, veiled, waiting only to be disclosed? For nothing is secret, that shall not be made manifest; neither anything hid, that shall not be known and come abroad.

†

He was a boy again, sitting next to his father in the Guild Chapel at Evening Prayer one late afternoon of summer. An assiduous observer, Will had noticed that members of the congregation, alternately pious and bored, devoutly attentive or irritably fidgeting, tended to look round in all directions during the service: now at the priest and the communion table, now up at the ceiling, now down at their feet, now at the church door. He had observed, however, that his father only ever looked in one direction, staring continually at the whitewashed wall above the nave. His eyes remained constantly fixed on that mark, while he kneeled and stood, while his lips moved soundlessly in prayer, while his hands were lifted frequently in supplication.

'O Lord, open thou our lips,' sang the priest.

'And our mouth shall shew forth thy praise,' raggedly responded the congregation.

Will had thought for a long time this was merely an idiosyncratic habit of personal devotion, but realizing how different was his father's physical attitude from that of his fellow-parishioners, curiosity at last moved him to speak.

'Father,' he asked, 'What is it that you see there?'

John's eyes were bright with tears. But he only sighed, and shook his head.

'I see nothing. Nothing but the light of the setting sun as it moves across the wall.'

And yet he continued to stare at nothing, to bend his eye on vacancy.

The choir intoned: 'My soul doth magnify the Lord …'

Will asked him again: 'Father, what is it you see there?'

'I see nothing. Nothing but the shadows of evening gathering round about us.'

'Please, father, tell me. You can tell me. I have to know.'

John Shakespeare heaved a great sigh, that seemed to shatter all his bulk and end his being. He leaned very close to his son and whispered in his ear.

'It is not nothing I see, child. It is everything. I see Christ in majesty, seated on a rainbow. I see Him judging all the peoples of the earth, the quick and the dead. The righteous he assigns to his kingdom, and the unrighteous he sends down to the pit. It is all there, on the wall, just behind the whitewash. We have covered it over because we had no choice. But God forgive us the deed of that day. God forgive me.'

He sat back in the pew and put an arm round his son's shoulders.

'Now it is all I can see. One day we will see it, with our own eyes. "For yet in my flesh, shall I see God."'

The service was ending.

'Now lettest thou thy servant depart in peace, according to thy word. For mine eyes have seen thy salvation …'

†

So there it was, the invisible writing on the wall. He turned his face towards the women and the priest. He could feel, under the tips of his fingers, the soft emollition of the unction. Slowly his hand moved down from his forehead, traversing his body to his chest, then up again to his left shoulder, and over to the right. The sign of the cross. The priest absolved him, and commended his soul to God. Through the mist of incense he could see three women, bowed and grieving, like weeping queens conducting the dying Arthur to Avalon. His pain had gone, and with it his fear.

Let it come. The readiness is all.

And so he died: a papist.

†

Shakespeare's Face: 'The mind's construction'

'There's no art to find the mind's construction in the face' (Macbeth)

King Duncan's observation, which reflects on his own experience of betrayal by a man whose character he misjudged, runs counter to the norms of common sense. In fact we rely on the face to identify a person, to distinguish him or her from others, and to tell us much, though not necessarily everything, about their personality. Certainly the art of biography would regard the subject's face as primary evidence, and most modern biographies display a gallery of images, photographs, drawings or paintings, delineating the subject's life, where possible, from infancy to death. 'A man's face,' observed Oscar Wilde, 'is his autobiography.'

The assumption of a natural connection between physiognomy and character applies equally to artists: but here the causal link can of course work in the opposite direction. As in the literary theory of the 'author-function,' an image of the writer may be derived from a reading of the work. George Orwell concludes his essay 'Charles Dickens' with this assertion:

> When one reads any strongly individual piece of writing, one has the impression of seeing a face somewhere behind the page. I feel this very strongly with Swift, with Defoe, with Fielding, Stendhal, Thackeray, Flaubert, though in several cases I do not know what these people looked like and do not want to know. What one sees is the face the writer *ought* to have. Well, in the case of Dickens I see a face that is not quite the face of Dickens's photographs, although it resembles it. It is the face of a man about forty, with a small beard and a high colour. He is laughing, with a touch of anger in his laughter, but no triumph, no malignity. It is the face of a man who is *generously angry* – in other words, of a nineteenth-century liberal, a free intelligence, a type hated by all the smelly little orthodoxies which are now contending for our souls.[1]

Physiognomy and literary response here coalesce, and Dickens' fiction is read in the light of a powerfully realized image of its author. This image is, however, perceived as an idealized construct, the face that the writer *ought* to have, and is dependent on a particular interpretation of the literary evidence. The critic's X-ray vision penetrates the patina of the text to reveal the author's true presence behind the writing, 'the face behind the page.'

But it can surely be no accident that the idealized portrait of the writer turns out to resemble so closely the face to be seen in surviving photographs of Dickens. Orwell's disclaimer, his lack of interest in what authors *actually* looked like, betrays an awareness that his critical response to Dickens' writing is drawing on two sources, the literary and the visual. Orwell's reading of Dickens' work prompts him not to create an entirely new image of Dickens, but rather to modify the familiar likeness, so that Dickens' own portrait, and Orwell's image of Dickens, lie side by side in the reader's mind. 'The mind's construction' is evident in both face and works, but each displays a somewhat different facet of the life's totality.

When Ben Jonson urged the reader of the First Folio to regard Shakespeare's writing, rather than his portrait, the engraving by Martin Droeshout that serves as frontispiece to the volume – 'Reader, looke/Not on his Picture, but his Book!'[2] – the injunction in a sense comes too late, since Jonson's poem lies on the page opposite the Droeshout engraving of Shakespeare's face. The image precedes the recommendation to ignore it. Indeed, if anything, Jonson's instruction to the reader draws attention to the portrait, even as it disclaims significance from it: the reader is compelled to look back at the portrait before embarking on the text. Word and image prove mutually dependent, each validating a critical judgment founded in part on both. At least one fictional contemporary reader of Shakespeare was persuaded by his enjoyment of the writing to defy this authorly purism, and to want to possess a portrait of the writer whose work he admired:

O sweet Mr Shakespeare, Ile have his picture in my study.[3]

Gullio in *The Return to Parnassus* clearly felt that being able to contemplate an image of the author would be a suitable extension of his delight in the works. He at least wanted to see the face behind the page.

When literary critics give attention to the portraits of writers they tend to follow Orwell rather than Ben Jonson. Here, for example, is Anne Barton, commenting on the image of Ben Jonson himself:

In the famous, and much copied, portrait of the mature Jonson attributed to Abraham van Blyenberch, the sitter almost seems to belong to a different race from Sidney, Spenser, Marlow, Raleigh and Donne – or even from Shakespeare who stares out from the woodenly inept Droeshout engraving. Jonson's broad, blunt, vigorously plain face dissociates itself oddly in any portrait gallery from the more elegant, attenuated faces of his Elizabethan contemporaries. His artistic detachment from them, during much of his life, was equally radical.[4]

Here a substantive critical evaluation is located in the physiognomic differences to be found in contemporary portraiture. Jonson's face mirrors the
character of his work. Caroline Spurgeon wanted to use the so-called 'Chess
Portrait'[5] of Shakespeare and Jonson as the cover illustration for her book
Shakespeare's Imagery, on the grounds that the image more closely resembled
her conception of Shakespeare:

> No other presentation I have yet seen of Shakespeare approaches it in
> satisfying quality. You will find in the face thought, imagination, great intel-
> lectual power, great sensitiveness and refinement, and altogether a feeling of
> strength and power behind sensitiveness which is remarkable.

These are of course precisely the qualities she detected in Shakespeare's
imagery. Spurgeon came close to admitting to a degree of wish fulfillment at
this coincidence, justified by a sense of incompatibility between the face in the
Droeshout engraving, and the image of Shakespeare in the reader's mind:

> If there is one thing certain in a world of uncertainties, it is that Shakespeare
> did not look like the Droeshout portrait. On the other hand he might have
> looked like the man to the right in the 'chess portrait'; so, for my part, I
> prefer to look at that.[6]

And this would also be the more generally held view today. Word and image
are no longer seen as alternatives, but as components of an artistic language
that fuse into intertextual combinations. Images are an essential element of
the material culture in which all works of art are generated and consumed.
The meanings produced by literary works are determined cumulatively by
a wide range of factors which include, as Gary Taylor puts it, 'how they are
edited, what kinds of commentary they generate, whether they are translated
into other languages, how often they are quoted, how they (and their author's
name) are spelled, *how they (and their author) are visually represented*'[7] (my italics).

Shakespeare's face is one of the most insistently reproduced icons in the
world. It adorns countless book covers, hotel and restaurant signs, beer mats,
tea caddies, confectionery packets, cigarette and playing cards, ceramics,
theatre and museum foyers, advertisements, and banknotes. Its currency is
based in large measure on the cachet of high culture (Shakespeare metaphorically authorizes those products he vicariously endorses), combined with its
instant recognisability. The high balding dome – 'what a forehead, what
a brain!'[8] – has been parodied by Picasso and innumerable other artists,
and stands as a guarantor of the author's unique genius. It is probable that
every English-speaking citizen of the UK is acquainted with Shakespeare;
not necessarily from plays and books, but from the visual images borne by
those ubiquitous advertisements, tourist attractions, pub signs, biscuit-tins,
credit-cards and calendars. An agency offering elocution lessons used to

advertise itself through a cartoon drawing of a puzzled Shakespeare, bewildered by a voice from a telephone receiver: to be understood by 'Shakespeare' would be a guarantee of correct speech. In the television series *Batman*, the entrance to the 'Batcave' was controlled by a switch concealed within a bust of Shakespeare: the decorative property of a millionaire's house opens to activate an exotic world of drama and costume, fantasy and adventure. The stimulant beverage *Red Bull* is advertised by a cartoon of Shakespeare, seeking inspiration in the can. Radio 4 once broadcast a programme on language, *The Story of English*, billed as 'the great adventure which transformed the island speech of Shakespeare into the world English of 1,000 million,' and entitled 'From Will to the World.' The *Radio Times* carried a cover design, showing a map of the world superimposed on Shakespeare's inflated forehead, in which the forehead of the Bard, set in an English pastoral landscape, had swelled like the British Empire to encompass 'the great globe itself.'

Facts

But where does this familiar received image of Shakespeare come from? There are only two portraits which have claim to authenticity, in the normal sense of being more or less closely derived from the subject's actual living appearance. These are Gheerart Janssen's bust in Holy Trinity Church, Stratford, and Martin Droeshout's title-page engraving to the 1623 First Folio. Both were commissioned some years after Shakespeare's death, and probably both relied on some form of preliminary sketch supplied by friends or relatives. They seem to have been acceptable to those who commissioned and viewed them, although this in no way guarantees any certainty of realism on the part of the artists. Although they depict what could be the same man, there are striking differences between them in their modes of representation. The Janssen bust, discussed earlier in Chapter 1, honours the well-to-do Stratford burgher, offering us a corpulent, older man with up-turned, trimmed moustaches, neatly bobbed side-locks, expensively tailored robes, who holds in his hands the stylized reminders of the source of his wealth in the foregrounded pen and sheet of paper. The image of the Droeshout Shakespeare, with its younger, more dishevelled appearance and encephalous forehead, has proved the more popular image of the artist, despite the engraver's obvious technical incompetence in such matters as relating the proportion of the head to that of the torso.

Tradition

Several other portraits have been identified as images of Shakespeare, including the Chandos, Felton and Grafton portraits. The Chandos portrait, which depicts a handsome and rather roguish Shakespeare with a gold ear-ring, is a preferred image for many: Erika Jong says of Shakespeare in her novel *Serenissima: 'I have gazed at the Chandos portrait of W.S. and felt that I knew and loved the man behind those luminous brown eyes ... '* (p. 38). Others have found a gentle, pensive expression in the Felton portrait, and a soulful gaze in the Grafton. In each case, the critic is searching for an image approximating to his or her own conception of the artist, trying to find the mind's construction in the face. Very recently a newly-discovered picture, the Cobbe portrait, has been promoted as a genuine and true likeness from the right period, around 1610: 'a far better picture' says Stanley Wells, 'of a really handsome man.'[9] Other, later versions of the same picture have long been extant, including the 'Janssen' portrait in the Folger Shakespeare Library, Washington DC, so the contemporary portrait, which may have belonged to the Earl of Southampton, naturally has a reasonable claim.

But equally naturally, the dating, provenance and authenticity of all these images of the poet have been strongly disputed within the scholarly community. And these arguments are only partly about dates and origins and historical probability. Readers of Shakespeare will prefer one portrait or another as their version of the true likeness of the poet, the image that arises from their particular response to the work, finding, in this image rather than in that, 'the mind's construction in the face.' In the past scholars would even find it legitimate to alter the primary visual images to bring them more closely into line with their received image of the Bard. Around 1770 the 'Janssen' portrait of Shakespeare was altered to make it balder. Edmond Malone persuaded the vicar of Holy Trinity Church to have the original gaudy paintwork of the Gheerart Janssen bust whitewashed, to make the image more like a classical bust, thus endorsing his own neo-classical conception of the plays. Both these revisions were subsequently reversed to restore the original features. Samuel Schoenbaum suggested that each portrait functions as a Rorschach blot onto which the critic 'projects the image of his own conceit.'[10]

Speculation

It is a matter of some importance that the best-known image of Shakespeare, the Droeshout engraving, appears as the frontispiece to the first collected edition of Shakespeare's works, the First Folio. The 1200 or so volumes printed sold at the premium price of £1, and came adorned with a full panoply of dedications and commendatory verses. The general tendency of these introductory materials is to link the plays to the dramatist, to *personalize* their provenance, to attach them firmly to the *author* rather than to the theatrical milieu in which they had been first produced. The early quartos of Shakespeare's plays had tended to stress theatrical rather than authorial origin. The title-page of the popular *Titus Andronicus*, for example, merely records that it was 'Plaide by the Right Honourable the Earle of *Darbie*, Earle of *Pembrooke*, and Earle of *Sussex* their *Servants*,' and not until 1598 was Shakespeare's name attached to a printed version of one of his plays, *Love's Labour's Lost*. Heminge and Condell, the editors of the First Folio, instead emphasize Shakespeare's 'authorly' status and the 'readerly,' literary nature of the texts: 'reade him, therefore; and againe and againe.'[11] The poet-contributors also focus on the author in their commendatory verses. Ben Jonson speaks of 'my beloved, The Author,' Hugh Holland of the 'Scenicke Poet,' Leonard Digges of 'the deceased Author' and I. M. simply of 'the memorie of M. W. Shakespeare.'

The Droeshout engraving, strategically placed on the title-page, is a personalizing, validating presence, literally authorizing the works that follow. Ben Jonson's accompanying epigram 'To the Reader' seems at first glance to direct attention away from the image of the author towards the works themselves, 'Reader, looke/Not on his Picture, but his Booke.' But, of course, it is impossible to obey this injunction. Jonson's lines appear on the verso, but Shakespeare's face dominates the recto; neither can be viewed without sight of the other. Engraving and epigram prove mutually dependent, constituting a unified design, the effect of which is to invite 'the Reader' to view the plays in the context of a formidable authorial presence. Early purchasers of the First Folio, that is, were at the beginning of a process all modern readers of Shakespeare must be familiar with, coming to the plays having first confronted a carefully constructed picture of their originator as a powerful authorial presence, indeed one of the greatest of all authors, a transcendent genius and an omniscient seer.

On the other hand the prefatory material gathered to open the First Folio also operates in a completely contrary way, to anonymize the author of the plays. The posthumously published First Folio was very explicitly a memorial tribute to the author Shakespeare, who did not live to gather together his own works. The dedication is defined as 'an office to the dead,' and throughout it echoes the language of the burial service: '*we most humbly consecrate to your H. H. these remaines of your servant Shakespeare …*' The address 'To the Great Variety of Readers' makes it clear that the editors saw themselves as executors to a will, undertaking on behalf of the deceased the tasks he himself was prevented by death from fulfilling.

The gathering of the works on behalf of the author announces his constitutive absence from the process, and renders the act of publication a posthumous service of commemoration. The Folio is also defined as a funeral monument, a tomb designed to contain the corpus of the author's writings, both to retain memory of them and to preserve them from violation (i.e. textual corruption, piracy etc.). It is therefore a culturally constructed artefact that inevitably seems detached from the originating author. Shakespeare the author is clearly absented from the scene of production, and the plays ritually called together in order to construct a new author-function that replaces the dead author. Shakespeare the author is uncoupled from Shakespeare the man. The portrait itself tends to endorse this absence, since it does not, for many observers, bring the author to life as some of the other portraits do.

This tendency of the Droeshout engraving to become anonymous through excessive familiarity can be illustrated from its use in a recent cultural context. In 1994 the Royal Shakespeare Company initiated a two-month Shakespeare extravaganza, focused on a major theatre season, with an associated series of events and exhibitions at London's Barbican Centre. The theatre festival was accompanied by a TV Shakespeare season entitled 'Bard on the Box.' The overall title of the festival was 'Everybody's Shakespeare.' There was something for everyone, the title suggested, in this broad-ranging and diversified, international and multi-cultural, celebration. In one sense the title was individualizing, speaking to the number and multiplicity of persons. In another sense it was universalizing, since the common ground on which this infinitely diversified constituency could meet, the global totality that contained all these individuals, was an abstraction, the one and only 'Shakespeare.' Thus 'Everybody's Shakespeare' was also 'the greatest ever celebration of the genius of Shakespeare.' What enables us collectively to inhabit 'Shakespeare' is not that which particularizes and differentiates us, but that which universalizes him. This immediate and contemporary availability of Shakespeare can be recognized as yet another manifestation of that universal genius proclaimed by Ben Jonson: 'He was not for an age, but for all time.'[12]

Shakespeare is everybody's. But the syntax allows for another reading: 'Everybody *is* Shakespeare.' This alternative interpretation was foregrounded in the festival's publicity leaflet, which exhibited a politically correct gallery of faces, black, white, yellow; male and female; young and old. Each face peeped cheerfully out from behind the mask of Shakespeare's face in its most familiar representation, the Droeshout engraving. Everybody then can become Shakespeare, or at least personify Shakespeare, for the mask is also of course the standard symbol of drama, the theatrical prototype for assuming a role, playing a part. We can all play Shakespeare, or play at being Shakespeare, by participation in this ritual of celebration. The Droeshout engraving is particularly appropriate to make this point, on account of its strange featurelessness and anonymity. 'No human being could possibly look like that,' claimed a contributor to the associated TV programme 'The Battle of Wills,' which was about rival claimants to authorship of the plays. Some of those concerned to question Shakespeare's true identity have suspected that the face in the Droeshout portrait is actually a mask (there is an odd line between the edge of the face and the background). Though it would seem improbable for an artist to depict someone in a mask, we can readily accept that the face *is* notoriously separable from its physical context, since it has become, through continuous familiar usage, an immediately recognizable cultural icon. That which is universal is also anonymous. Anthony Burgess, in the conclusion of his biography of Shakespeare, formulates this impossible paradox of genius and universality:[13]

> Martin Droeshout's engraving…has never been generally liked… the face is that of a commercial traveller growing bald in the service of an ungrateful firm … We need not repine at the lack of a satisfactory Shakespeare portrait. To see his face, we need only look in a mirror. He is ourselves, ordinary suffering humanity, fired by moderate ambitions, concerned with money, the victim of desire, all too mortal. To his back, like a hump, was strapped a miraculous but somehow irrelevant talent… we are all Will.

Any portrait is a transaction between the subject and the artist. The subject wants his picture; the artist wants to create a work of art. The two objectives may or may not coincide. The visual languages used to represent persons are not always concerned with accurate physical representation. Often they are also designed to represent, through the development of visual conventions, general categories of social type, historical contexts, ideas and values. The question of whether Shakespeare, by the time he died, actually *looked like* the bust in Holy Trinity church, is perhaps an anachronistic curiosity of the modern photographic imagination, rather than a proper concern of the seventeenth-century plastic artist, who was probably more interested in the question of whether the image 'looked like' whatever the individual's family and friends, the commissioners of the portrait, the commercial and professional middle-class of Stratford and the governors of the church wanted to *signify* by means of the statue.

In the seventeenth century, sculptural representations such as this one had already begun to *commemorate* rather than *imitate* the person, overtly using the person's physical attributes as a source for the direct communication of cultural meaning. This process was consolidated in the eighteenth century. We have seen that Malone wanted the bust in Holy Trinity Church to look more like a classical statue. The best-known sculpted representation of Shakespeare is the marble statue commissioned by public subscription, executed by Peter Scheemakers and erected in Westminster Abbey as a memorial to the national poet in 1741. It functioned both as a collective tribute, drawing on what was already a substantial fund of reverence and admiration; a memorialization of a pre-eminent genius of English culture; and an official emblematization of Shakespeare's reception into the structures of national authority and power, constituted by church, state and monarchy. Here representation is at its most impersonal, a lapidary codification of the signs of cultural power. The features of Shakespeare scarcely resemble any of the earlier portraits, but are constituted by those conventions of idealized depiction which transformed the eighteenth-century English aristocracy into a pantheon of classical characters. Within an impersonal and idealizing texture provided by the cold chastity of the medium, this figure etches the faces into the sharp, clean lines of an 'English' countenance; and a clear, candid spirituality further hints (especially in the shaping of the hair and beard) at a similarity to the icon of Christ.[14]

The semiotics of the statue also enact in microcosm a relation between the figure and its institutional space. The form of Shakespeare is shown leaning on a pedestal, embossed with the faces of a pantheon of English monarchs. The supportive pedestal expresses monumental authority, and links the image to its surrounding context of royal and state power. The figure by contrast expresses relaxed contemplation and nonchalant mastery; the pose is derived from the conventional Elizabethan image of the melancholy young man leaning against a tree (as in Nicholas Hillyard's miniature). Thus the artefact juxtaposes the weight and stability of the monumental context against an aristocratic insouciance, a relaxed grace and elegant langour appropriate to the eighteenth-century image of the man of letters. The pile of books surmounting the pedestal partakes of both dimensions: the solid, weighty, heavily-bound records of monumental achievement, they are merely a prop for the casual elbow of the leaning poet, rapt in an impassioned stillness of meditation.

This particular icon offered the perfect form for reproduction and circulation, and as a miniature souvenir became a standard souvenir item. The history of its reproduction actually began very early. A leaden copy, executed in a mass-production factory at Hyde Park corner, appeared as a centrepiece in David Garrick's Great Shakespeare Jubilee, held in Stratford in 1769. This event, at one level a genuine tribute to Shakespeare from a great man of the theatre, was the founding prototype of all subsequent festivals held around the name, fame and reputation of Shakespeare. Garrick's celebration was as much about Garrick as it was about Shakespeare: a contemporary illustration shows the actor-manager declaiming his *Ode to Shakespeare*, a great hymn of bardolatry, with the statue in the background. Garrick's Jubilee, in the words of one scholar, 'marks the point at which Shakespeare stopped being regarded as an increasingly popular and admirable dramatist, and became a god.'[15] At the same time, it employed as a central symbolic icon an image of Shakespeare which became, in a later age of mechanical reproduction, an instantly recognizable souvenir.

The contradictory apotheosis of this statuesque image was then its incorporation into the design of the British £20 note, which for a time featured Shakespeare's image. The device on the banknote transacted a complex exchange of values: the currency of Shakespeare as a cultural token, a symbol both of high art and national pride, enhanced the material worth of the promissory note, while the high value of the note itself conferred a corresponding richness on the symbol of national culture. Here the solid bulk of another major apparatus of British society, the Bank of England, was articulated with the marble gravity of Shakespeare and the immense solidity of Westminster Abbey in an institutional configuration grouped to link the strength of a currency with the power of traditional authority.

This paper portrait of Shakespeare probably represents the culmination of eighteenth-century bardolatry; but it represented also its terminal point. That which is specific, unique, supremely individual, here appeared in its most generalized, impersonal form. The incomparable, irreplaceable, unrepeatable genius of Shakespeare was fragmented by the process of mechanical reproduction into millions of identical simulacra. But the overriding premise of this ideological structure is that authority and power are vested in the material presence of a concrete substance. The banknote may be merely fragile paper, but it bears the signature of authority, the image of reliability, the stamp of power. The mysterious potency symbolized by the financial token is by definition absent (even a banknote is really abstract 'credit'; it declares itself explicitly to be a 'promise'), but it is a god with a countenance of marble, with feet of lead; and with printing presses of solid steel. What happens, however, when the identity of money as abstract value supersedes and obliterates the character of money as material substance?

In the contemporary social economy money is debt and credit, profit and investment, the cheque and the credit card, figures scrolling across a computer screen or printed on a bank-statement, as much for the private citizen as for the industrialist or commercial entrepreneur. Wealth is no longer piled up in greasy banknotes, or accumulated amid the clashing cacophony of industrial production, but amassed through the technological media of computers and mobile phones, realized in the vacuous non-existence of the futures market. Commercial exchange, even at the simplest level, is as likely to proceed via the paper or plastic authorization of credit, as through an exchange of physical tokens like coins or notes. Clearly if the traditional resources of culture are to be mobilized in support of these developments, they will require new forms of representation.

The traditional iconography of Shakespeare reproduction traded in effects of mass and solidity, gravity and substance. This was replaced by the 'Bardcard,' product of a new 'post-modern' iconography, appropriate to a society where money can be referred to as 'plastic.' Like the £20 note, cheque guarantee cards, issued by some banks, for a time bore a picture of Shakespeare. Where on the banknote the bardic image only symbolically authorized value, on the Bardcard it did so literally, since the image was depicted in the form of a high-technology visual hologram, designed to inhibit fraudulent use and reproduction. The hologram was developed from a photograph, which is not (as one might reasonably expect) a copy of one of the standard Shakespeare portraits, but a photo of a costumed actor pretending to look like Shakespeare.

The authenticity of the card was thus demonstrated not by a display of cultural power, but by a technological *coup d'oeil*. In terms of content, the image approached grotesque self-parody, since the proof of individual ownership, by the cardholder, of certain resources of credit held by a bank, was attested by the most fraudulent and artificial means imaginable: a hologram of a photograph of an actor pretending to be ... Shakespeare. Where the traditional imagery of the Scheemakers statue invoked cultural and economic solidity, the image of the Bardcard was pure post-modernist surface, yielding to the efforts of interpretation only a ludicrous self-reflexive playfulness. Where the £20 note pointed to the legitimate state ownership and control of both economic and cultural power, the Bardcard proved its holder's title to credit by displaying the image of the one major author whose responsibility for the cultural productions attributed to him has been consistently and systematically questioned. This quality was compounded by the reverse of the card, where the holder's signature authorized individual ownership of its power, irresistibly recalling the illegible scrawl of the six signatures attributed to Shakespeare, which some experts have described as apparently belonging to six different people, at least three of them illiterate or terminally ill. One wonders how the bank would react to a cardholder who signed his name with the flexible and cavalier approach to spelling also visible in those 'Shakespearean' autographs.

Shakespeare's face went to the grave having been copied, so far as we know, in only one or two pictures, which don't even resemble one another all that much. The desire to have 'sweet Master Shakespeare's picture' did not stop there, and many people have wanted to have Shakespeare's remains exhumed to find out what he really looked like, despite the inscription on the tomb that forbids its violation.

At the close of the nineteenth century there was a vigorous public debate about whether Shakespeare's tomb should or should not be opened. The motivation of those willing to transgress the tomb's exhortation and open the grave was either to prove that the grave's occupant (if it has one) is someone other than Shakespeare; or to confirm details of Shakespeare's appearance, so elusively recorded by the various extant portraits; These contradictory motives enthused Stratfordians and anti-Stratfordians respectively: if the bones in the grave match the Droeshout engraving, then a link between man and work is established; if the grave were empty or otherwise occupied, this would fuel the mystery around theories of alternative authorship. Fantasies about finding manuscripts buried in the tomb are held in common: they might confirm once and for all Shakespeare's authorship, or they might be in someone else's handwriting. James Rigney finds in this tomb-raiding curiosity 'an archaeological concern to locate the authentic remains of the author and flesh them out in the lineaments of the artefact.'[16]

Supporters advocated exhumation as a means of testing the portraits, and even photographing the remains before their inevitable dissolution. 'Think of a photograph of Shakespeare,' mused J. Parker Norris: "in habit as he lived". Would not such a relic be of inestimable value to the world?'[17] 'If we could get even a photograph of Shakespeare's skull it would be a great thing.'[18] Very old exhumed corpses have been found to retain their form and the garments they were buried in intact, though these corrupt quickly once exposed to air. But Norris echoes a description of the Ghost in *Hamlet* ('in his habit, as he lived'). Shakespeare himself of course is reputed to have played the Ghost on stage, so it would be in keeping for his 'Canonized bones/Hearsed in death' to 'burst their cerements' as he returns to resolve our questions. 'If we had but Shakespeare's skull before us,' wrote Clement Ingleby, a Trustee of the

Shakespeare Birthplace Trust, 'most of these questions would be set at rest for ever.'[19] Even the anticipated photograph of the remains would, in Norris's phrase, be a 'relic of inestimable value.' Ingleby argued for disinterment, 'a respectful examination of the grave,' on grounds of a legitimate 'desire, by exhumation, to set at rest a reasonable or important issue respecting the person of the deceased while he was yet a living man':[20]

> Beyond question, the skull of Shakespeare, might we but discern in it anything like its condition at the time of interment, would be of still greater interest and value (p. 29).

Ingleby's proposals were vilified as vandalism and sacrilege. Local Stratford dignitaries were clearly concerned about the Stratford monopoly on Shakespeare's remains: 'Photographs of Shakespeare's skull' complained Stratford councillor Alderman Gibbs 'would, doubtless, have a large sale all over the world.'[21] J. O. Halliwell-Phillips argued that if the skull were found and compared to the Holy Trinity bust, any discrepancy would suggest that the skull could not be Shakespeare's. This would in turn confirm the earlier rumour that Shakespeare's skull had in reality been stolen from the grave, acquired by a 'Resurrection Man' and taken to America by phrenologist Johann Kaspar Spurzheim. A phrenological drawing, dated 1807 and attributed to Georges Cuvier, and which can be held to match the Chandos and Droeshout portraits, purports to have been taken from Shakespeare's skull. And who would pay 6d to view a tomb that had been proven not to contain the authentic skull of Shakespeare?

In any case, Gibbs asserted, the portraits of Shakespeare were obviously accurate, as they showed a man with a huge skull capable of containing the Shakespearean brain:

> It is quite clear to all physiologists and phrenologists that the brain of Shakespeare must be enclosed in the skull of a fully developed man, the structure of whose head must be similar to that shown by the bust in the chancel.[22]

As Mary Thomas Crane has recently observed, 'Portraits of Shakespeare emphasize the large dome of his forehead, accentuated by a receding hairline; he must have had a brain.'[23] Gibbs may also have been aware of the story that John Milton's skull proved on exhumation to be disappointingly flat and low-browed, lacking the distinctive 'supra-orbital development' marking the skulls of both Shakespeare (and Sherlock Holmes)[24] as repositories of unusual brains. Recently Petrarch's grave has been opened and found to be occupied by the skull of a woman. Ironically this is exactly what happens in Belgrave Titmarsh's Victorian burlesque play *Shakspere's Skull and Falstaff's Nose*.[25] The hero Dryasdustus, a Shakespeare scholar bent on proving Shakespeare's plays were written by his ancestor Dryasdust, hires grave-robbers to open Shakespeare's tomb. They find and produce the skull – 'His fame was crumbled into dust,/Except the skull' (p. 23) – but it proves in reality to be 'feminine.' This displacement of the overdeveloped, high-browed skull of the cultural hero by an inferior specimen – that of a low-brow, or even a woman – represents the kind of risk to cultural stereotypes entailed in exhumation. Charles Dickens during an earlier exhumation campaign was grateful that the Stratford grave remained inviolate, that Shakespeare's tomb 'remained a fine mystery,' and no bardic skull had been produced and exposed in 'the phrenological shop windows.'[26]

These stories continually enact and re-enact a dialectic of desire and disappointment. Although by this stage articulated in modern scientific terms of phrenological mapping and photographic commemoration, this appetite for discovery remains recognizable as that familiar old hunger for the restoration of a lost presence, the necrophiliac desire for 'conference with the dead.' These Victorian scholars and enthusiasts coveted Shakespeare's skull with the reverence usually afforded to the relics of saints. Their aspiration to refit the authentic skull back into the portraits was not just to test the accuracy of portraiture, but to reassemble Shakespeare's fragmented parts into something resembling the living man. The prospect of finding in the grave not the true remains but a substitute, such as the skull of a woman, provoked in them profound anxieties of potential disappointment and disenchantment. Most chilling of all was the possibility of finding nothing: proof that no-one had ever been buried there, or simply evidence of the inexorable universality of decay. As Clement Ingleby recorded, the latter was a distinct possibility:

> I am informed, on the authority of a Free and Accepted Mason, that a Brother-Mason of his had explored the grave which purports to be Shakespeare's, and had found nothing in it but dust (Ingleby, pp. 31–2).

Shakespeare's face went to the grave, possibly remembered, but mostly unrecorded, by those who knew him, or had seen him act, or had dealt with him as writers, actors, businessmen, lovers, butchers or Catholics. Dust to dust, as the burial service reminds us. The pictures made after his death consistently defy expectation and disappoint desire. They float free of the man's life and his works and become graven images that could never truly represent the dramatist 'in habit as he lived.' Or they are even taken to be pictures of someone else altogether. Whether or not there really is an art to find the mind's construction in the face, without the face itself, the mind eludes us. Once again, as with every aspect of Shakespeare's life, we are left with facts, traditions and speculations that manifestly fail to answer our questions or resolve our uncertainties.

Fable: 'An Account of a Voyage to Bardolo'

This fable is based on models such as Jonathan Swift's *Gulliver's Travels* (1726), but also echoes later 'island' stories such as H.G. Wells's *The Island of Dr. Moreau* (1896), William Golding's *Lord of the Flies* (1954) and James's Hawes's *Speak for England* (2006). It uses historical material, but stretches it as far as it will go. Captain William Keeling did exist, and was responsible for staging Shakespeare plays on the deck of his ship. His great-grandson Thomas Keeling is wholly invented. Rowe's 1709 edition of Shakespeare was not one 'book' but six volumes, and did not contain an illustration of the Droeshout engraving (though it did use images derived from the Chandos portrait and the Janssen bust, which latter appears, as it did in Dugdale's work, with a woolsack rather than a pen). Nor would the people of Bardolo have derived a full-blown Bardolotry from Rowe's work alone. But this story is wholly fictitious, and any resemblance to a person or persons, living or dead, is wholly coincidental. As there never has been a society with a culture based exclusively on Shakespeare's work, there is no means of knowing whether or not it would be a genuine Utopia.

An Account of A Voyage to Bardolo

It was one of the most intriguing and notorious cases in the annals of maritime history, involving, in the year 1710, the complete and mysterious disappearance, somewhere in the scattered archipelagos between South-East Asia and Northern Australia, of a boatload of young English children. The story had been largely forgotten, but I had occasion, some two centuries later, to be grateful that my curiosity had prompted me, during my training as a naval officer, to study it well. Most of the information lay in the archives of the East India Company, in the form of minutes and transcripts of hearings and inquiries, and were not easy to obtain or to decipher. But the facts, so far as I could collate and interpret them, seem to have been as follows.

At the beginning of the eighteenth century, a ship of the East India Company, the *Rachel*, embarked on a voyage to Japan, via Socotra and Malacca, as Malaya was then called. There was nothing unusual about the expedition in most respects, since the ship carried the normal freight of trade goods to exchange for silks and spices in the Orient. But there was one exception to this normality: the ship carried a cargo of children. The presence, on board, of six young boys, and six young girls, would not in itself perhaps have occasioned so much notice, since all were orphans without family or connections, had not all of them been inexplicably lost at sea before the ship returned to port.

The captain of the *Rachel*, one Thomas Keeling, came from a long line of distinguished East India Company mariners. His great grandfather was the famous William Keeling who had led many expeditions to the Far East, discovered the Keeling Islands in the Indian Ocean, and ended his days as keeper of Cowes Castle on the Isle of Wight. But William Keeling was no ordinary ship's captain. Through his acquaintance with the then Earl of Southampton, who as Governor of the Isle of Wight conferred on him his sinecure, he developed a taste for the theatre, and in particular for the work of Southampton's protégé, the renowned dramatist William Shakespeare. Keeling became famous for his sponsorship of theatricals, performed on board ship by members of his crew, and was known to posterity as the man who devised a performance of Shakespeare's tragedies of *Hamlet* and *Richard II*, on board the ship the *Red Dragon* off the coast of Socotra in 1609. His great-grandson Thomas maintained this family tradition, and was a formidable enthusiast for the works of Shakespeare, and an avid sponsor of the drama. Which is why he was taking a cargo of children half way around the world.

His objective in carrying these youngsters was twofold. He harboured an ambition to revive the dramatic customs of an earlier day, in which companies of child actors dominated the theatrical profession; and he wished to promote the glories of the British theatre across the globe. To further these objectives, he arranged to transport a company of young children, six of each sex, to the imperial court of Japan, where he hoped to entertain the Emperor with their thespian talents. The children were taken from various orphanages, and were all characterized by their beauty of appearance, and the remarkable capacity of their talents in singing, dancing, acting and speaking verse. The boys had all had experience on the stage, and the girls were accustomed to perform, mostly in musical shows in their institutions, or at charitable events in the concert halls of London. Keeling hoped so to impress the Emperor with the dramatic and musical abilities of these fledgling performers that the palmy days of the British theatre would live again, and his own reputation as an ambassador of British culture would become unassailable.

The ship made good progress around the Cape, meeting no foul weather, and was proceeding through the straits of Malacca, when a great tropical storm broke over her decks, and captain and crew feared the worst. Every effort to maintain an even keel, and keep the vessel from shipping water, failed. There was no abating of the storm, and the ship was helplessly adrift, being pressed inexorably towards a reef of treacherous rocks fringing an uncharted island. The captain took the decision to abandon ship, and the crew managed to lower one of the boats, hoping thereby to reach the safety of the island. Abiding by the rule of 'women and children first,' the twelve youngsters were huddled swiftly into the lifeboat, and cast adrift. The captain tossed down his chest, containing his books, navigational instruments and other tools, and made way for members of the crew to leap down into the vessel. But at that moment a great storm-blast broke the mooring, and before there was any remedy, the boat was taken by the winds and soon lost from sight.

As the men were struggling to fit the other boats to take to safety captain and crew, they were all suddenly battered from their feet by a huge wave that swamped the decks, and turned the ship back again towards the Indian Ocean. The crew lay helpless before the onslaught of wind and waves, and the ship ran free of its own accord, leaving the island far behind. By the time the men could regain control of the vessel, the spot where they had launched the single lifeboat lay somewhere on the unfathomable, unmapped oceans behind them.

In the calm of the next morning, captain and crew vowed to do everything they could to find the lost children. They crossed and criss-crossed the seas for leagues around, exploring every island, but found no trace. Eventually, all their stores expended, and all their hopes dashed, they set sail for home. The sorrowful captain read over the waves of the unmoved ocean a memorial tribute from the words of the prophet Jeremiah: 'a voice was heard in Rama, Rachel weeping for her children, because they were not.'

It was a strange story, and occasioned some controversy once the ship was back in port, for no-one could understand how captain and crew could return home unscathed, while a whole boatload of children had been given up like sacrifices to some monster of the deep, or some tribe of head-hunting cannibals. People who cared nothing for the children while they were in their institutions, became filled with concern for them now they were lost. The company conducted stringent and exhaustive inquiries, but such was captain Keeling's reputation as a man of charity, as well as an exemplary sailor, that in the end no charges were proffered, and the matter was left as a tragic case of accidental loss, 'missing, presumed dead.' In the ensuing years, many boats travelling the same route had kept an eye out for signs of their survival, but nothing had ever been found. Until, that is, some two hundred years later, when I stumbled upon the solution to the mystery, by enduring my own casting away in the very same spot where these 'Children of the Revels' had been lost from the eye of man.

I had received a sound education as a boy, but drifted from career to career, trying the law, school-teaching and for a time acting in a London theatre before joining the service. My career in the Royal Navy was not a distinguished one, since our respective temperaments could not agree. I cared nothing for the brutality of naval discipline, and the arbitrariness of their punishments, and they cared even less for my capacity for administering them as an officer. We parted company on bad terms. But I was fitted for no career but that of the sea. Hence I found myself aboard a tramp steamer, carrying machinery for some mining expedition, which was making through the Straits of Malacca when it was surprised, not by a storm, but by attack from a body of pirates, who managed to board under cover of darkness, and overpower the entire crew. I happened to be sleeping in one of the lifeboats that hung over the ship's side, being unable to endure the stifling heat of my cabin, and woke to hear the commotion, without being immediately detected. I knew instantly what was afoot, and determined, if I could, to get off the ship and seek help. We could not be far from shore. It was a matter of minutes to release the rigging that held the boat, to lower it into the sea, and to make my escape. I could see nothing in the darkness except the flash of an occasional shot, so I knew things were going badly with my companions. So I hoisted the little sail, lay down in the hull of the boat, and let wind and tide take me where they would.

As day dawned, I peered above the gunwale, and observed that I was making fast for an island I could not recall seeing on the charts. It lay black and low on the horizon, reddened by the light of the rising sun, its shape conical with a flattened top, as if it were the shell of an extinct volcano. As I drew closer and the light grew stronger, I could see a bright green of tropical vegetation clothing the sides of the mountain, and around its base a long fringe of white sandy beach. What may have been a thin plume of smoke issued from the summit of the mountain, as if the fires of the volcano were not entirely extinguished. It was not civilization, but my chances of survival were considerably greater there than back on the ship and at the mercy of the pirates. I let the boat run towards the outlying reef, then steered along it till I found an inlet and made landfall. The white breakers carried me easily up the beach, and I was able, with some effort, to drag the little boat to a line of palm trees that marked the landward edge of the beach and cover it loosely with palm fronds and wild grass. I had no idea whether the island was inhabited or not, and my fear of death at the hands of the pirates was gradually being replaced by anxieties about the nature of my new island hosts, who might for all I knew be even more savage than the buccaneers I had eluded.

I made a rough shelter from palm fronds and driftwood, and then, exhausted by my exertions, slept in the shade of the palms through the rest of that day and most of the night, waking only when the cold of the tropical darkness reached its chilly nadir. I had used up the small store of provisions kept in the boat, so as soon as it was light cast about me for a source of fresh water. Fortunately, not far from my makeshift camp, a rivulet ran down from the mountain and emptied into a creek. Here I was able to slake my thirst. I hunted around in the cool shade and found a grove of mango trees, the fruit of which satisfied my hunger. I felt I had stumbled upon a veritable earthly paradise, but soon detected a serpent in the garden. Watching a cloud of flies dancing over the still green surface, I noticed the blunt snout of a crocodile jutting from the water, and realized that I would have to penetrate further inland to find safety on higher ground. I left my boat in its place of concealment, took a careful sighting of all visible landmarks, so I would have some hope of finding the place again, and set off for the interior.

At first the going was easy, though steep, through a forest of tall palm trees whose broad fringed leaves admitted thick bars of sunlight. Gradually the shade grew darker, the cover of foliage denser, and I found myself in the fastness of a tropical rainforest. The vegetation was thick and unyielding, almost impenetrable in parts, and I had no tools with which to cut my way through, so it was hard going. Attempts to worm my way between the intertwined branches and lianas left me very quickly exhausted, as well as scratched and bleeding. I rested for a while in a clearing, where I worked out a more rational and scientific approach, and hunted around for some kind of natural channel through the undergrowth. For a while, I followed the course of the stream, but its declivity soon became steeper and harder to traverse. I came then, however, upon a sort of flat terrace on the slope of the mountain, where the stream ran out into a little pool, and there on the edge were signs, in the form of trampled earth and hoof-prints, that this was a watering-hole where animals came down to drink. Sure enough, nearby I found a kind of tunnel in the forest that ran upwards, and had evidently been shaped by some species of deer or wild pig. The prospect of meeting some fierce beast at a turning of his own tunnel was not inviting, but I had no other means of mounting the slope. My only alternative was to return to the crocodile-infested waters I had left far below me. So I picked out a strong stick as a weapon, took to the animals' run, and by dint of stooping, and in parts creeping along on all fours, made good progress towards the summit.

At last I emerged from the tunnel and found myself on clearer ground, near the peak of the mountain. Just above me, a grassy slope ended abruptly with a sharp edge, which I guessed to be the lip of the volcano's crater. I rested there for a while, intending to mount and survey the interior of the island. But as I lay in a thicket, looking up at the cloudless blue of the tropical sky and the waving green fronds of the palm trees, my heart was virtually stopped by the sound of human voices. The island was, after all, inhabited, and all my efforts to reach safety had merely brought me within the grasp of whatever savage tribe it was that peopled this unknown place. I wriggled closer into the thicket and listened intently. The timbre of the voices was strange, not guttural or heavily inflected, but musical and modulated. Some of the words I thought I recognized, as if the speakers were conversing in a European tongue. The more I heard, the more convinced I was that the language being spoken, on the inaccessible peak of this unvisited shore, was my own native English. I crept up towards the lip of the cone, and peeped over the edge, before swiftly ducking down again. What I glimpsed there will be hard for the reader to credit, but I swear that this was truly what I heard and saw.

The interior of the island was indeed the gigantic crater of an old volcano. Inside its green, fertile cup the vegetation was much thinner, and sloped down easily to a valley bottom that contained a decent-sized lake. This was something like what I had expected to find. Far more unexpected was what I appeared to see down below in the valley, which was nothing less than a large human habitation, resembling a small town. All around the lake there were buildings, some of substantial size and distinctive shape. Though they were oddly made, of local materials and unusual proportions, there could be no doubt that they had been constructed in the style of a medieval or Tudor English town. The smoke I had seen drifting from the peak had its source in the domestic fireplaces of this odd little city.

But before I could recover from my astonishment and take a proper survey of this impossible apparition, the speakers I had heard conversing caught a glimpse of me observing them, and if anything more surprised than I was, stopped in their tracks. They were two young men of European appearance, as white as myself, but partly dressed in the fashion of two or three hundred years before. Above the waist each wore a crudely tailored doublet, black in colour, with the protruding collar of a white shirt, while below their legs were swathed in a kind of raffia skirt. Their feet were bare. Both men looked curiously alike. Each had his hair partly shaved above the forehead to confer a kind premature baldness, while the rest curled long around the shoulders. Each face was lined with a small beard, and the lips shaded with a moustache. Each of them wore a small gold ring in the left ear. I was beginning seriously to doubt the evidence of my senses, since what I thought I was looking at was the spectacle of two men who both bore a remarkable resemblance to William Shakespeare.

Ducked down within the thicket, I heard them conversing in low tones, but could not decipher their words. Then one of them called out to me, his voice ringing most incongruously around the crater's edge: 'Come forth to where we can see thee.'

Reluctantly I moved out from the shelter of the thicket and into plain sight, holding my hands before me in a gesture of submission. They stared at me with great curiosity, though without the incomprehension I felt towards them.

One of them said to the other: 'This is most strange.'

'Then as a stranger,' said the one who had called out to me, 'give it welcome.'

'Why dost hide thyself?,' said the other man to me, using the same oddly archaic diction and phrasing. 'We will do thee no harm.'

Then they both bowed towards me with an old-world courtesy, and said in unison, 'We are honoured to make your acquaintance. We are Orsino and Marcellus. How art thou called?'

I told them my name was Edward, a name they seemed to recognize. 'You are the first stranger to visit us for many years,' said the one who called himself Orsino. 'You are a survivor. No doubt you have been shipwrecked on our shore.'

I nodded assent, since the diagnosis was close enough. But my mind was full of unsatisfied curiosity. If these people had encountered strangers, how could they still be dwelling in some unchanged Tudor England? How did they know about shipwrecks?

The two men looked at one another. 'You are puzzled, Edward,' said Orsino. 'We know of survivors, and of storms at sea.'

'It is all in the Book,' put in Marcellus, trying to be helpful, but mystifying me even further.

'But you are only the second survivor to have chanced upon our island,' explained Orsino.

'Who was the first?' I asked.

'A man came to us in the ninth generation. He was from the land known as Dutch, but lost upon the waters like all mankind. He did not speak as we do, and there was little understanding between us. He stayed here with us a while, but was unhappy. Then he … disappeared, and was never seen again. But come, we must return to the city and present you to our king. You will be most welcome.'

And so they led me, still struck with amazement, but at least now without fear, down towards the town.

'What is the name of your city?' I asked, automatically assuming their orotund style of speech.

'It is the City of Bardolo,' replied Orsino. 'And the island is known by the same name.'

'And the name of your king?'

'Our king is always called William. After the Bard.'

'Immense is his genius',' added Marcellus.

'Extraordinary his power of invention,' intoned Orsino, as if joining in a kind of liturgy.

'Inexhaustible his knowledge of the human heart.'

'The Bard?,' I repeated, beginning to glimpse something of the strange truth that lay behind all this mystery, though it was long before I understood it fully.

'The Bard' they replied, again in unison, and in a tone of reverent adoration that silenced me for a while.

As we talked, we approached the outskirts of the town, which I could now see much more clearly. It was built around the waters of the lake, which the people called Thames. The buildings were made of wood and volcanic stone, and whitewashed in the style of Tudor buildings in English towns, and their roofs thatched over with the reeds that grew abundantly by the lakeshore. Most were dwelling houses of a few rooms, but in the centre was a much larger building, that I took correctly to be their civic centre. It was high and circular, with a thatched roof. From the roof jutted a flagpole carrying a banner that flapped idly in the windless air. All round the circumference of the building there were doors through which people passed in and out. By now, my astonishment had decreased to manageable proportions, so it seemed only natural to me that the central edifice of the City of Bardolo should be this replica of an Elizabethan theatre.

As we passed along, men, women and children stopped in the street, and emerged from their houses to stare at me. The men all looked very similar to my two companions, all shaved semi-bald, and with the same facial hair, and all dressed alike. The women were dressed quite differently, all in long thin robes that resembled the clothing on classical statues. All were evidently curious to see me, but not in any way hostile or alarmed. Many greeted me with gestures of friendship and courtesy. Soon we reached the main door of the theatre building, which I afterwards learned was known as the Globe. Inside I found the structure to be much like drawings I had seen of the theatres of Shakespeare's time. A big platform stage dominated the interior, while the inside of the round building consisted of a series of galleries. At the back of the stage stood a large wooden throne, such as one would often see in a dramatic production. But sitting on it, and bearing what looked like a theatrical costume for a stage king, with a crown of leaves and a sceptre of wood, was the King of Bardolo himself. Like all the other men, he displayed the forehead and beard, the black doublet and white shirt collar, of an effigy of William Shakespeare.

I was brought before him, and he greeted me with the same courtesy and generosity of feeling I had found everywhere among these strange people, though he also conversed in that strangely archaic tongue. He asked me how I came there and where I was from, questions to which I delivered carefully guarded answers. He asked me if I had known of the Island of Bardolo before I was 'cast adrift on the rough rude seas,' and I explained to him that nothing at all was known, even of its very existence. He seemed surprised, though not particularly displeased, by this. He asked me what were my first impressions of the city and its people, and I professed a great admiration for the beauty and ingenuity of the buildings, and the hospitality and gracefulness of the people. I indicated further that I would be very glad of some instruction in the history of his state, since I knew nothing of it. He indicated that he would be pleased to arrange for me to visit the Academy of Bardolo, and to meet with the most learned and knowledgeable of their scholars, who would be able to instruct me fully in the civilization and culture of his kingdom. Such a visit would take a day to two to arrange, and in the meantime, officers of his household would care for me.

I kept my counsel, and avoided asking his majesty any awkward questions about his peculiar kingdom, utterly cut off from the world, yet apparently constructed entirely in the image of one of the world's great writers. Every man looked like Shakespeare; every man, woman and child bore a single name from one of Shakespeare's plays; and all spoke like Shakespearean characters. But they never displayed any awareness of this strange anomaly, as if they knew of no other way of living. They often alluded to 'the Bard' and 'the Book,' but with religious fervour rather than literary appreciation. I could not begin to understand them, but had no intention of offending or alarming their sensibilities by any imprudent challenging of their unconscious assumptions and cherished beliefs.

I was given comfortable lodgings in a house adjoining the theatre, and during the following day my slight wounds were dressed by physicians, and my ragged clothes replaced by the uniform of doublet and grass skirt. I was bathed in the waters of the lake, and clad in clean garments. In the afternoon, I was visited by the king's own barber, who spent some time carefully tending my hair and beard. At the end of this process, happening to catch a glimpse of myself in the surface of a vessel of water, I realized that I now looked exactly like the rest of them, and had been turned into another replica of William Shakespeare.

On the next day a messenger from the king took me from my lodging to a large building that lay behind the theatre, and which I had not noticed on my first entrance into Bardolo. The building was evidently of some capacity, since it stretched all the way to the edge of the crater and, as I afterwards learned, had chambers built into the mountain around a system of natural caves. This was their Academy, which housed all their institutions of education and research. I was introduced to its director, an elderly man of distinguished appearance, who wore the usual Shakespearean hair and beard, but in his case they were a snowy white. His name was Dr. Pericles. In conversations that lasted several days, he inducted me into the history of Bardolo, and to its customs and manners. It was in the course of this discussion that at length I made the connection with my memory of the lost children from the voyage of the *Rachel.*

The culture of Bardolo was a most curious mixture of intellectual sophistication and superstitious ignorance. In some branches of learning and science, they were singularly advanced, while in others manifestly retarded. Clearly, they had mastered the arts of building sufficiently to construct, from poor and unpromising material, a town, that supported a population of some thousands. Their practical abilities were most remarkable, and they made full use of all that nature supplied. Their living was provided for by their own husbandry in the growing and harvesting of fruit and vegetable foodstuffs, and by the abundant wild life of the island. They caught fish, snared birds and hunted wild pig. In the arts, music and dance, they seemed highly proficient, though in literature they seemed to know nothing beyond the works of Shakespeare. They excelled in mathematics and physics, but they knew nothing of biology or chemistry, and had only the vaguest idea of geography. They seemed to know of other countries and peoples, yet had no inkling of where they were, and seemed to think of them as belonging to the past. They knew little of astronomy, and nothing at all of mechanics. Their medicine was of the crudest kind, but surprisingly effective, since they had learned how to derive, from numerous plants and herbs, their properties of physic. Their government was of the simplest kind, since they all owed willing obedience to the king, and ideas of resistance to his authority seemed repugnant to them. They married and had children very young.

Their ideas of time were most unusual. They spoke of their history as consisting of thirteen generations, which I computed, by their very early reproductive habits, to be about 200 years. But they spoke of the first generation as belonging to the beginning of time. They spoke often of 'the Twelve,' as if their race had been founded by some lineage of patriarchs. They referred frequently and reverentially to 'the Book,' but I did not betray my ignorance as to what this scripture might be.

At the end of each day, I had been given far more information, but remained none the wiser as to any true understanding of the civilization of Bardolo. It was on the third day of my meetings with Pericles that the truth at last dawned on me. He clearly felt that I was an apt and attentive pupil, and had made sufficient progress in my understanding to move on to the next stage of my education. To this end, he conducted me deeper into the Academy building, through a series of corridors with rooms on either side. From these various chambers, I could hear the sound of voices, sometimes the noise of tools, sometimes notes of music, but could not see what was in them.

At last, Pericles paused before a great door that appeared to mark the end of the building, but was in fact the entrance to a great chamber inside the rock. The door was guarded by two men, which struck me as odd, since I had seen no other signs of security anywhere on the island. At a sign from Pericles, they stepped aside and permitted us to pass. The chamber was a cave of very large proportions, lit by torches, and at one end a natural alcove curving into the rock. In the centre of this recess there lay a boat, fashioned from planks of oak that had never been grown in this climate and soil. Above, around the curving wall of the alcove, were three pictures, drawn with immense skill, but with crude materials, using charcoal on animal skin. All three were pictures of William Shakespeare. In the centre was a design that resembled Shakespeare's funeral effigy in Holy Trinity Church, Stratford; to the left a copy of the Chandos portrait; and to the right a facsimile of the Droeshout engraving from the First Folio. Inside the boat, on one of the plank seats, lay an old seaman's chest, with the lid open to reveal an old book, encased in a leather binding, with faded gilt lettering. I knew of course, before inspecting it more closely, what it was, for the revelation had fallen on me like a hammer-blow, in that very instant. The book was a collected edition of Shakespeare's works, dating from the year 1709. I guessed that within its pages, along with Shakespeare's plays and poems, would be found the three pictures of Shakespeare, the copies of which now adorned the walls of this extraordinary shrine. 'The Twelve' were none other than the children who had been lost at sea in 1710. And the people of Bardolo were all their descendants.

'The Bard,' said Pericles simply, indicating the images above the boat. 'These are his three manifestations, of Plenty, Love and Wisdom. In the centre is Bard the Father, who holds the Woolsack of Abundance. To his left is Bard the Lover, who brings us Passion and Fertility. To his right is Bard the Wise, who opens to us the Book of Knowledge.'

'And this is the Book itself?' I asked, glad at last to be seeing the light.

'That is the Book. The Book rests in the Ark that brought the Twelve to Bardolo. The world was destroyed, save for a few wandering strangers like yourself. But we multiplied and prospered, and lived faithfully, as the People of the Book of the Bard.'

I nodded assent. What could I say? The evidence for his faith was before us, in the book and its icons. He knew no better, and I at the moment I had no thought of disabusing him. It would have been far better for me if I had stuck to that resolve and never sought to challenge their innocence or disturb the peace of their paradise. For it was I who introduced the snake of scepticism into that eastern garden, and though I made good my own escape, I fear now for whatever may have happened, as a direct consequence of my interference, to the people of Bardolo.

I was able at last to piece together the whole story of this remarkable island. The six boys and six girls, set adrift from the *Rachel* in 1710, had landed safely on this island, and with nothing more than their own abilities, and the few tools and instruments stowed in the captain's chest, had managed to establish a society. They must have begun to breed among themselves very quickly once they had realized that the law and morality they had left behind no longer applied to them. But far from descending into barbarism, these extraordinary children not only maintained the values of the civilization they could barely remember, but founded a new one on the old basis.

Over the generations, the knowledge these survivors possessed of who they were and whence they came disappeared, and was replaced by the mythology of 'The Twelve,' in which legendary story their boat became the Ark of the Covenant, and their survival a deliverance from some Great Flood. The most extraordinary feature of their history was, however, the pure accident of the presence, in that chest that went with them to the island, of a copy of Shakespeare's works. This book had become their scripture, their mythology, the source of all their information about the world. The extravagant bardolatry of the eighteenth century had led them to believe that William Shakespeare's life on earth was a kind of Incarnation, and that he was truly the manifestation of God temporarily come among mankind. Shakespeare had bestowed upon mankind the law, the prophets and the gospel, all revealed in his poetry. The Twelve had brought his book to the island as a chosen people who survived a great global catastrophe, and their descendants lived by the Book, and adored the image.

I stayed with these people above a year, before the final, cataclysmic events that will close my narrative took place. During that time I grew in understanding of their faith and their morality. Shakespeare was their God, and his book their Bible. In the Globe theatre that formed the centre of their civic life, the plays of Shakespeare were read out, from a makeshift lectern, in cycles throughout the year, to the gathered population. Shakespeare's language penetrated deep into their being, so it became natural for them to respond to every situation with a saying from 'the Book,' or to manage every difficulty of social life with some piece of wisdom from 'the Bard.' I had noticed that they seemed to have no incidence of crime, and no mechanisms for dealing with it: no police, no courts, no prisons. This systematic avoidance of wrongdoing did really seem to derive from their internalization of the ethical values to be found in Shakespeare. None of them harboured any inclination towards political power, as they had read in the History plays of the miseries it brings to those who seek it. None of them was inclined towards falsehood or dishonesty or fraud, since they knew from the Comedies how absurd such pretensions are. None of them was tempted towards anger or jealousy or violence, since they knew only too well from the Tragedies how such passions invariably end. They seemed free from all the customary moral problems that arise from sex, since they were able, as soon as the sexual impulse arose in them, to satisfy their desires in a free mutual coupling, followed by a kind of marriage, always conducted in the early morning, in a cave in the rocks, by a priest who always bore the name of Friar Laurence. Any member of the little commonwealth who transgressed the norms of the community was not punished, but only sent back to school to be re-educated in the Wisdom of the Bard.

It was in many ways an ideal society, a kind of Utopia in which the most destructive passions of mankind were regulated and managed by the pervasive influence of a kind of literary scripture that served for ethics, politics and religion. And though I could appreciate the value of this almost perfect model of human society, I suffered under the constant disquiet of concealment, growing more and more restless in the poisonous, gnawing knowledge that it was all based upon a misunderstanding. Gradually I became more and more determined to expose the absurdity of their beliefs, and to bring these idolatrous people to their senses. I burned with evangelical zeal, like some reformer from the Middle Ages, to bring these people out of the darkness of their superstition and into the cold light of modern scientific truth.

I had established a firm friendship with Dr Pericles, who seemed the wisest man among them, and we met and conversed almost on a daily basis. We talked mostly of Shakespeare, and it was fortunate that I remembered, from my days as a jobbing actor, a fair smattering of knowledge about the author and his plays. But where most of the Bardolians were like devotees of some fundamentalist religion, he seemed to me to have a kind of sly comic wit and a knowing scepticism that would surely make him a willing auditor to what I had to say. So at last, on one memorable day, I screwed my courage to the sticking place, and ventured to tell him everything.

I cautioned him that what I had to tell would be very difficult for him to hear, perhaps even more difficult to comprehend. and I swore on everything I held sacred that what I had to say was nothing less than the absolute truth. He was mildly astonished at the vehemence of my assurances, for since the Bardolians would never think of telling a lie, such protestations of honesty were unknown among them. And he listened, with every appearance of interest and curiosity, to my account of my world, which had the potentiality to bring his world crashing down in ruins around us.

I explained to him that Bardolo was merely an island in the Pacific Ocean, and that the rest of the world had not been destroyed in any Deluge, but persisted, in a greatly enlarged and hugely populated condition, all around them. I told him about the children of the *Rachel,* and conveyed to him my settled belief that these were the 'Twelve' from whom all his citizens derived. I told him about Shakespeare, and tried to convince him that although this dramatist was the object of great adulation and hero-worship among many cultures, he had never been more than a remarkably talented man, flesh and blood like ourselves. I told him the little I knew about Shakespeare scholarship, explaining that there were now many editions of all the plays, often quite different from the original texts, and that the plays flourished in the theatres around the world, but were often changed radically into performance texts for different venues. I told him what I knew about the three portraits of Shakespeare and where they came from. I pointed out that their style of dress, with its incongruous coupling of Elizabeth doublet and tropical grass skirt, arose from the fact that all these portraits showed only the head and torso of the Bardic body, and not the legs; and that the dress of their women was copied from an image, in the old Shakespeare edition, that designated merely symbolic figures, and did not represent any actual style of clothing. And I explained that some people had even ventured to doubt whether Shakespeare himself was author of the plays, and to propose that they may have been written by some else. This and much more I conveyed to him through the course of that long hot day, and at the end of it he sat for a while in silence. Then he raised his eyes to me with a smile, and signalled that all this new information would take him some time to absorb and digest. He would ponder on what I had told him, and see me again on the morrow.

That night I was awoken from sleep by the faintest of sounds, which nonetheless, by their breaching the customary silence of the black tropical night, gave me an instinct of danger. I crept from my straw mattress, and peered over the ledge of my window. Outside there was gathered a small group of young men, some of whom I recognized from their posts of guarding the sacred Book. They were whispering together, and I knew instantly that I was to be seized and arrested as a heretic and blasphemer. What they intended to do with me I could not guess. Would they imprison and torture me? Or impound me and subject me to ever stronger doses of Shakespearean moral teaching? Either way, I did not intend to stay to discover their intentions. In a back corner of the little house I occupied I knew the stone wall had crumbled, and would provide a rear exit. It was the work of seconds to wriggle through this aperture, and to creep silently, and under cover of the darkness, around the back of the town. I managed to do this without raising any suspicion, and navigating by the stars, climbed the inside of the crater to a spot I thought must be reasonably close to the point where I had entered. I knew I would not be able to make my way down the outside of the mountain in darkness, so lay up in a thicket to wait for the sunrise. As the faint traces of early light streaked the sky with orient pearl, I peered down towards the town, to see if I could see any sign of pursuit. From that distance, I could not see anything, but as the light grew in strength, I could hear sounds of consternation, and the noise of people moving among the buildings. Shortly after, as I expected, I saw a group of men issue from the town and start to climb the hill towards my hiding place. I delayed no longer, but casting around for the pig's tunnel, by good luck hit upon it, and scrambled down the slope far more rapidly than I had climbed it a year before. By the time I heard the noise of my pursuers crashing down through the thick undergrowth, I had reached the beach, and found my boat safe in its hiding place. As luck would have it the tide was in, so I was able to push the little boat easily into the waves. I rowed hard, and was some hundred yards off in the bay when the Bardolians reached the edge of the water.

There they stood, in a scattered line through the surf, in complete silence, and made no attempt to follow me, as if it did not occur to them that they could pursue me across the water. In the early morning light I could not see the expressions on their faces, so to this day it remains a mystery to me how they regarded my escape from the island. Did they feel resentful over the escape from punishment of a heretic, who had forsworn their most cherished beliefs? Did they feel sorrow at losing the opportunity to bring a lost sheep back into the fold? Or were they rather gratified at my departure, even if it meant my almost certain death on the unpeopled waters, since they would at least have succeeded in ejecting one who could so brazenly offend their sacred faith?

I drifted at sea for a few days, and would have perished there, under that burning sun and on the waves of that pitiless sea, had I not been spotted by a ship, and rescued from my ordeal. I told them my story, and they of course thought me a madman, or at least one who had been driven crazy by the ordeal of my sojourn on the waters. As I recovered from the ill effects of that exposure, I realized that it would be far better to withhold my true story, and so laughed it off as a delusion brought about by hunger and thirst. Once I was safely back home, I continued to keep my counsel, and told no one the full tale of my voyage to Bardolo.

It took me a long time to get used to modern civilized life once more, and to this day I retain many difficulties of adjustment. I can hardly bear the noise and traffic of the city, and find the pressure of London's crowds, with their diversity of population, almost intolerable. Men seemed to me over-dressed in the costume of the twentieth century, and women grotesquely imprisoned within their elaborate encasing garments. Everyone seemed to carry a low forehead, and their clean-shaven faces seemed bland and repulsive. The speech of the modern day seemed to me intolerably harsh and crude, accustomed as I had become to the musical and mellifluous cadences of the people of Bardolo.

Everywhere in the city, I saw the signs of human depravity and the complex mechanisms established to counteract it: everywhere there were police and soldiers, everywhere men and women committing crimes, and being hauled off to prisons and workhouses. I even missed that strange and ludicrous religion of Bardolo, by contrast with the churches of my own civilization. At least theirs was a rational and humane belief system, while here people go to church to listen to speeches of hatred against other nations and to sing hymns of glory to their brutal Empire. How often have I found myself, standing on a street corner, afraid to dash in among the crowds and traffic, longing for the peace and tranquillity of that distant island!

But I knew I could never go back. Even if I could find it again, they would never accept me. I had betrayed them. Perhaps Bardolo was no longer even there, since my ambition to disillusion them of their idolatry might well have introduced, into that little Utopia, the germ of its ultimate dissolution. Perhaps the people had begun to realize that their society was founded on a grotesque untruth, that they were victims of a colossal illusion. Perhaps they had fallen to fighting among themselves, even to destroying the very fabric of their civilization. I might find my way back there and find nothing but a few charred ruins among the eternal silence of the rainforest.

But at night, in dreams, I often travelled back to Bardolo, carried there on the slow dark tide of sleep. I would glimpse it from afar across the ocean, a precious stone set in a dark blue sea, and the city was always much larger than I had seen it in reality, with lofty spires and great theatres. I would be almost there, urged by the green swell landwards, seeing the people waiting for me on the sand, stretching their arms towards me in welcome, when suddenly the tide would beat me back, and in a mist of spray I would wake to the hard grey light of modern London. Everything would collapse, the cloud-capped towers, the gorgeous palaces, the great Globe itself, would all vanish, and dissolving, leave not a rack behind. And this is all I have left of Bardolo: such stuff as dreams are made on. There it is, far away over the untroubled waves, resting quietly on that far horizon; for ever rounded with a sleep.

Notes

1 Introduction

1 *Shakespeare in Love, dir.* John Madden (1998). Performers Joseph Fiennes, Geoffrey Rush, Tom Wilkinson, Anthony Sher, Judi Dench, Gwyneth Paltrow. USA: Miramax.
2 Caryl Brahms and S. J. Simon, *No Bed for Bacon* (London: Michael Joseph, 1941; London: Black Swan, 1999).
3 Nicholas Rowe, 'Some Account of the Life &c. of Mr William Shakespear,' preface to Rowe's *The Works of William Shakespear in Six Volumes* (London: Jacob Tonson, 1709), vol. 1, p. i.
4 Brahms and Simon, *No Bed*, p. 27.
5 Bill Bryson, *Shakespeare* (London: Harper, 2007), p. 17.
6 W. H. Auden, 'Who's Who,' *Collected Shorter Poems 1927–1957* (London: Faber and Faber, 1966), p. 78.
7 Katherine Duncan-Jones, *Ungentle Shakespeare: Scenes from His Life* (London: Arden Shakespeare, 2001), p. ix.
8 Rowe, 'Some Account,' p. vi.
9 Rowe, 'Some Account,' p. xxxiv.
10 Jonathan Bate, *Soul of the Age: the Life, Mind and World of William Shakespeare* (London: Penguin, 2009).
11 Peter Ackroyd, *Shakespeare: the Biography* (London: Chatto and Windus, 2005).
12 Peter Ackroyd, *London:the Biography* (London: Vintage, 2001).
13 Bate, *Soul*, p. 428.
14 Samuel Schoenbaum, *Shakespeare: A Compact Documentary Life* (Oxford: Oxford University Press, 1977), pp. 296–7 (a condensation of Schoenbaum's *Shakespeare: a Documentary Life* [1974]). Schoenbaum considers this story a myth.
15 Park Honan, *Shakespeare: A Life* (Oxford: Oxford University Press, 1999), p. 409.
16 Wells, Stanley, *Shakespeare: for all time* (London: Macmillan, 2002), p. 45.
17 Ackroyd, *Shakespeare*, p. 485.
18 Michael Wood, *In Search of Shakespeare* (London: BBC, 2003), p. 377.
19 Duncan-Jones, *Ungentle*, p. 266.
20 Ben Jonson, *The Devil is An Ass* (1616).
21 Germaine Greer, *Shakespeare's Wife* (London: Bloomsbury Publishing, 2007), p. 304.
22 Bate, *Soul*, p. 428.
23 Samuel Schoenbaum, Shakespeare's Lives (Oxford: Oxford University Press, 1970), p. ix.
24 Stephen Greenblatt, *Will in the World: How Shakespeare Became Shakespeare* (New York: Norton, 2004).
25 While others praised it for exactly the same reasons.
26 Greenblatt, *Will*, p. 108.
27 Greenblatt, *Will*, p. 312.
28 Stephen Greenblatt, *Hamlet in Purgatory* (Princeton: Princeton University Press, 2001), pp. 6–7.
29 Greenblatt, *Will*, p. 317.

30 Greenblatt, *Purgatory*, p. 7.
31 Gary Taylor, 'Stephen, Will, and Gary too,' review of *Will in the World*, by Stephen Greenblatt, *The Guardian* (9 October, 2004), p. 9.
32 Greenblatt, *Will*, p. 321.
33 Diane Middlebrook, 'The Role of the Narrator in Literary Biography,' *South Central Review* 23.3 (2005), p. 16.
34 Alastair Fowler, 'Enter Speed,' review of *Will in the World*, by Stephen Greenblatt, *Times Literary Supplement* (4 February 2005), pp. 3–5.
35 Colin Burrow, 'Who Wouldn't Buy It?,' review of *Will in the World*, by Stephen Greenblatt, *London Review of Books*, 27.2 (20 January 2005), pp. 9–11.
36 Richard Jenkyns, 'Bad Will Hunting,' review of *Will in the World*, by Stephen Greenblatt, *The New Republic* (22 November 2004), pp. 21–4.
37 Fowler, 'Enter Speed,' p. 5.
38 M. G. Aune, 'Crossing the Border: Shakespeare Biography, Academic Celebrity, and the Reception of *Will in the World*,' *Borrowers and Lenders 2:2* (2006), n.p.
39 Lois Potter, 'Review of *Will in the World*, by Stephen Greenblatt,' *Shakespeare Quarterly* 56.3 (2005), p. 375.
40 Charles Marowitz, 'Stephen Greenblatt's *Will in the World*,' *Swans Commentary* (25 April 2005). http://www.swans.com/library/art11/cmarow16.html
41 Charles Nicholls, *The Lodger: Shakespeare on Silver Street* (London: Allen Lane, 2007; London: Penguin, 2008); James Shapiro, *Contested Will* (London: Faber and Faber, 2010).
42 Jorge Luis Borges, '*Everything and Nothing*'and 'Shakespeare's Memory,' in *Collected Fictions* (London: Penguin, 1999), pp. 319–320 and pp. 508–516.

Life One

1 John Heminge and Henry Condell, 'To the Great Variety of Readers,' prefatory matter to the 'First Folio': *Mr William Shakespeares Comedies, Histories and Tragedies* (London: Isaac Jaggard, 1623), p. 7. References are to *A Facsimile of the First Folio, 1623* (New York and London: Routledge, 1998).
2 Ben Jonson, cited Schoenbaum, *Documentary*, p. 259.
3 Heminge and Condell, 'Great Variety,' p. 7.
4 See Schoenbaum, *Documentary*, pp. 214–19.
5 Sir William Dugdale, *Antiquities of Warwickshire Illustrated* (1656). See Schoenbaum, *Documentary*, pp. 311–13, which reproduces the Dugdale illustration of the monument.
6 Wells, *For All Time*, p. 105.
7 Robert Greene, cited in Schoenbaum, *Documentary*, p. 151.
8 Henry Chettle, cited in Schoenbaum, *Documentary*, p. 151.
9 *Venus and Adonis* (London: Richard Field, 1594).
10 Francis Meres, *Palladis Tamia*, cited in Schoenbaum, *Documentary*, p. 190.
11 'Bold lover, never, never canst thou kiss,/Though winning near the goal.' John Keats, 'Ode on a Grecian Urn,' *Lamia, Isabella, The Eve of St. Agnes and Other Poems* (London: Taylor and Hessey, 1820), p. 114.
12 Wells, *For All Time*, p. 101.
13 Ackroyd, *Shakespeare*, p. 256.

Life Two

1 Schoenbaum, *Documentary*, p. 183.
2 Schoenbaum, *Documentary*, p. 254.
3 See Bate, *Soul*, p. 376.
4 Schoenbaum, *Documentary*, pp. 250–1.
5 Schoenbaum, *Documentary*, pp. 251–2.

6   Schoenbaum, *Documentary*, p. 254.
7   'The Names of the Principall Actors in all these Playes,' *Facsimile of the First Folio*, p. 15.
8   Bate, *Soul*, p. 356.
9   Bate, *Soul*, p. 356.
10 Aubrey, cited in Ackroyd, *Shakespeare*, p. 221.
11 See Ackroyd, *Shakespeare*, p. 221.
12 Rowe, 'Some Account,' p. vi.
13 Sir William Oldys, cited in Schoenbaum, *Documentary*, pp. 201–2.
14 John Davies, *The Scourge of Folly* (1610) in *The Complete Works of John Davies of Hereford* (1618), ed. A. B. Grosart (1878), vol. 2, p. 26.
15 Schoenbaum, *Documentary*, pp. 205–6.
16 This interpretation is explicit in another, independent version of the story, produced in 1759 by Thomas Wilkes, before Manningham's diary had become available. See Schoenbaum, *Documentary*, p. 206.
17 Bate, *Soul*, p. 186.
18 Alexander Pope, Preface to his edition *The Works of Mr William Shakespeare*, 6 volumes (London: Jacob Tonson, 1725). Quoted from *William Shakespeare: the Critical Heritage, vol 2: 1693–1733* ed. Brian Vickers (London: Routledge, 1974), p. 298.
19 Wells, *For All Time*, p. 36.
20 Greenblatt, *Will*, pp. 190–1.
21 Bate, *Soul*, p. 166.
22 Wood, *In Search*, p. 116.
23 Bate, *Soul*, p. 366.
24 Greenblatt, *Will*, p. 322.
25 John Aubrey, cited in Schoenbaum, *Documentary*, p. 74. See also Ackroyd, *Shakespeare*, p. 50.
26 See Bate, *Soul*, pp. 355–6.
27 Bate, *Soul*, p. 355.
28 Greenblatt, *Will*, p. 249.
29 I. M. [James Mabbes], 'To the Memorie of M. W. Shake-speare,' Dedicatory Poem in *Facsimile of the First Folio*, p. 13.

Life Three

1   Schoenbaum, *Documentary*, pp. 73–4.
2   Schoenbaum, *Documentary*, p. 109.
3   Schoenbaum, *Documentary*, pp. 30–1.
4   Schoenbaum, *Documentary*, p. 30.
5   Schoenbaum, *Documentary*, pp. 98–9.
6   Rowe, 'Some Account,' p. v.
7   Schoenbaum, *Documentary*, pp. viii.
8   Schoenbaum, *Documentary*, pp. 73–4.
9   John Dover Wilson, *The Essential Shakespeare: a Biographical Adventure* (Cambridge: Cambridge University Press, 1932).
10 Rowe, 'Some Account,' p. vi.
11 Schoenbaum, *Documentary*, pp. 143–4.

Life Four

1   Greenblatt, *Will*, p. 58.
2   Bate, *Soul*, p. 174.
3   Schoenbaum, *Documentary*, pp. 21–2.
4   Schoenbaum, *Documentary*, pp. 30–44.

5 Schoenbaum, *Documentary*, pp. 210–12.
6 Schoenbaum, *Documentary*, p. 232.
7 Schoenbaum, *Documentary*, pp. 234–48.
8 Schoenbaum, *Documentary*, pp. 272–5.
9 Schoenbaum, *Documentary*, pp. 220–3.
10 Schoenbaum, *Documentary*, pp. 238–9.
11 Schoenbaum, *Documentary*, pp. 297–306
12 Wells, *For All Time*, p. 43.
13 Schoenbaum, *Documentary*, pp. 144–5.
14 Rowe, 'Some Account,' p. x.
15 Schoenbaum, *Documentary*, pp. 260–4.
16 Duncan-Jones, *Ungentle*, p. 248.
17 Schoenbaum, *Documentary*, p. 283.
18 Schoenbaum, *Documentary*, p. 285.
19 Wells, *For All Time*, p. 36.
20 Duncan-Jones, *Ungentle*, p. 262.
21 Bate, *Soul*, p. 172.
22 It cannot be coincidental that Jonathan Bate is Director of 'Bardbiz,' registered at Companies House under the number 4477996.
23 Ackroyd, *Shakespeare*, p. 385.
24 Greenblatt, *Will*, p. 330.
25 *King Lear*, 3.4.28–36.
26 Edward Bond, *Bingo* (London: Eyre Methuen, 1974).

Life Five

1 Alice Fairfax-Lucy, *Charlecote and the Lucys: the Chronicle of an English Family* (1958), p. 5.
2 Dedication to *Lucrece* (1594).
3 Schoenbaum, *Documentary*, pp. 76–9.
4 Schoenbaum, *Documentary*, p. 93.
5 Frank Harris, *The Man Shakespeare and his Tragic Life Story* (London, 1898).
6 Anthony Burgess, *Shakespeare* (London: Penguin, 1972.), p. 56.
7 Schoenbaum, *Documentary*, p. 94.
8 Sir William Oldys, cited in Schoenbaum, *Documentary*, p. 225.
9 John Aubrey, cited in Schoenbaum, *Documentary*, p. 224.
10 Wells, *For All Time*, p. 17.
11 Bate, *Soul*, p. 162.
12 Greenblatt, *Will*, p 119.
13 Burgess, *Shakespeare*, p. 58.
14 Bate, *Soul*, p. 164.
15 Ackroyd, *Shakespeare*, p. 83.
16 Wells, *For All Time*, p. 20.
17 Ackroyd, *Shakespeare*, p. 86.

Life Six

1 Dedication to *Venus and Adonis* (London: Richard Field, 1593).
2 Dedication to *Lucrece* (London: Richard Field, 1594).
3 Rowe, 'Some Account,' p. x.
4 *Shakespeare's Sonnets* (London: G. Elde for T.T., 1609).
5 Heminge and Condell, 'To the Most Incomparable Paire of Brethren,' *Facsimile of the First Folio*, p. 5.
6 Wells, *For All Time*, p. 87

7 *Willobie his Avisa* (Oxford, 1594).
8 Wells, *For All Time,* p. 155.
9 Greenblatt, *Will,* p. 228.
10 Bate, *Soul,* p. 209.
11 Ackroyd, *Shakespeare,* p. 196.
12 Anthony Burgess, *Nothing Like the Sun* (London: Heinemann, 1964; London: Alisson and Busby, 2001), p. 110.
13 Erika Jong, *Serenissima: a novel of Venice* (New York: Houghton Mifflin, 1987), p. 9. Later republished under the title *Shylock's Daughter* (Harper Collins, 1995).

Life Seven

1 Sonnet 152.
2 Schoenbaum, *Documentary,* p. 224.
3 Schoenbaum, *Documentary,* p. 224.
4 Duncan-Jones, *Ungentle,* p. 131.
5 Greenblatt, *Will,* p. 233.
6 Wood, *In Search,* p. 203.
7 Sonnet 137.
8 Sonnet 137.
9 Burgess, *Nothing Like,* p. 139.
10 Bate, *Soul,* 208.
11 Wells, *For All Time,* p. 87.
12 Ackroyd, *Shakespeare,* p. 288.

Life Eight

1 Schoenbaum, *Documentary,* p. 55.
2 From the Roman Catholic 'Sacrament of Extreme Unction.'
3 See Eamon Duffy, *The Stripping of the Altars: Traditional Religion in England 1400–1580* (New Haven and London: Yale University Press, 1992), pp. 568–9.
4 Schoenbaum, *Documentary,* pp. 53–4.
5 Schoenbaum, *Documentary,* p. 41.
6 Schoenbaum, *Documentary,* p. 45–53.
7 Schoenbaum, *Documentary,* p. 46.
8 Wood, *In Search,* p. 57.
9 Wood, *In Search,* p. 38.
10 Wood, *In Search,* pp. 148–51.
11 Wood, *In Search,* p. 341.
12 Wood, *In Search,* pp. 76–80.
13 Wood, *In Search,* p. 377.
14 Richard Wilson, *Secret Shakespeare: studies in theatre, religion and resistance* (Manchester: Manchester University Press, 2004), p. 297.

Life Nine

1 George Orwell, 'Charles Dickens,' in *Collected Essays, Journalism and Letters,* edited by Sonia Orwell and Ian Angus, vol. 1 (London: Harcourt Brace Jovanovich, 1968), p. 460.
2 Ben Jonson, 'To the memory of my beloued, The Avthor Mr. William Shakespeare: And what he hath left vs,' facing the Droeshout titlepage engraving to the First Folio, *Facsimile of the First Folio,* pp. 2–3.

3 The first part of *The Return to Parnassus,* in *The Three Parnassus Plays,* edited by J. B. Leishman (London: Nicholson and Watson, 1949), pp. 192–3.

4 Anne Barton, *Ben Jonson, Dramatist* (Cambridge: Cambridge University Press, 1984), p. 3.

5 For details of this portrait see Bryan Loughrey and Neil Taylor, 'Shakespeare and Jonson at Chess?,' *Shakespeare Quarterly,* 34:4 (Winter 1983), pp. 440–8.

6 Unpublished Appendix IX of *Shakespeare's Imagery,* pp. 385–6, in the Folger Shakespeare Library. Spurgeon was eventually persuaded that to use the chess portrait as her cover illustration might distract from the force of her argument.

7 Gary Taylor, *Reinventing Shakespeare: a Cultural History from the Restoration to the Present* (Oxford: Oxford University Press, 1991), p. 6.

8 A. L. Rowse, *The English Spirit: Essays in History and Literature* (London: Macmillan, 1945, 1966), pp. 5–6.

9 Stanley Wells, 'Handsome Shakespeare,' *Blogging Shakespeare* [bloggingshakespeare. com/?s=cobbe+portrait&submit.x=0&submit.y=0&submit=Search]

10 Schoenbaum, *Shakespeare's Lives,* pp.13–14.

11 Heminge and Condell, 'Great Variety,' *Facsimile of the First Folio,* p. 7.

12 See the 1994 programme for the International Festival, *Everybody's Shakespeare,* The Barbican Centre and Royal Shakespeare Company (October/November 1994). 'Everybody's Shakespeare is the first event of its kind in this country and probably the world: an international multi-disciplined celebration of the work and influence of Shakespeare' (Adrian Noble).

13 Burgess, *Shakespeare,* p. 261.

14 The Folger Shakespeare Library has a Victorian 'Bible-Shakespeare Calendar,' the cover of which features a Shakespearean visage assimilated to the traditional iconographic conventions used for representing Christ.

15 Christian Deelman, The *Great Shakespeare Jubilee* (London: Michael Jospeh, 1964), pp. 69–70.

16 James Rigney '"Worse than Malone or Sacrilege": The Exhumation of Shakespeare's Remain,' *Critical Survey* 9 (1997), p. 78.

17 J. Parker Norris, 'Shall we open Shakespeare's Grave?,' *Manhattan Illustrated Monthly Magazine,* XIX (July 1884), p. 73.

18 Norris, from the *American Bibliopolist* (April 1876), quoted by C. M. Ingleby, *Shakespeare's Bones: the proposal to disinter them considered in relation to their possible bearing on his portraiture* (London: Trubner and Co., 1883), p. 41.

19 Ingleby, *Shakespeare's Bones,* p. 34.

20 Ingleby, *Shakespeare's Bones,* p. 41.

21 Reported in the *Stratford upon Avon Herald* (5 October 1883).

22 Quoted in Rigney '"Malone or Sacrilege",' p. 78.

23 Mary Thomas Crane, *Shakespeare's Brain: reading with cognitive theory* (Princeton: Princeton University Press, 2000), 14. See also Sir Arthur Keith. 'Shakespeare's Skull and Brain,' in *Tenements of Clay: an Anthology of Biographical Medical Essays,* ed. Arnold Sorsby (New York: Charles Scribner's Sons, 1975).

24 Sherlock Holmes also had the inflated forehead that conventionally denotes supreme intelligence. In *The Hound of the Baskervilles,* Dr Mortimer says: 'You interest me very much, Mr. Holmes. I had hardly expected so dolichocephalic a skull or such well-marked supra-orbital development. Would you have any objection to my running my finger along your parietal fissure? A cast of your skull, sir, until the original is available, would be an ornament to any anthropological museum. It is not my intention to be fulsome, but I confess that I covet your skull.' Arthur Conan Doyle, *The Hound of the Baskervilles* (London: George Newnes, Ltd.: 1902), p. 13.

25 Belgrave Titmarsh, *Shakespeare's Skull and Falstaff's Nose* (000).

26 *The Letters of Charles Dickens,* ed. Georgiana Hogarth and Mamie Dickens (London: Macmillan, 1893), 111.

Index

SHAKESPEARE NOW!

Series Editors: Ewan Fernie, The Shakespeare Institute, University of Birmingham, UK and Simon Palfrey, University of Oxford, UK

Philippa Kelly

THE KING AND I

Shakespeare NOW!

'An innovative new series ...
Series editors Simon Palfrey
and Ewan Fernie have rejected
the notion of business as usual
in order to pursue a distinctive
strategy that aims to put
"cutting-edge scholarship"
in front of a broad audience.
With its insistent appeal to
the contemporary, this is
fresh Shakespeare for readers
turned off by the prospect
of dry-as-dust scholarship'
- Shakespeare Quarterly

Shakespeare Now! is a series of short books that engage imaginatively and often provocatively with the possibilities of Shakespeare's plays. It goes back to the source - the most living language imaginable - and recaptures the excitement, audacity and surprise of Shakespeare. It will return you to the plays with opened eyes.

continuum

For further details visit
www.continuumbooks.com